Mrs. Appleyard's Kitchen

BOOKS BY LOUISE ANDREWS KENT

Novels

THE TERRACE

PAUL REVERE SQUARE

MRS. APPLEYARD'S YEAR

———————

MRS. APPLEYARD'S KITCHEN

Stories for Young People

DOUGLAS OF PORCUPINE

THE RED RAJAH

TWO CHILDREN OF TYRE

HE WENT WITH MARCO POLO

HE WENT WITH VASCO DA GAMA

HE WENT WITH CHRISTOPHER COLUMBUS

JO ANN, TOMBOY (with Ellis Parker Butler)

IN GOOD OLD COLONY TIMES (with Elizabeth Kent Tarshis)

Mrs. Appleyard's Kitchen

LOUISE ANDREWS KENT

Keats Publishing, Inc. New Canaan, Connecticut

TO

M. W.

with whom some of the
best meals were eaten

Preface

A SLIGHT BATTLE took place between Mrs. Appleyard and her Editor as to whether there should be a Preface to this book. Mrs. Appleyard, who had become interested in a chicken curry, felt that her duty was at the stove. The Editor maintained that a book without a Preface was like a dinner without hors d'oeuvres. Luckily for the Editor, this well-directed simile coincided with the moment when Mrs. Appleyard dropped the last grain of rice into the violently boiling water, and she was at leisure for a moment.

'Just a few words about what sort of book it is,' said the Editor, in the sweetly persuasive editorial tones of one who conceals a whip behind his back.

'I thought you were writing the Preface,' said Mrs. Appleyard vaguely, beginning to peel an onion.

The Editor, with praiseworthy firmness, took the knife away.

Thus badgered, Mrs. Appleyard made the following statement:

'This book will never displace real cookbooks — books like the Hesseltine and Dow *Good Cooking*, for instance. I don't know how brides got along without that, because it has everything in it that anyone ever heard of cooking, and it's practical. If I'd had it when I was a bride everything might have been different. I might never have made those choke-dogs, for instance. . . .'

'Brooding never did anyone any good,' said the Editor tersely, 'and please talk about your own book.'

'Oh, yes — well, I still think there's room for the smaller, more personal book, for the kind that is based on one person's experience, rather than the encyclopaedia of cooking that has all the wisdom of the ages in it. The smaller ones are fun to read, too, even if you never cook out of them.'

'Is your book for wartime?' asked the Editor.

'Not specifically,' said Mrs. Appleyard, 'but I think it might be helpful. Its point of view is that you eat things when they are at their best rather than dragging them over the country when they are out of season. And that you have a few things and take pains in making them, rather than many and give them only part of your attention.

'I hope it makes cooking seem like something that's fun for a family to do together. I have no patience with the martyred mother who loves her martyrdom more than she does her family — the kind that monopolizes all the unselfishness and comes to the table too tired to eat, or faints just before the meal because she has been standing over the hot stove on the hottest day in summer, making three different kinds of pie when the family would much rather have her look cool and comfortable while they eat some plain raspberries. We're all going to have some cooking as part of our war work and we might as well enjoy it and let our families enjoy it with us. It's a challenge to our ingenuity to get the most out of what we have.

'I didn't leave out the things that took sugar, because I don't think the war is going to last forever, and I think we're going to win it and there will come a time when someone says, "How was it we used to make that foamy sauce?" Imagine if everyone had forgotten! I learned how to make that sauce from my husband's mother, and she'll always be remembered while it's made — just as no one eats fish chowder in our house without thinking of my grandmother. Don't you think a chowder is a lot nicer than a bronze tablet?'

The Editor agreed to that and asked if the recipes were mostly family ones.

'In our family we say "receipts,"' said Mrs. Appleyard, 'and I'll tell you why. It's a question of Latin. "Recipe" is the imperative form of the verb — what I'd say to you if I wanted to tell you how to make cornstarch pudding, for instance, or cough syrup, or any other unlikely substance. "Take — *recipe*," I'd say, "two tablespoonfuls of cornstarch and throw it into the sink." Those directions would be the *receipt* — the instructions that you received from me, because the word is derived from the past participle — is that clear?'

'As clear as imitation Hollandaise sauce,' murmured the Editor.

'I'm glad,' said Mrs. Appleyard, 'because I just made it up. Of course when we don't want to embarrass anyone we just call them "rules,"' she continued. 'Yes, a good many of them are family receipts and others came from friends, and some are things we worked out ourselves. There isn't anything in the book that we haven't made at some time or other, and when we get something so that we think it's right, we have always written down just what we did at the time, including warnings about the difficulties. I think it's almost as important to know what not to do in certain things you cook as it is to have the positive instructions you need. Having made a good many peculiar mistakes in my time I can at least serve as a horrible warning if not as an example. I've tried to tell you about the various dishes so that you can cook them even if you haven't done much cooking before.'

'Do you call these recipes — I mean receipts — economical as well as practical?'

'In the larger sense of the word — yes. If you mean that I suggest lots of perfectly delicious ways of making things without eggs, butter, flour, or sugar — no. I'd always rather save up until I could make the thing properly, and in the meantime eat bread and cheese. There's nothing so wasteful as an "economical" dish that the family won't eat. It wastes time and temper as well as materials. Cut down on the number of things you serve but use the best materials for those you make. Remember that if you serve dried beef instead of porterhouse steak, you can afford cream for it and still be away ahead; that if you will bake your potatoes perfectly to go with it, making the family wait for the potatoes instead of the other way, and take pains with the other vegetables you serve, you will have a good meal instead of a poor one.

'Don't serve the family's favorite kind of meat, vegetable, and dessert all at the same meal. Stagger them (not the family, the favorites!). Have strawberry shortcake the day you have meat loaf instead of the day you have broiled chicken. Of course it's a poor heart that never rejoices, and there will be times when you produce all the treasures for one meal; but for everyday menu planning it's good management — which is economy, as I seem to remember being told — to have some favorite food at every meal rather than all the dull ones at once and all the more interesting ones at another time. And don't forget that a good hot bowl of soup with people you like tastes a lot better than chicken croquettes with béchamel sauce and warm ice cream, with after-dinner speeches ahead of you; and that cooking for your family is Family Fun, if you will make it so, and that we're all lucky if we have families to cook for.'

'You mean that your book won't be much help unless you do your own cooking?'

'I think the people who do their own cooking will use it most, but, you know, even if we have people to help us, there are likely to be gaps. There are Thursday and Sunday evenings when you can have your kitchen to yourself, and there are those periods when the children say, "When Hilda is on her vacation will you make cream puffs with chocolate sauce?" And there are picnics. Besides, I hope it's going to be partly for my convenience. People keep saying to me, "Mrs. Appleyard, I do wish you would give me your rule for oatmeal cookies." And then, poor idiot that I am, I do, knowing well that they will lose the paper before they get home and then try to do it out of their heads, and then blame me because the cookies didn't come out right. Now I shall just say, "Look on page 69 of my book," and that will end the discussion.'

'Your point is well taken,' said the Editor. 'Perhaps they'll stop writing to me about green peas and things too. I hope that in your book you have told about all the things to eat that were in *Mrs. Appleyard's Year.*'

'I think we have. May I go back to my curry now?'

'Yes, indeed,' said the Editor, who was beginning to be hungry. 'Will you give me the recipe — excuse me, receipt?'

'Look on page 162,' said Mrs. Appleyard firmly, and went on cutting up onions.

Contents

1

A Cook in spite of Herself. Some of the best reading in the world, Mrs. Appleyard says, is found in cookbooks. She ought to know because she began to read them as literature long before she took to wielding the egg beater. There have been frequent periods in Mrs. Appleyard's life when she was on short rations. Her doctor has told her to lose three hundred pounds and she has. No, she has not vanished in the process. She is still moderately substantial. She has merely lost ten pounds thirty times. During those periods when her too, too solid flesh was melting, she has learned to sublimate her yearnings for chocolate cake and lobster Newburg by reading cookbooks. She has fortunately discovered that she can get a pleasantly stuffed feeling simply by moving her eyes rapidly from left to right over menus that begin with twenty assorted appetizers and end with Baked Alaska.

Mrs. Appleyard is the reader all writers have been looking for. If the hero of a book climbs a peak only slightly lower than Mount Everest — some cone as hard to negotiate as lemon sherbet with stars like spun sugar fizzing around it against a sky as dark as a Concord grape (the similes are Mrs. Appleyard's) — there she is panting and puffing behind him. Probably he is saved only by her hot breath blowing down his neck. When the heroine takes to the tropics and acts like a langorous panther, Mrs. Appleyard lies limply — though lumpily — on a couch draped with hibiscus blooms and mosquito netting. Her laugh becomes low, thrilling, and just slightly sinister as it hisses from between lips that are a scarlet gash in her gardenia-white face. Her eyes lengthen and narrow. She wears a sarong....

What she can do with a cape when the hero is a bullfighter would delight Mr. Hemingway. How crisply witty she was during her Jane Austen period only Mrs. Appleyard knows. It was perhaps her happiest phase, although she also enjoyed her life in Barchester when she was the Archdeacon and Mrs. Proudie both at once. Sometimes, too, she thinks back wistfully to the days when she was Becky Sharp, decked with diamonds, and waltzed wickedly at Waterloo — with Rhett Butler or somebody.

When Mrs. Appleyard reads a cookbook she eats.

Having now eaten her way through cookbooks where everything is smothered in whipped cream, through the kind that lets no innocent piece of meat escape without an overcoat of sauce, through helpful advice about garnishing pheasants with artichoke bottoms, through the spirally bound collection of the Appleyard Centre Woman's Club (twenty rules for doughnuts, four for green tomato mincemeat, six versions of sour-cream cookies, for any one of which the owner will pull hair!), through books dainty and delectable, books hearty and homely, Mrs. Appleyard has naturally decided to give the book of her own kitchen to the world.

There are good reasons for this step.

Mrs. Appleyard had not read more than twenty or thirty cookbooks when she began to have an uneasy feeling about this form of literature. Cookbooks, she thought, ought to tell someone who does not know how to cook something how to cook it. Yet frequently the writer approaches the subject assuming airily that the reader knows all about it anyway. In that case, Mrs. Appleyard thinks it would be better for the writer to tell about her trip to the Gaspé or how to crochet an openwork afghan. There are also writers about cooking who, from pure malice, Mrs. Appleyard thinks, deceive the trusting reader about some simple process — cooking string beans, for instance.

In book after book the reader is told to break string beans into inch pieces and cook them for various lengths of time ranging from twenty to sixty minutes. Beans broken in this way and cooked an hour look and taste like pieces of some-body's ski boots, Mrs. Appleyard says. If you cook them twenty minutes, they may look and taste better, but as you can't chew them the improvement in appearance and flavor is of somewhat academic interest. Mrs. Appleyard here states, and is willing to have her book judged at this point by what she says, that the cooking of string beans depends greatly on how they are cut. If you do not care to take the trouble to cut them on a long diagonal so that a large amount of cut surface is exposed to rapidly boiling water, why don't you have squash or open a nice can of corn? Furthermore, all the water that you use ought to cook into the beans so that all their flavor and minerals and vitamines are in them and not thrown down the sink or on the petunias. They should cook in this way in about half an hour. They will be tender, a delicate shade of natural olive green, and all they need on them is a little butter and salt. If you like them with cream, be sure they stand in it long enough so that they absorb some of it.

Now, it seems that the writers of cookbooks must know this simple fact about cutting string beans, yet they blithely advise you to break them into inch pieces, and then they begin to chatter about sultana roll. Yet string beans have to be eaten frequently and if you really want sultana roll, you can get it from the caterer. He is a lot more deft about imitation green coloring, and combining glue with raspberry and claret extract than — for instance — Mrs. Appleyard.

'The trouble with most cookbooks,' she says, 'is that they assume that people live the way they don't live. They talk as if you still made soup by cooking a knuckle of veal for three days when as a matter of fact you open a red-and-white can in three seconds. Cookbooks are often very good about telling you what to do — generally something you don't want to do — but they don't tell you what not to do, which is sometimes just as important. I don't know that I have much to contribute,' she added, in one of her rare moments of modesty, 'but at least when I think I know anything I am going to Tell All.'

Mrs. Appleyard began by speaking of her qualifications as a cook. They seemed to consist chiefly of the fact that when she was married, her mind was a blank page upon which any receipt could be written. She had never even made fudge. Because as a child she had always had her nose in a book, her family had decided to make a librarian of her. They did not know that reading books is no more a virtue in a librarian than drinking cocktails is in a bartender. Mrs. Appleyard found it out the first week, but was too lethargic to say so. She decided that if she were supposed to be leading an intellectual life she would not have to be domestic. She thought, poor moron, that she didn't like domesticity. She just didn't like it without Mr. Appleyard. In his society, she discovered, opening a can of corned-beef hash became a romantic gesture. So was mending his socks.

'Unless,' Mrs. Appleyard has been heard to remark (Record 4567 B), 'you think it would be fun to mend his socks, don't marry him.'

Mr. Appleyard adapted himself to his wife's cooking with extraordinary amiability. He did, it is true, murmur at times about the sour-cream johnnycake that his grandmother used to make, and he would occasionally speak in a homesick fashion of the salt pork with sour-cream gravy that his mother made. Still, as Overbrook Hill was far outside the sour-cream zone, Mrs. Appleyard never had to do much but listen sympathetically while she planned whether Cicely's spring coat had better be pink or blue. Of course Mr. Appleyard was one of those men who 'had that for lunch,' but what man hasn't?

Besides, Mrs. Appleyard soon checkmated that dinner-table gambit. She got a job testing receipts for a magazine.

That phase of her career has always needed some explaining. Why, it has been asked, would a magazine pay for the materials and also pay, for testing things, someone who had never cooked anything more complicated than tomato soup — the condensed kind — and canned peaches?

'That was why,' Mrs. Appleyard explains. 'If I could cook it, so could anyone. Those rules just had to be good.'

It must have been nervous work for Mr. Appleyard. Rare indeed were those times when he was able to anticipate and duplicate at noon what he was going to have for dinner. Those pungent curries, those weird and wonderful desserts full of marshmallows and maraschino cherries, those thirty-nine ways of disguising eggs so that their own mother would never know them, those soufflés that rose only to fall again, those casseroles with pretty nearly anything in them — no man ever had those for lunch!

Then there was the seasonal rhythm. Much has been written about how editors read Christmas stories in June, and in December have to writhe in their chairs while poets make the exciting discovery that June rhymes with moon — approximately. It remained, however, for the Appleyards to discover how strange life can be when you eat suet pudding on the Fourth of July and revel in cooling drinks and ice cream at Christmas.

Mr. Appleyard bore it all nobly. It is true that he did say once with a patient expression — it was while Mrs. Appleyard was trying out 'twenty new thoughts about spinach,' a good many of the thoughts containing garlic — that perhaps it would be better if Mrs. Appleyard would try it on the dog instead of on the visiting economist who was coming to dinner. He said there was no such thing as a little garlic. . . . Still, for the most part he ate what was set before him in the silence that — in a man — implies praise.

Mrs. Appleyard still has an interesting little collection of scrawls on paper that she 'hasn't got around to trying yet.' She will not include any of them in her book. Neither is she going to put in any rules for economical cakes. When she feels economical she does not make cake. She prefers a raw carrot stick to any cake that has been constructed from motives of economy. She also states that, while this is not an advertising pamphlet, she will call things by their trade names if she feels like it. This is her book and it is going to tell the way she cooks — and inspires cooking in others. Luckily there have always been adventurous souls who seemed to like to help in the Appleyard kitchen. This book should really belong to them. Perhaps also to Hugh.

He was standing beside his mother looking over her shoulder while she was copying some rules into her private cookbook. He was ten years old, perhaps. After a while he said, 'Mother, when I am married, will you give my wife that book?'

Mrs. Appleyard considered the question, realized with gratitude how unassertive her mother-in-law had been in the matter of that salt pork with cream gravy, and answered: 'Well, I don't know if I would, Hugh. I could show it to her, of course, and tell her she could copy anything she liked out of it, but I don't believe I'd give her the book.'

'That's all right, mother,' Hugh said kindly. 'I expect the kind of girl I'm planning to marry will have a cookbook of her own.'

This is Mrs. Appleyard's own book, and anyone is welcome to copy anything out of it.

2

Weights and Measures. Mrs. Appleyard believes in weighing and measuring. She has deep admiration for the cook who operates on inspiration, but she herself is not gifted that way and she clings to the measuring cup. Unfortunately, all cookbooks do not use the same system. Some chat in terms of ounces and others in cups. In unravelling these directions — including her own — Mrs. Appleyard has found the following facts helpful.

3 teaspoonfuls (t.)	equals	1 tablespoonful (T.)
16 T.	equals	1 cup (c.)
½ c. butter	equals	¼ pound (lb.)
2 T. butter	equals	1 ounce (oz.)
2 c. butter	equals	1 lb.
2 c. granulated sugar	equals	1 lb.

It takes almost three cups of powdered or light-brown

sugar to make a pound, so always measure them by cups
instead of dumping in a package at a time.

4 c. pastry flour	equals	1 lb.
2 T. flour	equals	1 oz.
4⅓ c. coffee	equals	1 lb.
1 sq. Baker's chocolate	equals	1 oz.
9 large eggs	equals	1 lb.
2 c. Hamburg steak	equals	1 lb.
Pinch of salt	equals	⅛ t.

3

'*Beverages*.' Why are things to drink always called beverages in cookbooks? Mrs. Appleyard says she has no idea. Perhaps it's refined or something. Anyway, far be it from her to flout tradition. A glass of water is a beverage; so is a glass of champagne. Mrs. Appleyard is fond of both, though her experience has been chiefly with water.

She sometimes feels that not enough attention is paid to water. There seems to be an idea that all water is alike. Nonsense! Water varies just as much as wine. It doesn't cost enough so that it pays to advertise it, that's all.

Fond of water though she is, she never appreciated it so much anywhere as in England. English waiters do not approve of the nervous American habit of water-drinking. Probably they know the water is needed to season the potatoes or else they think that if you drink it, you will have no room for cabbage. At any rate when you sit down at the table you are invited to slake your thirst on some good sturdy bread. Mrs. Appleyard soon discovered that if she wanted water at all, she must be firm.

She learned to brave the pitying look with which the waiters said to themselves, 'Ah, an American!' and also that it was not enough to say, 'May we have some water?' but that, in order to save the whole family from desiccation, she must add: 'Six glasses, please. One for each of us.'

A further complication was that the Appleyards, although they like water cold, do not like ice in it. They want it the way it comes out of the springhouse at Appleyard Centre — as when Mrs. Appleyard says: 'Dinner's almost ready. Get the water from the spring. Don't dip it. Hold the pitcher under the pipe.'

Realizing, because they are an adaptable family, that Simpson's-in-the-Strand probably did not have a springhouse with thimbleberries growing around it, they were willing to drink London water in its native lukewarmness. Mr. Appleyard was even detected fishing out lumps of ice with a spoon. The most elegant-looking of the waiters had just put it in. He had heard Mrs. Appleyard's American accent and went to work at once. Mrs. Appleyard felt sorry for his honest perplexity at the capriciousness of Americans. 'All Americans drink ice water' was an article of faith with him, and here were six who didn't.

Mrs. Appleyard also felt drawn to the waiter because he was wearing a frock coat like the one Mr. Appleyard was wearing the first time she ever saw him. This reminded her so pleasantly of her courtship that she actually ate most of her broad beans. She did not wish to hurt the feelings of anyone in a coat like that. She also prevented Mr. Appleyard from asking maliciously if the beef were really English, thus averting a split of no mean proportions in Anglo-American relations.

Ah, that beef! Was there ever anything better? or half so good? Except possibly the saddle of mutton. Is there a better dessert than English strawberries in a punnet — which is a small round basket, lined and covered with fresh strawberry leaves — and Devonshire cream? Except perhaps the raspberries. Appleyard Centre raspberries are no better even when you pick them off the bush yourself. What is so good to eat with cheese as English biscuits? What fish is better than English sole eaten at a restaurant that has been looking out over Piccadilly for a couple of centuries?

There is plenty of poor cooking in England — just as there is in America — but some of the best food in the world is English, if you know where to look for it. English writers have a genius for describing terrible meals, Mrs. Appleyard says, and she thinks they don't spend enough of their time telling about the good ones that you may have: the wonderful teas, the breakfast with bacon that makes you realize you never ate bacon before, the Yorkshire hams, the salmon that was swimming up the river that morning —— But she was supposed to be talking about things to drink, wasn't she? All right, all right!

WATER

Water should be cold, but it should not be cold enough to paralyze the palate. If you are not lucky enough to have a cold spring piped into your front yard, you can help to make the outside of the pitcher agreeably frosty by putting in a few ice cubes and after a few minutes, fishing them out. Or you can leave them in if Mr. Appleyard is not one of the guests. Or, as far as Mrs. Appleyard is concerned, you can serve the water lukewarm. She really doesn't care so long as it's wet.

TEA

By exerting immense self-control, Mrs. Appleyard will not say what she thinks of tea made with tea bags. Why should she blast a great industry, the product of American ingenuity? She simply declines to mention how to manipulate those little mechanisms known to some as the mouse in the teacup. Merely saying that she would as soon think of making lobster soup by boiling a lobster buoy, she passes on to the making of tea.

For four people:

A quart teapot — earthenware	2 qts. boiling water
Another quart teapot	5 t. of the best tea
A tea-strainer	you can afford

Into a quart earthenware teapot that is *hot* and *dry* put the tea. Set the teapot on the stove near the kettle. Never bring the kettle to the teapot: always the teapot to the kettle. Run two quarts of fresh cold water into the kettle and bring it rapidly to a real bubbling boil. As soon as it is boiling hard, pour enough water over the tea to fill the teapot nearly full. Cover the teapot. An English tea cozy is the best thing, but anything that will keep it warm will do — a towel folded several times, for instance. Let it stand at least five minutes, never more than seven. If you want it stronger, use more tea, not longer steeping. Now strain it into another warm teapot, which may be silver if you like. Put the rest of the hot water into another teapot or into a silver teakettle, or into anything you have handy, according to the degree of elegance that you are maintaining at the moment. This is for the feeble souls who like hot water flavored with tea. There are always some of these around — Mrs. Appleyard is ashamed to admit being one of them — and it's just as well to face the fact. Of course the pleasantest thing is to have a silver teakettle with an alcohol lamp under it that really works, but this is a rare sight in these times, and you can have good tea without it.

The point of these manoeuvres, Mrs. Appleyard says, is this: The fragrance of tea is best extracted by steeping it as near the boiling point as you can get it without its actually boiling. If you leave it on the grounds too long, you get bitterness instead of fragrance.

Making tea is so simple that it is amazing how much bad tea there is available. Even a moderately priced tea is good to drink if it is carefully made, and the most expensive kinds can be ruined by water that is not freshly boiled, or not really boiling when it hits the tea, or by being steeped too long, or not long enough.

Mrs. Appleyard likes several kinds of tea: Lapsang Souchong, Ming Cha, Earl Grey's Mixture, Flowery Tip Orange Pekoe are all good — and so is your favorite brand, whatever it is. And as we are lucky to have any tea at all, it's worth taking pains to make it right.

COFFEE

Mrs. Appleyard approaches the subject of coffee with a certain amount of nervousness. Theoretically she knows how to produce a good cup of coffee. In practice she is always sure that it might have been better. She has tried various methods, and as she has probably had her worst results with percolators, she will leave that subject to those who know how to dominate them.

On one or two points she is fairly sure. Coffee should be freshly roasted, freshly ground, and served as soon as it is ready. Why is coffee always so good on a picnic? Partly because you are on a beach or a hilltop, and because the air is fresh and you are hungry — yes; but also because everyone is gathered around the fire, breathing in the smell of coffee and wood smoke, and as soon as the coffee is cleared and the grounds have settled, it is poured out and you drink it. It has no chance to stand around and get bitter.

Also on a picnic there is generally someone who is particular about his coffee and he is asked to make it and gives his whole soul to it. Give him a cooking space to himself — a fire between four stones will do — a new enamel coffee-pot, a vacuum tin of coffee that he opens on the spot, water from the spring, an egg right out of the henhouse, and he will produce something that makes everyone say, 'That's the *best* coffee!'

One of these picnic coffee chefs told Mrs. Appleyard how he did it and it sounds simple. (If it were, hers would probably taste more like it.)

Use plenty of coffee, he says, at least two tablespoonfuls to a cup of water. You can weaken it with cream or milk, you know, but you can't make it stronger after you've once started. Crush the egg, shell and all, with the grounds and put in no more than five *grains* of salt to a cup of water. Stand right over it so that you know when it comes to the boil, and time it with your watch. Let it boil exactly one

minute, dash a little cold water into it, and let it stand just
five minutes for the grounds to settle. Be sure that it keeps
hot but that it doesn't boil again. Under his supervision
coffee never boils over and wastes all its goodness on stones,
ants, and grasshoppers, but keeps it where it belongs — in
the pot.

Probably in these days when coffee is not ground or
roasted at home, the best coffee comes out of a freshly
opened vacuum tin. People sometimes forget that once
a vacuum is broken, there is no more magic to that can
than there is to any other open can of coffee. Buy coffee
in small quantities and from a shop that sells a large
amount so that you know the stock is frequently replaced.
Wash and scald and sun everything that you use in coffee-
making. Always use enough coffee.

Even with these precautions the picnic coffee is still perhaps better than the coffee made in the kitchen, because it
is served out of the pot in which it was made instead of being decanted into that handsome Georgian silver coffee-pot.
Coffee made in a glass coffee maker in sight of the guests
also has the virtue of being served as soon as it is ready.
However, it is possible to produce with one of these ap-
pliances something that tastes as if the grapes of wrath had
been squeezed into it. Mrs. Appleyard has done so and
knows of what she speaks.

Perhaps drip coffee is safest for the amateur. An earthenware pot is better than a metal one. Neither coffee nor tea
is really at home in metal. Like any other sort of coffee-pot,
all parts of the drip pot should be scalded and dried in the
sunshine. Always use plenty of coffee and be sure it is
ground right for drip coffee. The water must be freshly
boiled and boiling hard when it is poured over the coffee.

Have the pot warmed before you put in the coffee and plug the spout with tissue paper so that the fragrance stays in the coffee instead of rising to the attic. Pour over a few tablespoonfuls of water at first and then let it stand a minute before you add the rest. Keep the water boiling and do not pour it on too fast. The water should be in contact with the grounds for about seven minutes. Put the pot where it will keep hot while the water is dripping through the grounds, but never let it boil. If your sense of beauty or vanity requires you to serve it in another pot, be sure that the second pot is freshly scalded and hot enough to take the shellac off your table. (It won't hurt Mrs. Appleyard's, because hers is finished with linseed oil — a substance she really knows how to use. Perhaps it would be better if she stuck to it and let Mr. Appleyard make the coffee....)

ICED COFFEE

Never use left-over coffee for iced coffee. If your hand and arm become paralyzed when you think of pouring coffee away, make coffee jelly with it; or learn to make the right amount.

For iced coffee use at least two tablespoons of coffee to each cup of water. Make it your favorite way — boiled, dripped, or percolated — and pour it over cracked ice in tall glasses just before you are ready to serve it. People vary so much in their ideas about sugar and cream that it is better to serve them separately. Cream may be whipped, but Mr. Appleyard has views on whipped cream of such a firm nature that in Appleyard Centre the substance is pretty nearly illegal. Rich yellow cream that has the taste of June grass in it is what he prefers — and why not? Leave enough room in the glasses for the cream to be poured in. Those who like it generally like plenty. Long spoons for stirring in cream and sugar are almost an essential for iced coffee. There are few drearier sensations than being confronted with a glass of iced coffee with the cream and sugar all at the top and a limp cellophane straw.

COFFEE FOR TWENTY

There comes a time in most lives when a lot of coffee has to be made and no ordinary pot is big enough. You can produce something that most of your guests will accept as coffee by putting a gallon of water on to boil in a large enamelware saucepan and three quarters of a pound of coffee into a cheesecloth bag. The bag must be big enough so that there is room in it for nearly twice as much coffee as you put in. Be sure it is tied tightly at the top. Crush a whole egg, shell and all, with the ground coffee — if you like it made with egg — and add a few grains of salt.

Just as the water comes to a full bubbling boil, put in the bag and let it boil one minute. Then cover the kettle tightly and let it stand where it will keep very hot but not boil for six minutes longer. Remove the bag and pour the coffee into a freshly scalded coffee-urn.

If you are serving forty people do not try to double the quantity in the bag, but make a second batch while the first one is being served. If you have the water ready in the teakettle, you will have time before the first lot is used up. Use a new bag, because you will not have time to wash and scald the first one properly and if you do not, your second lot of coffee will be bitter. Be sure your kettle is thoroughly scalded in between times, too.

CHOCOLATE

Chocolate, Mrs. Appleyard says, is usually cocoa, and weak at that. This is a slander on a noble drink. Cocoa is a nice drink for children, and you will be quite safe in making it if you follow the directions on the package. You may use powdered chocolate, if you like, or you may even brew a drink out of cocoa shells — and Mrs. Appleyard will say nothing against it; at least she won't if she does not have to drink any of these concoctions under the name of chocolate. She means *chocolate*.

It's a nuisance to make real chocolate. It uses more dishes than tea or coffee. It's fattening. It keeps you awake at night — if it happens to. Nevertheless there's something about a well-made cup of hot chocolate that is very cheering on a cold January afternoon. It is associated in Mrs. Appleyard's mind with frosty moonlight nights, sleighbells, straw around your feet, a chinchilla muff — you could blow holes in the fur — the creak of runners on the crisp snow, the steam from the horses' breath, the driver humped in bearskin with big mittened hands and earlaps on his peaked cap, bare elms against a green-and-silver sky. You sang — whether you could sing or not. Everyone can sing on a sleigh ride. 'Jingle bells' ... 'Nelly Gray' ... 'Over the River' ... 'She's got rings on her fingers' ... 'Old Black Joe' ... 'The Merry Widow' ... 'Up the Street' ...

And afterward you stamped your numb feet and laughed a good deal at nothing special and the hot chocolate made you warm again down to the tips of your fingers and toes.

And here's how it was made.

For twelve people:

6 sqs. Baker's cooking chocolate   6 T. sugar
1 c. water   8 c. rich milk
¼ t. salt   ½ pt. cream, whipped
                    1 T. brandy (or 2 t. vanilla)

Grate the chocolate and put it into the top of a large double boiler with the water, salt, and brandy. Stir until the chocolate is melted and when the mixture is smooth, add the sugar and keep stirring. Stir in the milk and when it is scalding hot, beat the chocolate with an egg-beater until it froths. It must be served at once or there will be skin on the top. It will not taste of the brandy, which simply makes it extra smooth and rich. Serve the whipped cream separately for those who have no regard at all for their silhouettes. Some deceive the eye though not the palate by floating marshmallows — or compounds thereof — on top of chocolate. Of this subterfuge Mrs. Appleyard says little, but that is not because she has no opinions about it.

Coffee Chocolate is good if you don't mind staying awake at night. Even if chocolate does not keep you awake, you can be pretty nearly sure of a clear-minded night by substituting a cup of strong coffee for the water in this rule. Either of these drinks is good iced. Put cracked ice in tall glasses, make the chocolate or coffee chocolate fresh, pour it over the ice. Put a tablespoon of thick cream — or of whipped cream if you prefer it — on top, stick in a sprig of mint, and relax. For iced chocolate you may need to add extra sugar, as cold drinks taste less sweet than hot ones.

For Mint Chocolate add six drops of peppermint extract for each glass of iced chocolate to be served. Plenty of mint in the top, of course — enough to make a real bouquet to smell.

Iced Chocolate may also be made by shaking cold milk and chocolate syrup together in a glass shaker with some ice cubes. Chocolate syrup may be bought readymade, but it is easy to make it at home and it is convenient to have it on hand in the refrigerator.

CHOCOLATE SYRUP

4 sqs. Baker's unsweetened chocolate   ⅛ t. salt
       6 T. sugar

2 c. water

Grate the chocolate and put it into the top of the double boiler with the water. Stir it over the direct flame until the chocolate is melted, then add the salt and sugar and cook it over hot water three minutes longer. Cool it, put it into a jar with a tight cover, and keep it in the refrigerator until you need it.

To make a Chocolate Milk Shake put two tablespoonfuls of this syrup and eight ounces of rich milk into a glass shaker with an ice cube. Add whatever flavor your customer likes — two drops of peppermint extract, two drops of almond, or one quarter teaspoon of vanilla. Let him shake it himself and give him a tall glass for it. This is a good way to make some of the skinny members of the family take extra milk.

CIDER

Cider with preservative in it is often a beautiful clear dark amber color and comes in a jug of exotic shape with a handsome label printed in seven different tints. It looks fine on a fruit stand and, according to Mr. Appleyard, should be left right there.

Cider should be bought the day it is made from the mill where it is made. The right kind of mill can generally be identified by its unprofessional appearance. The roof slants at various interesting angles. There is a smell of apples with overtones of vinegar. (Mills where they use preservative never let any cider turn to vinegar.) The jugs in the right kind of mill are clean, but there are no seductive labels on them picturing an apple the size of a large turnip and colored like a peach and probably, Mr. Appleyard says, tasting like a turnip and having the same amount of juice. It is the sort of apple that Adam would have immediately handed over to Eve, he says.

He seems to imply that it would serve her right, but Mrs. Appleyard, who is sampling the day's run of cider from a paper cup, fails to snatch up the insult. Fresh cider must have a soothing effect on her. . . . She also likes it as it mellows to the happy stage where the cork comes out of the jug with a resounding pop and the cider fizzes a little as it is poured into the glasses.

She always puts most of it into the refrigerator, where it will slowly reach the fizzy state, but also leaves out a gallon or two in a warm place where it will turn to vinegar. It is much better in watermelon pickle or mincemeat or raspberry shrub than vinegar that is made in vinegar works.

She can, however, in recommendation of commercial vinegar, honestly say that when poured over some rusty nails and left standing for a few days, it makes a very fine wart-remover. There are various charms that you are supposed to say as you apply the black and sticky result, and it is a good idea to get someone — a grandmother is a likely philanthropist — to buy your warts. They will vanish in about two weeks. . . . Used straight, bottled vinegar can be applied to your table top to bleach it — if you were ever silly enough to darken it with ammonia. Combined with salt it helps in cleaning an old brass kettle. Probably Mrs. Appleyard could think of other uses for it, but she would rather talk about cider.

There is nothing especially technical about serving cider if you bought it at the right place and kept it cold long enough for it to harden a little. A sixteen-pound turkey from Craftsbury, Vermont, makes a very nice background for a few glasses of cider. So do mince and pumpkin pie.

There are also occasions when *Hot Spiced Cider* is a pleasant drink. Either sweet cider or some that is beginning to harden may be used for this.

For twelve people:

12 c. cider	2 T. stick cinnamon, broken fine
12 whole cloves	¼ t. nutmeg

Put the cider into a saucepan with the spices. Bring it slowly to the boiling point. Strain it. Serve it hot with toasted cheese and chutney appetizers (see page 145).

RUM PUNCH

Anyone who comes into the kitchen and finds Mrs. Appleyard removing the peel from several dozen lemons is correct in guessing that something exciting is going on in the family. It takes at least an engagement to stir her to this particular activity.

For sixty people she takes:

24 lemons	4 oz. yellow Chartreuse
4 lbs. lump sugar	2 T. Orange Pekoe tea
2 gal. water	4 oz. apricot brandy
2 c. New England rum	2 oz. orange curaçao

Take the thin peel off the lemons. She says you ought to cut it so thin that you can see through it. Put it into a large bowl with the sugar. If possible get the old-fashioned roughly cut kind of lump sugar instead of the too civilized package variety. Put the water into a large kettle and bring it to a boil as quickly as possible. While it is heating, squeeze the lemons and pour the juice over the peel and sugar. Just as the water reaches a full bubbling boil, toss the tea into it and let it boil *exactly* one minute — no more and no less. Use your watch to time it. Too long boiling makes it bitter; too short cooking fails to bring out the flavor. Remove it at once from the fire and strain it over the lemons and sugar. Stir it hard until the sugar is melted. Add the rum, apricot brandy, Chartreuse, and orange curaçao. Keep on stirring.

Now put it away in a cool place — not the refrigerator — for at least a day to blend and ripen. It may then be strained into scalded jugs until you are ready to use it. If it is not to be used within a day or two add a little more rum to the top of each jug.

When serving the punch put ice cubes — a block of ice is better, if you can get it — into a large punch bowl. Add diced fresh pineapple and maraschino cherries. Strawberries or raspberries may be added if they are in season or a few stoned black cherries, or some slices of banana or of fresh peach. Freshly sliced lemon and orange may be used.

too. But not too much fruit, please. You aren't making
fruit compote! Decorate the bowl with some sprays of
fresh mint.

CIDER AND RUM PUNCH — HOT

Half spiced cider (see page 23) and half this rum punch
heated together makes a good drink after skiing. Mrs.
Appleyard sometimes adds a little raspberry vinegar to it.
Not bad a bit, is the verdict.

TEA PUNCH (NO ALCOHOL) NO. 1

1 gal. boiling water	2 qts. pale dry ginger ale
16 lemons	1 qt. purple grape juice
1 T. tea	Cut-up fruit
4 oranges	Fresh mint
	2 c. sugar

Put the water on to boil. Slice the oranges and lemons
very thin. Add the sugar and pound it into the fruit with a
pestle until it makes a thick syrup with the fruit juice. Do
not pound it too long or you will bring out the bitterness
in the rind. When the water is boiling, throw in the tea.
(Mrs. Appleyard likes Earl Grey's mixture for this, but
Orange Pekoe will do.) Let it boil exactly one minute.
Strain it over the fruit juice and sugar mixture. Put it
away to cool and ripen. When it is cool, add the grape
juice. When serving, strain it over a chunk of ice in a punch
bowl and add some fruit — sliced orange, strawberries,
peaches, and bananas — and a few very thin slices of
cucumber. Last of all add the chilled ginger ale and the
mint.

TEA PUNCH (NO ALCOHOL) NO. 2

1 gal. boiling water	2 qts. pale dry ginger ale
16 lemons	1 qt. white grape juice
1 T. tea	or pineapple juice
4 oranges	2 c. sugar

Make this just as you do Tea Punch No. **1**. A good combination of fruit to put into the punch bowl for this version is freshly sliced lemon, strawberries, and diced pineapple. Decorate it with mint.

Either of these rules serves thirty people, only you have to keep the small boys from coming back for seconds before their less enterprising elders are served. Mrs. Appleyard would be glad to hear from anyone who has a real solution for this problem. She doesn't consider muzzling them is hospitable.

LEMONADE

Mrs. Appleyard and her friend Mrs. Teasdale are rivals in the construction of lemonade. Each dallies appreciatively with a long cool glass of the other lady's beverage, and they frequently say to each other, 'Now do tell me just once more how you do it.' Each is completely sincere but when confronted with lemons and sugar she always reverts to type. It is difficult to get precise instructions from either of the rivals, but Mrs. Teasdale is especially abstruse. Can it be that she does not really wish to give away her secret? She has a good deal to say about how it is impossible to be sure, now that the green glass pitcher is broken and she thinks the sugar scoop she has in Overbrook Hill isn't the same as the Appleyard Centre one. However, spies sent into her kitchen disguised as thirsty tennis players have reported that the formula is about like this:

3 lemons	4 c. cold spring water
1 orange	Ice
1 lime	1 c. sugar

This makes enough for three tall glasses of lemonade and enough to fill them again before they are empty. 'What's the use of a small glass of lemonade?' Mrs. Teasdale says — a very sound remark, according to Mrs. Appleyard.

Put the sugar in the pink glass pitcher (the green one, alas, being broken). Pour the strained fruit juices over it and stir until they are thoroughly dissolved. Add part of the water and stir some more, then the ice and the rest of the water. If you have any doubt about its being well mixed, pour it into something else and then back into the pitcher. (This may be how pitchers get broken.)

Some people, Mrs. Teasdale says, might like this sweeter, but this combination has always been perfectly acceptable to Mrs. Appleyard while the two friends are sitting in a shaded room with a breeze blowing through it on a hot day, and saying how remarkable each other's children are.

LEMONADE WITH SUGAR SYRUP

There are people so prudent that they have sugar syrup on hand in the refrigerator for making lemonade. Mrs. Appleyard is not one of these. The presence of sugar syrup merely inspires her to make a lot more lemonade than usual and have the neighbors in. When an emergency arises she is just where she would have been anyway. However, for those who have the strength of character to make the syrup and put it away in case Uncle Roswell, Aunt

Cynthia, and three thirsty little Haliburtons drive into the
front yard it is a good thing, and this is how you make it.

4 c. granulated sugar   4 c. water

Boil the sugar and the water together for ten minutes.
Pour it into jars that have been boiled and are still hot, and
seal them. Keep it on hand if you can and remember to
make some more when you use it up.

The juice of six lemons, three cups of water, and one and
a half cups of sugar syrup make a good smooth lemonade
that will not be sour on top and with unmelted sugar at
the bottom of the glass. If the syrup is kept in the refrigerator, one or two ice cubes will be enough to chill it. If
you are making a fruit drink to be used later the same day,
shave off the thin yellow peel of the lemons and drop it into
the boiling syrup for a few minutes. The syrup should then
be cooled and the lemons can be squeezed when you are
ready to serve the lemonade. If you have used the peel
when you cooked the syrup, you can use slightly more water
when you mix the drink. This is very good with a cup of
strawberries, crushed and carefully strained, added to it
when you add the lemon juice.

For her final word on the subject of lemonade, Mrs.
Appleyard now reveals to a waiting world the secret of

GRANDMOTHER APPLEYARD'S LEMONADE

Grandmother Appleyard left behind her many happy
memories. She was an unequalled teller of the tales of the
countryside. She could always think of some ingenious way
to use something for a purpose for which the maker of it was
a lot too unenterprising to intend it. She was generous.
The expression 'She would take her dress off her back and

give it to you, if she thought you needed it' will always describe Grandmother Appleyard to her daughter-in-law, who once actually saw her mother-in-law do just that. She had clever fingers. Two bedspreads with quilted patterns of shells and feathers among the pink and green roses and tulips show how skillful she was with her needle. But even if the quilts were not there, even if she had not once broken up an old stove with a grindstone, she would still be remembered for her lemonade.

The big yellow mixing bowl that she used is still there. Into it she used to put:

12 lemons	4 c. granulated sugar
4 oranges	16 c. water

Slice the lemons and the oranges — the thinner the better, she said. Have the sugar beside you as you work and sprinkle it over the slices from time to time. When all the fruit and all the sugar are used, take a wooden pestle and crush them. 'Scrunch' is a better word for the process, perhaps. It consists of grinding the juice out of the fruit with the sharp sugar crystals and the dissolving of the sugar in the juice. Do not work over this too long. The idea is to get the juice out of the slices and the flavor out of the rind. Pounding it too long or too hard will only bring out the bitterness of the white skin under the rind. The result should be a thick lemony syrup that has the flavor of rind and juice but no bitter taste. Three or four minutes of crushing is about enough if you have cut the lemons really thin. If you don't mind an occasional seed in your lemonade, all you need to do now is to put in some ice, pour in the spring water, stir it well, and skim off any seeds that come at once to the top.

If there are city folks around who might be made nervous by seeds, you have Mrs. Appleyard's permission to strain it over a chunk of ice into your best punch bowl.

This scrunched-up lemon and sugar is used in Appleyard Centre as the basis for several kinds of fruit punch.

Around Fourth of July a box of ripe strawberries is always crushed along with the lemons and pale dry ginger ale takes the place of part of the water. Sometimes the added liquid is a third water, a third pineapple juice, and a third ginger ale; or white grape juice may be used in place of the pineapple juice. In raspberry season there are always raspberries floating around in it. Once in a while there are a few mint leaves crushed with the fruit, and there are almost always sprigs of mint stuck into the bowl.

It is hard to specify how many people can be served with this lemonade because there has never yet been any left. All Mrs. Appleyard generally gets is a somewhat feeble decoction made by adding some more water to what is left in the bottom of the bowl. A gallon is supposed to serve twenty people (caterers allow thirty), but as small sticky hands always appear under Mrs. Appleyard's elbow before she finishes serving the first round she is pretty vague about the numbers. She swears every year to make more next time.

For hot August evenings a good thirst-quencher is:

MRS. APPLEYARD'S RASPBERRY SHRUB

2 qts. raspberries	2 c. cider vinegar
4 c. sugar	2 c. boiling water

The vinegar you make yourself by leaving some cider around in a warm place is the best kind to use.

Crush the fruit with the sugar, pour the vinegar over it, and heat it until the sugar and the vinegar are well blended. Do not boil it. Set it aside to cool. Cover it and let it stand in a cool place for two days. Cook it again gently for twenty minutes, adding a little water if it seems too thick. Strain it through a very fine sieve, pouring the two cups of boiling water slowly through it to get all the color and flavor out of the pulp.

Water and ice cubes may be added to this amount of shrub — there should be about two quarts — enough to make a gallon of liquid. The Appleyards, however, like to use it in the kind of lemonade made by crushing lemons and sugar together (see page 28) — about a cupful of shrub to a gallon of lemonade.

Or if the raspberry flavor is to predominate, Mrs. Appleyard crushes three thinly sliced lemons with one cup of sugar and adds two quarts of the raspberry shrub, two quarts of water, and a few fresh raspberries. Ginger ale may be substituted for part of the water. It is a good idea to taste this frequently, Mrs. Appleyard says, as the shrub has a good deal of tang to it and you may like it a little sweeter or diluted further. After all, the person who constructs the drinks ought to be allowed to sample them, as that may be all she'll ever get anyway. To any and all rules that contain lemon, Mrs. Appleyard is apt to add a lime or two if they are handy.

Mr. Appleyard is fond of *Vermouth Cassis*, and he makes it by putting into a highball glass two ice cubes, an ounce of dry vermouth, and half an ounce of crème de Cassis, and filling the glass with club soda. (Mrs. Appleyard wonders if when the Cassis is gone — and it won't be long now — she can't do a little good in the world with some of the red currants by the carriagehouse and the black raspberries by the springhouse. There may just possibly be something in it.)

Fortunately there are still likely to be cranberries, so that Mr. Appleyard can still make

THE MAGIC COCKTAIL (J. H. C.)

This is called the Magic Cocktail, because the formula came from a famous magician to a distinguished surgeon, who revealed the secret to his friend Mr. Appleyard, and gave him permission to tell Mrs. Appleyard, and thus bestow it on a thirsty and appreciative world.

First catch your cranberry cider. This project presents certain difficulties as there is apparently only one place in Massachusetts where it is made. If you happen to take any other route than 128 to the Cape, you are not in the least likely to find it. However, you may be able to get pretty good results with a bottle of cranberry juice from the grocery store. Whichever you use, begin by pouring out a quarter of it. This need not be thrown away; your wife can drink it. Substitute for it an equal amount of pure grain alcohol, shake it up and let it stand for a few days to blend.

For each cocktail Mr. Appleyard uses three ounces of the fortified cranberry cider, one ounce of Jamaica rum, and a dash of lime juice. He shakes it well with ice and when he pours it out, it is a handsome pale pink. There is enough for a 'dividend.'

4

Brides Must Bake. Most cooks like to bake, and Mrs. Appleyard is no exception. There is probably no more thrilling moment than the one when the broom straw (sterilized, of course, in these aseptic times) is thrust into the cake and comes out clean and shining without the least hint of stickiness. Then that wonderful smell just as the biscuits are done and before they begin to scorch — why has Chanel never bottled it? What a boon it would be to a young bride if she could sprinkle a little on her flowered Austrian skiing-folk-dancing-and-cooking apron so that at least she would be a pleasant advertisement for her baking — no matter what the facts in the case might be.

Mrs. Appleyard, like all other cooks who studied in the school of experience, has turned out her quota of biscuits that were better for throwing than for eating. She offers her rule for them with some hesitation because making biscuits, like riding a bicycle, is one of those things that come all at once. No amount of telling how it is done seems to have much effect. However, there has to be a first time and you might as well try it this way, and don't blame Mrs. Appleyard if your husband implies that any members of his family tree constructed them differently. Even brides' husbands' ancestors had to learn.

BAKING–POWDER BISCUIT

2 c. flour	1 t. salt
4 t. baking powder	2 T. butter
¾ c. milk (more if needed)	

Mix the dry ingredients. Mrs. Appleyard always sifts them four times and measures the flour after the first sifting. Work in the butter with your fingertips — or cut it in with a pastry blender if you'd rather — until it is all through the flour in lumps that are almost too small to see. Use an extra tablespoon of butter if you like them very short. Cut the milk in with a table knife. Toss the dough on a floured board, pat it into the shape of a fat pincushion, roll it out lightly not too thin, three quarters of an inch is about right. Shape the biscuits with a cutter and put them into a tin pan or on a baking-sheet. Bake them in a hot oven (450° F.) about twelve minutes.

If they are baked in too slow an oven, the gas from the baking powder will escape without having raised the biscuits. The less biscuits are handled the better, and the emergency kind is often the lightest. These are made with the above mixture, only more milk is added and they are not rolled out, but pushed from the end of a large spoon onto the baking-sheet one and a half inches apart, brushed lightly with thick cream, and baked in a hot oven from eight to ten minutes.

MRS. APPLEYARD'S DATE-NUT BREAD

This is a very adhesive kind of bread. It sticks to the fingers, to the ribs, and to the sides of the pan unless precautions are taken. It is generally eaten slightly warm with plenty of butter. The addition of some cottage cheese and some fruit is considered a satisfactory dessert by the simple dwellers in Appleyard Centre.

1 c. dark molasses	½ c. nuts, chopped
2 c. graham flour	1 c. sour cream
2 large eggs	1 c. white flour
1 t. baking powder	1 t. baking soda
1 c. dates, cut in pieces and floured	½ t. salt

Sift the dry ingredients. This does not mean that the bran is discarded from the graham. It will stay in the sifter, but it must be stirred back into the flour. Mrs. Appleyard mentions this because once one of her pupils carefully removed the bran. She also repeats that she always sifts the flour once before she measures it, then adds the salt and baking soda and baking powder and sifts everything together three times more. Some people add soda to the cream or molasses — probably because it's fun to see it fizz. Mrs. Appleyard believes that the fizzing ought to go on during the baking and not be wasted beforehand. The careful sifting distributes the soda through the bread, and it is all ready to combine with the acid in the cream and help to raise the bread during the baking. Soda and baking powder are two different substances. You'd better take Mrs. Appleyard's word for this or you will get some only too interesting results. (She knows a young lady who thought they were interchangeable. She is the same one

who cut out an opera cape with a pair of nail scissors.)
There is no use going into the chemistry of the matter any
further, because Mrs. Appleyard's ignorance on the subject would probably embarrass you.

Stir the molasses and the cream together and add the
eggs, well beaten. Next add the dry ingredients, beating
them in well. Then stir in quickly the floured dates and
nuts. These may be walnuts, pecans, or — if you are lucky
— butternuts. Put the mixture into a bread tin that has
been buttered, lightly floured, and lined with heavy waxed
paper. Bake the bread in a moderate oven (375° F.) one
hour. This makes one large loaf.

SOUR–CREAM GRAHAM BREAD

2 eggs, well beaten	1½ c. sour milk
1⅛ c. maple syrup	2 c. graham flour
½ c. thick sour cream	1½ t. salt
2 c. white flour	2 t. soda
2 t. baking powder	

Sift the dry ingredients together. Beat the eggs well and
stir them into the cream, milk, and syrup. Beat in the dry
ingredients. The batter should be quite stiff. Add a little
more of the graham flour if necessary. Butter bread tins
and line them with heavy waxed paper. Fill them two-
thirds full with the mixture. Bake in a moderate oven
(375° F.) for one hour, reducing the heat the last part of
the time. Test with a broom straw. When it comes out
clean, the bread is done.

Mr. Appleyard likes this for dessert with butter, powdered maple sugar (see page 82), and thick cream.

Why wouldn't he?

PUFFED MONTPELIER CRACKERS

These are a nuisance but the customers say it's worth it. 'Worth it to whom?' Mrs. Appleyard has been heard to inquire, when in one of her less melting moods, for even she can sometimes resist flattery.

Boston Common crackers may be used in those benighted regions where Montpelier crackers have not yet penetrated. What is so wonderful, cynical outlanders have been known to ask, about an ordinary soda cracker?

To be sure they have no exotic flavor. No one pretends they are Camembert, caviar, or Bar-le-Duc. Yet for all three — and for many other things — they are the perfect background. They are larger than an ordinary soda cracker and at once crisper, fluffier, and flakier. There is a story told in Montpelier that a big baking company in the West once hired away the baker from the Montpelier firm that made the crackers, offered him a large salary, and provided him with everything that he asked for: the specially ground flour, the soapstone ovens — everything that was part of his secret.

But the first batch of crackers was a failure, and so was the second — and so on. They had everything — the money, the secret rule, the baker, the ovens — everything but the Vermont water. Water for Montpelier crackers, it seems, has to run out of those special hills. Out of special clouds, too, perhaps. Snow and hail and sleet and thunder all have their part in it. Maple trees, too, that are powdery gilt in the spring and hot gold in the fall hold it around their roots, and it trickles under the roots of pasture apple trees loaded with pink drifts of blossom, and under pointed firs like church steeples when the snow is on them. It filters through limestone and around granite boulders and slate. It chuckles in brooks where there are trout, and quietly washes a bank where there are freshwater clams with pearls in them, and tells no one about them. It reflects gentian and jewel weed and the pointed wings of swallows. The sun draws it up in straight gold bands behind Hunger Mountain and lets it fall again — and they make crackers with it. Like all other good Vermonters in the region of the Winooski (or Onion) River, the Appleyards always have a box on hand.

The crackers are good broken into a bowl of rich Guernsey milk and eaten with Vermont cheese. They are good split, buttered, and put into the oven for a few minutes. They take kindly to having almost anything spread on them. Mixed with French bread crumbs they make the best cracker crumbs in the world for stuffing, for scalloped oysters, for anything au gratin. In fact the only way that Mrs. Appleyard cannot conscientiously recommend them is the way one fifteen-year-old six-footer ate them. He was the type of boy with hollow legs, and always went off to bed with a large sandwich or two to help him through the night. One night he was heard rummaging in the pantry, but others had been before him. For once everything was scraped clean — no forgotten hunk of Washington pie, no peanut butter, no sardines, no marshmallows — in fact none of those substances that would produce a restful night, either in combination or singly. However, he emerged with his sandwich just the same. It consisted of a Montpelier cracker, split, with another Montpelier cracker in between.

This type of sandwich would be best consumed, if at all, under water, Mrs. Appleyard says. It makes her thirsty just to think about it.

It may seem like painting the lily to soufflé them, but here's how you do it. The materials are simple:

Montpelier crackers   Butter
Ice water

Be sure to split enough crackers. Allow at least two whole crackers apiece.

Put ice cubes into a large bowl of cold spring water. When the water is very cold, put in the split halves of crackers. Have ready some clean damask napkins — the kind that are getting a few thin places in them. At the end of three minutes — or sooner, if they seem to be getting too soft — remove the crackers from the ice water. A pan-cake-turner with holes in it is best for this gesture. If the crackers stay in too long, they will fall to pieces; if not long enough, they will not puff.

When they have drained for a few minutes — five, per-haps — put them into iron dripping-pans and dot them over thickly with soft butter. Dust them with paprika, if you like it. Have the oven hot (450°–500° F.) and bake them until they are puffed, crisp, and golden brown. They should be done in from twenty-five to thirty-five minutes. It is hard to get on too much butter. Always allow at least an hour for the whole process, as nothing is less attractive than a puffed cracker that has changed its mind and de-cided to be a wet blotter. It should show no symptoms of ever having been near the water. If you didn't put on enough butter the first time, add some more halfway through the baking. There is no use making them if you are not going to be reckless with butter. If you are feeling cautious, why not have a few prunes? They might be just as good for you.

BOSTON BROWN BREAD

1 c. rye flour	1 c. graham flour
¾ t. soda	¾ c. molasses
1 c. corn meal	¾ t. salt
1¾ c. sweet milk	

Sift the dry ingredients together thoroughly. Mix the milk and molasses together, make a hollow in the flour mixture, and pour in the other mixture, beating it in well as you do so. Put the batter into greased tins that can be covered tightly. The tins should be taller than they are wide. A half-pound coffee tin of some brands is a good size and proportion. Do not fill the tins more than two-thirds full. Steam the bread for three hours. Be sure that the tins do not rest on the bottom of the kettle; there must be a chance for the water to circulate freely underneath them. Cover the kettle tightly so that as little steam as possible escapes. A lot of water can vanish in three hours and it is important for the kettle not to cook dry. The bread will steam more evenly if you do not have to uncover the kettle and add water during the steaming process. At the end of three hours, uncover the tins and set them in the oven for from five to ten minutes to dry out.

Add raisins if you like them: the Appleyards don't. Half a cup would be about right, Mrs. Appleyard thinks, but her opinion on this point is not worth much. Of course the usual place for this bread is alongside baked beans, but don't forget that when it is cold sandwiches of it, cut thin and either buttered or spread with a combination of butter and horse-radish, are good with any kind of shellfish. If you are going to use it for this purpose, a baking-powder tin is a nice size to steam the brown bread in.

BLUEBERRY MUFFINS

Bakery blueberry muffins are generally trying to make up their minds whether to be muffins or cake. Mrs. Appleyard's are frankly and honestly muffins, and if you prefer the cake variety, ask someone else how to make them. Hers have lots of berries in them and are never likely to be mistaken for currant cakes that have been in a fight.

¼ c. butter	2⅔ c. flour
½ t. salt	1 c. milk
⅓ c. sugar	4 t. baking powder
1 egg	1 heaping c. blueberries

Heated iron gem pans with plenty of melted butter in them are the secret of baking these muffins so that they are beautifully browned all over.

Cream the butter, work in the sugar, and add the egg, well beaten. Put in two eggs if they are small, and leave out a little of the milk. Save out about a quarter of a cup of the flour. The rest you have, of course, sifted with the baking powder and the salt. Did you measure the flour after the first sifting? Mrs. Appleyard hates to keep nagging about this, but feels that it is her duty.

Put the berries into a bowl with the flour you saved out and roll the berries around in the flour until each one looks like Couching Lion seen through heat haze in August. Beat the rest of the dry ingredients into the butter-and-sugar mixture, alternating with the milk. Last of all add the berries, stirring and folding them in. A spoon with holes in it is good for this process.

Fill the hot buttered gem pans two-thirds full. Have the oven hot — 475° F. Bake until the muffins have risen above the tops of the pans and are a handsome tan, punctured here and there with spots of Tyrian purple.

SOUR–CREAM BISCUIT

It is sad to think that there are a great many people in the world who never see sour cream rolled off a pan of milk that has just turned to clabber. Mrs. Appleyard enjoys taking the skimmer that was her husband's grandmother's from the nail where it has hung for a hundred years, and with it removing the thick old-ivory cream and revealing the quivering alabaster below. Biscuits made with cream and clabber are tender and light. Be sure not to get in too much soda. Biscuits that taste of it are, perhaps, appreciated by the family pig, but no other eater for them has yet been discovered. Mrs. Appleyard learned from Mr. Appleyard's mother to use only enough soda to neutralize the acidity of the milk and to add baking powder to help with the rising process. For freshly soured milk and cream the proportions are about like this:

1 c. thick sour milk	1 t. baking powder
½ c. sour cream	½ t. salt
¾ t. soda	2 c. flour

You may need a little more flour than this. The dough should be rather stiff, as it is not to be rolled out and there is no butter to melt in the baking. Mix the soda and baking powder with the milk and cream. Taste it to be sure you have not put in too much soda. If there is the least taste of soda, add a little more milk or cream until you are sure that there is no taste of soda and also that the sour taste of the milk is neutralized. This takes courage but it is the only way you can learn. It is difficult to judge the exact amount of acid in sour milk, and even women who have used it all their lives will, if they depend on luck, turn out an occasional batch of biscuits that taste of soda. The only sure way to tell what you are doing is to taste the milk after you have mixed the soda with it. Or — if you sifted the dry ingredients together and then worked in the milk and cream — to taste the dough. In either case, correct it, if necessary by working in a bit more milk and cream. This of course will make more flour necessary — and you can keep this up far into the night. When the dough is just right, push it off the end of a large spoon onto a baking-sheet. Bake the biscuits in a hot oven (475°–500° F.) for ten minutes.

You may have a failure, but suppose you do? The whole process only takes about fifteen minutes: you can start all over again and next time it will come right. When you once get the hang of it, you will wish you always had sour milk for your biscuits.

POPOVERS

What makes popovers pop is one of those crucial questions that is often asked by the young and never answered by the old — probably because their mouths are too hot to speak.

Mrs. Appleyard thinks this desirable chemical change is produced by starting the popovers in hissing hot iron gem pans in a hot oven, but there is another school of thought that advises starting them in cold pans in a cold oven and letting everything heat up together. Frankly Mrs. Appleyard believes that this is just folklore, but of course she can't stop any adventurous spirit from trying it; in fact she means to try it herself some day. Anyway, the batter is the same. The lightness is given by the eggs and lots of beating.

| 1 c. milk | ¼ t. salt |
| 1 c. flour | 2 eggs, well beaten |

Sift the flour with the salt four times. Add the milk slowly and then the beaten eggs. Beat the batter for two minutes. Pour the mixture into hot buttered iron gem pans and bake in a hot oven (450° F.) for twenty minutes. Then reduce the heat to 350° F. and bake fifteen to twenty minutes longer. Serve at once with plenty of butter. With maple syrup or with hot chocolate sauce, they make a good cold-weather dessert.

YORKSHIRE PUDDING

Yorkshire pudding is really only a popover batter treated a little differently. What is better with roast beef? No one needs to turn up his nose at English cooking until he has tasted English roast beef with Yorkshire pudding — and then he certainly won't. All right — suppose they do have four vegetables, three of which are cabbage. A lot worse things can happen to you than some well-cooked cabbage (gooseberry tart with custard made of imitation eggs, for instance, or, nearer home, doughnuts that have soaked fat, or pale, tough piecrust).

Batter for Yorkshire pudding is made of

| 1 c. milk | 3 eggs, well beaten |
| 1 c. flour | ½ t. salt |

Sift the flour and salt four times. Add the milk slowly, then beat in the eggs. Beat the batter two minutes with an egg-beater. Into an iron dripping-pan pour fat from the roasting beef half an inch deep. Pour in the batter and bake it for twenty minutes at 400° F. Cut it into squares and put it around the beef. Baste it with the drippings from the roast and let it cook ten to fifteen minutes longer. It should be light and crisp and a dark golden brown.

CORN MEAL IN BAKING

Mrs. Appleyard remembers several things about the war once innocently called the Great War with some disfavor. She had an experience with whale meat that she has been known to mention to her family — probably not more than twenty or thirty times (see the Appleyard children's under-the-table notebook for accurate statistics on this point). Whale meat, she says, is all very well as described by Herman Melville in *Moby Dick*. As cooked by Mrs. Appleyard it resembled tough round steak that had been in swimming with a mackerel — all her fault, no doubt.

It was, however, no pang to the Appleyards to eat their ration of corn meal instead of white flour. They liked it already. When the young Appleyards learn to cook, they always begin with:

CORN-MEAL MUFFINS

1 c. corn meal	¼ c. sugar
½ t. salt	2 T. melted butter
2 eggs	1 c. milk
1 c. white flour	4 t. baking powder

Mix and sift the dry ingredients. Add the milk, the well-beaten eggs, and the melted butter. When you start to mix the batter, light the oven and put into it your iron gem pans with a dab of butter in each compartment. Fill them half full of the batter and bake the muffins twenty to twenty-five minutes at 400°–425° F. If the pans are large this makes a dozen muffins. They should be crusty at top and bottom, soft inside, golden brown all over. Honey and butter disappear rapidly in their presence, also marmalade.

SCALDED JOHNNYCAKE

One charm of scalded johnnycake is that it is an entirely different thing according to the pan in which it is baked and the thickness to which it is spread. The first version is a rugged one for hearty appetites.

1 c. corn meal, yellow or white	1 c. boiling water
1 t. salt	¼ c. milk
1 T. butter	2 T. fat — for browning

Put the fat — it may be sausage fat, bacon fat, or butter if you prefer — into a medium-sized iron frying-pan, and put the pan where the fat will melt slowly while you are scalding the meal. Boil your water in a saucepan and when it is boiling hard, pour it over the corn meal, to which you have added the salt and the butter. Always bring the bowl of meal to the stove, never the water to the meal. The water should be as near boiling as possible when it strikes the meal. Stir thoroughly until you are sure that the meal has absorbed all the water that it will take. Then add the milk. You may find that you have to add more water. It is hard to give the amount of water accurately as different kinds of meal absorb different amounts of liquid. The batter may seem too wet at first, but it will swell and take up water as it stands. It should not be thin and sloppy, but do not worry if you have made it a little too wet: it will simply take a bit longer to bake. Do not make the mistake of adding more corn meal after you start the scalding process unless you scald it separately and add more butter.

Now pour the batter into the pan containing the melted fat. Let it get hot for a few minutes on the top of the stove. When the batter begins to bubble up around the edges put the pan into the oven — 475° F. — and bake the johnnycake for half an hour. After the top has crusted over, which it should do in about ten minutes, put some more dabs of butter on top.

It should be a glazed golden brown underneath, rough and brown on top, rather soft inside. Like the cocoon, it makes the butterfly (an ancient joke sometimes served with this johnnycake in the Appleyard family). Cut it in wedge-shaped pieces. There is no harm in putting maple syrup on it.

THIN SCALDED JOHNNYCAKE

Use the same mixture given above. When it has absorbed all the liquid it will take, spread it very thin on a greased cooky-sheet. Use a spatula or a round-bladed knife and wet it from time to time as you spread. Either spread the johnnycake in a whole sheet and mark if off in squares, or drop it in dabs and spread them out in circles. Bake it in a hot oven (475° F.) for ten minutes. At the end of five minutes, put a small dab of butter in the middle of each square or round. The result to be desired is something like cassava cakes. The cakes should crumble in your fingers. They are good either hot or cold.

There are variations. One substitutes a teaspoonful of celery salt for the salt. This gives an interesting flavor that arouses curiosity in the consumer. There is also the trick of sprinkling grated cheese over the cakes during the last five minutes of their career in the oven. Mrs. Appleyard advises starting with them plain. Getting the plain ones right is enough of a trick without introducing foreign substances. If you add too much water, they will be leathery; if not enough, they will not stay together. Don't, Mrs. Appleyard says, be discouraged if the first batch is not just right. It does not take long to make them, and even Mrs. Appleyard herself has been known to throw away a whole panful and start over. In both kinds of scalded johnnycake, rather coarsely ground corn meal gives the best results. It's not much use trying to make it of the very finely ground kind, she says. She adds that the directions seem more dismaying than is really necessary. When you get the hang of it, you can make it in your sleep.

RHODE ISLAND JOHNNYCAKE (S. W. E.)

Mrs. Appleyard writes the name rather hesitantly. She means it as a compliment to one of her favorite states, but she realizes that some of its inhabitants may have some other formula for this most delicious of corn-meal dishes. All she can be perfectly sure of is that a good Rhode Island neighbor gave the rule to Mrs. Appleyard's grandmother and that the resulting johnnycakes have tempered many a cold morning when she was about to start for her morning trudge to school. This is how they were made.

2 c. white Rhode Island meal	2 T. butter
1 t. salt	2 c. boiling water (about)
½ c. milk	Extra butter for frying

Put the meal, mixed with the salt and butter, into a bowl and set it on the stove. When the water is boiling hard pour it over the meal. Be sure it is really boiling as it strikes the meal. Two cups of water should be enough, but it must absorb all it will take. Add the milk and let the mixture stand for two or three minutes so that you are sure it is wet enough. If you have to add more boiling water do so in very small quantities.

The batter should be soft but not wet. Drop it by large tablespoonfuls on a well-buttered griddle. When the cakes look brown around the edges, add a little more butter, turn the cakes, and brown them on the other side. Have the oven warm and have a dripping-pan ready in it. As the cakes brown put them into the pan. A little baking improves them but do not have the oven so hot that it dries them up. They should be a crisp brown outside, white and soft inside. Serve them with anything you like.

Mr. Appleyard, feeling that Vermont and Rhode Island ought to combine their talents, demands maple syrup — and gets it, of course. Mrs. Appleyard, a natural purist, thinks plain butter is sufficient dissipation.

SPOON BREAD

Wandering still farther afield Mrs. Appleyard thinks about spoon bread. This rule was given to her under the name of Southern Spoon Bread. Not having collected it on the spot she merely asserts that this is the way they make it in the southern part of Appleyard Centre — south of the millpond, the elm tree, and the old stage road to Canada. She generally makes double the amount given below in a four-quart milk pan and finds that recent mountain-climbers will not leave a scraping. Probably the quantity given would be enough for six ordinary appetites.

1 c. corn meal (white is best but yellow will do)	1 c. milk
	3 eggs
2 c. boiling water	2 t. baking powder
6 T. melted butter	½ t. salt

Scald the meal mixed with the salt and baking powder. Add four tablespoons of the melted butter, the milk, and the eggs, well beaten. Put the rest of the butter into a hot baking-dish, pour in the batter. Bake until the spoon bread is brown — about thirty-five minutes in a moderate oven (375° F.).

It's good instead of potatoes with either chicken or fish. Serve it in the dish in which it was cooked. You will want plenty of butter with it. If there is no maple syrup on the table Mr. Appleyard will ask plaintively if the sap didn't run last spring. However, it is not necessary to pattern your conduct after that of a man who can eat maple syrup with a spoon from a saucer.

SPIDER CORN CAKE

This is halfway between johnnycake and spoon bread. Like all things made with sour milk, it takes judgment, but if you get it right, your husband will rise up and call you blessed

1½ c. sour milk — part cream	½ c. white flour
1⅛ c. corn meal	1 t. salt
3 t. baking powder	1 egg
¼ c. sweet cream	1¼ c. sweet milk
1½ t. soda	2 T. melted butter

Sift the dry ingredients together. Pour in the sour milk

and half the sweet milk. Beat well. Stir in the egg, well
beaten. Melt the butter in a large iron frying-pan, pour in
the mixture, add the rest of the milk and the cream. Do
not stir. Bake thirty minutes at 350° F., or until it is well
browned.

This corn cake will have a soft layer in the middle.
Serve it with butter and tart jelly — raspberry and currant,
for instance — or maple syrup.

CORN PUDDING

Mrs. Appleyard is slightly confused as to whether this is
a kind of bread or a vegetable. She ought to know because
she invented it one day when there was not enough corn to
go around for some unexpected visitors. Perhaps they had
some theory about it, but all she knows is that they ate it.
In times of stress she has also made it with canned whole-
grain corn or with frozen corn instead of corn on the cob.

1 c. yellow corn meal	3 eggs
2 c. boiling water	2 t. baking powder
6 T. melted butter	½ t. salt
1 c. milk	1 c. corn, cut from the cob

Melt two tablespoons of the butter in a baking-dish.
Mix the baking powder and the salt with the meal, add
the rest of the butter. Scald the meal with the boiling water.
Add the milk and the beaten eggs. Beat. Add the cut corn.

Bake thirty-five minutes in a moderately hot oven —
about 400° F. Especially good with ham or sausage.

Even the scrapings are, among the Appleyards, a subject
of keen competition. They like it baked long enough so that
there is plenty of brown crust on the bottom.

CORN AND CHEESE SOUFFLÉ

3 T. butter	½ t. salt
3 T. flour	¼ t. paprika
1 c. milk	3 eggs, separated
1 c. corn, cut from the cob	½ c. grated cheese

Make a white sauce (see page 251) of the butter, flour, milk, and seasonings. Add the corn and the grated cheese. Then add the three egg yolks, beaten light. Last, fold in the stiffly beaten egg whites. Put the mixture into a greased baking-dish. Set the dish on a rack in a pan of hot water. Bake slowly at 375° F. for half an hour, or until puffed and brown. Serve at once. Guests must wait for the soufflé because the soufflé won't wait for them.

Supper is a good time to serve it — with a green salad and tomato marmalade.

Perhaps this soufflé ought not to have wandered into this section. Somehow one thing led to another. Mrs. Appleyard hastily wrenches the conversation back to

CREAM OF WHEAT SPOON BREAD

2½ c. boiling water	1½ c. milk
⅔ c. Cream of Wheat	1 t. salt
4 T. butter	3 t. baking powder
3 eggs, separated	2 T. flour

Add the Cream of Wheat to the boiling water so slowly that it never stops boiling. Cook over hot water for five minutes. Add butter. Let cool slightly and add milk, flour mixed with the salt, and the well-beaten egg yolks. Last of all fold in the stiffly beaten egg whites. Put the mixture into a well-buttered baking-dish. Dot more butter on top. Bake it in a moderate oven (375°–400° F.) for from thirty-five to forty-five minutes. Serve it from the dish in which you baked it as a vegetable instead of potatoes.

This is also delicious made with hominy but is a little more trouble, as the hominy needs longer cooking. Use about three cups of cooked hominy grits in place of the Cream of Wheat and boiling water.

5

Cakes — and Cookies, too. After baking a successful batch of muffins, it was generally only a matter of days before the thoughts of the young Appleyard novices turned toward cake. No blame attaches to them for this impulse: it is as natural as the thrusting green of the skunk cabbage in the spring woods, as inevitable as the auction purchase by young Appleyard boys of pairs of polished buffalo horns, as spontaneous as the combination of Mrs. Appleyard, a crescent of broken glass, and a tavern table with red paint on it.

However, the impulse, although powerful, can be guided, and it had better be guided toward sponge cake. Before beginning to sift the flour, the impatient cook has to hear Mrs. Appleyard's thoughts on cake.

'Don't make cake at all, if you feel economical. Toast yourself a Montpelier cracker or make some hot biscuits to have with maple syrup, or eat some raisins. There is nothing especially noble about having your cake cover the largest possible area with the smallest number of eggs. It is all right for a dachshund to be low slung, because that is his nature, but sponge cake should rise. If you want your

cake to rise, it's got to have eggs in it. Most economizing on
eggs is done in the country — where eggs are plentiful.
That is because they are taken to the store and exchanged
for some instantaneous cereal that tastes like last year's
mullein stalks and a pineapple cherry cake wrapped in
cellophane and made with baking powder and chicken fat.
This keeps the wheels of business turning.'

Mrs. Appleyard had plenty more to say on this subject,
but seeing a yawn, she simply added in a solemn tone,
'Never put baking powder in a sponge cake.'

Being assured by her pupils that they would avoid any
such social error, she proceeded to give forth her knowledge
on this vital topic.

SPONGE CAKE

6 eggs, separated	1 T. lemon juice
1 c. sugar	¼ t. salt
1 c. flour, measured	Grated rind of
after sifting	1 lemon

Sift the flour and measure it. Add the salt, sift three
times more. Separate the eggs and beat the yolks until
they are thick and lemon colored. Sift the sugar twice and
add it gradually to the egg yolks, beating it in well. Add
the lemon juice and the grated rind. Beat the egg whites
until they are stiff but not dry. Fold them into the yolks
and sugar, alternating with the flour. Do not beat at this
stage. Put the batter into a large ungreased angel-cake tin
and bake one hour at 325° F. After ten minutes sprinkle
the top of the cake with a little granulated sugar. This will
melt and combine with the batter to form a sugary crust.
The cake is done when it springs back when lightly pressed

with the fingertip. Turn it out onto a cake-cooler and let it stand until cold. Loosen it with a spatula, and it will slide from the pan with its own lightness.

ANGEL CAKE

The great problem with angel cake is what you do with the egg yolks. There is Hollandaise sauce, to be sure, but even Mrs. Appleyard, who likes it on everything but ice cream, feels that the lake of Hollandaise resulting from ten egg yolks would be a little difficult to dispose of. Still, it is not necessary to use them all at once, and there is foamy sauce to go with blueberry pudding, and velvet sauce to go with lemon soufflé, and perhaps you can work one or two into custard for chocolate ice cream. After all, it isn't Mrs. Appleyard's business what you do with them. You may buy from the bakery a cake made of powdered chalk for all she cares.

10 egg whites	1 c. sugar
⅛ t. salt	1 t. cream of tartar
⅞ c. flour	1 t. vanilla

Sift the flour and measure it. Add the salt and sift four times more. Sift the sugar twice. Beat the egg whites until they are stiff but not dry. Remember that even a very small bit of the yolk in them will keep them from beating stiff. Never beat them until everything else is ready, because the air bubbles go out of them quickly and it is the imprisoned air bubbles that are going to hold up the cake. Add the sugar, gradually beating it in. Add the vanilla. Fold in the sifted flour. Put the mixture into a large, well-greased angel-cake tin and bake it fifty minutes at 325° F. Do not slam the oven door or let the younger set play leapfrog around the stove while the cake is baking. This might be a good time for them to go in swimming.

When the cake is done, turn the pan upside down on a wire cake-cooler. After a while the cake will fall out. You can put some ice cubes wrapped in wax paper on top of the tin if you want to hurry things, but it is better to allow enough time for the cake to drop out of its own weight.

APPLEYARD CENTRE GINGERBREAD

Gingerbread is a good transition between sponge cake and the more difficult butter cakes. Mrs. Appleyard generally bakes it in two large layer-cake tins. When the first cake is done, it is removed from the pan and placed on the dish on which it is to be served. A large earthenware platter with crinkled blue edges is much esteemed for this purpose. The gingerbread is spread lightly with butter. Marshmallows torn in pieces — a dozen or so — are scattered over it, the second layer of gingerbread is laid over the first, and the dish is set into the oven with the door open. The gingerbread keeps hot and the marshmallows melt while the family are eating their fish chowder. This is a filling dessert and goes well with a meal that is not too heavy. Sometimes whipped cream and shredded crystallized ginger are served with the gingerbread, and there are some epicures who like thick sour cream with it.

1 c. sugar	½ t. ginger
1 c. dark molasses	½ t. nutmeg
⅔ c. melted butter	½ t. salt
1 c. thick sour milk, part cream	2½ c. flour
1 t. soda	2 eggs, well beaten
1 t. cinnamon	

Sift the flour and measure. Add the salt and spices and sift three times more. Mix together the sugar, molasses, butter, and milk. Beat the dry ingredients into the wet mixture, and add the well-beaten eggs. Fill buttered layer-cake tins half full. Bake twenty minutes at 400° F.

It may also be baked in heated, buttered iron gem pans for twenty minutes at 425° F.

CAKES WITH BUTTER IN THEM

Mrs. Appleyard thoroughly agrees with a piece of advice that she read in a French cookbook. If you must use two grades of butter, it said, use the better one in cooking and put the inferior one on the table where people can avoid it. Mrs. Appleyard solves the problem by using only one grade. If you feel you cannot use the best butter in cake, better express yourself in junket, or boiled rice, or go without something else — monogrammed playing-cards or peculiar hats.

In mixing butter cakes be sure that your eggs are fresh and cold. If they are to be separated, keep the whites in the refrigerator until you are ready to beat them. Have your butter soft but not melted, your sugar sifted and free of lumps; your flour dry and sifted four times. Be sure your pans are well buttered. If the rule calls for waxed paper, use plenty. Use a strong wooden spoon for creaming the butter, and a deep bowl. Never mix or bake a cake in a hurry. Cake mixtures are very sensitive to temper and haste.

Baking is as important as mixing. Well-mixed cakes — even of the best materials — can be spoiled by being shoved into the oven and neglected. Never try to bake a cake while you are baking something else in the oven. It would be a pleasant coincidence if both things needed the same temperature at the same moment, but it is as unlikely as a Jersey cow with a wreath of gardenias around her neck. It could happen, but it doesn't.

Divide the baking into four periods. In the first quarter the cake is rising. In the second quarter it keeps rising and starts browning. In the third it goes on browning. In the fourth it is getting baked inside, it browns more, it shrinks away from the sides of the pan. Reduce the heat during the second half of the time if the cake seems to be browning too quickly. It is all right to look at the cake frequently during baking so long as you do not move the pan until the cake has finished rising, and you handle the oven door gently. If the oven is too cold at first, the cake may rise too fast and run over the sides of the pan. If it is too hot, the cake may brown too quickly and split on top. This will also happen if you have used too much flour. If you use bread flour for making cake, take a little less than if you use cake flour.

Turn the cake upside down on a wire cake-cooler as soon as you take it from the oven. If it seems as if it were going to stick to the pan — and that happens to everyone sooner or later — keep calm, loosen it around the edges with a spatula, put ice cubes wrapped in wax paper on top of the pan, and hope for the best. If the misfortune occurs of the cake's coming out and leaving a piece behind, look upon it as a picture puzzle. Remove the broken piece gently with a spatula, tailor it neatly into the yawning gap, and give the cake a good thick coat of frosting.

If your frosting is the uncooked kind, put it on while the cake is still slightly warm. If you use cooked frosting, the cake may just as well be cool.

Cupcakes are easier to bake than loaf cakes, and take a

slightly hotter oven and a shorter time to bake than larger cakes. With these thoughts in mind, Mrs. Appleyard remarks to her panting listeners, you had better begin with:

MADELEINES

4 eggs	½ c. butter, melted
1 c. sugar, sifted	1 t. vanilla
1 c. cake flour	1 t. baking powder

These are small light cakes that are easy to make because the baking powder makes them pretty sure to rise well. Also because the butter is melted and the eggs are put in whole. They are not rich cakes and their charm is partly in their appearance — the way they are frosted and decorated.

Sift the flour and measure it. Add the baking powder and sift three times more. Beat the eggs well. Add the sugar and keep beating. Add the melted butter and the flavoring. Have the cake tins buttered — always use your smallest ones — and lightly sprinkled with flour. Fill them half full. Bake in a fairly hot oven (375°–400° F.) for fifteen minutes.

Frost with Seven-Minute Frosting (page 78) or with Almond-Butter Frosting (page 76). Decorate with candied cherries, almonds, or pecans.

When you have conquered these try:

LEMON QUEENS

1 c. sugar	1 T. lemon juice
½ c. butter	1¼ c. flour
¼ t. soda	4 eggs, separated
Grated rind of 1 lemon	

Sift the flour and measure it. Add the soda and sift three times more. Cream the butter, add the sugar, beat it in well, and add the lemon rind and juice. Keep beating. Add the yolks of the eggs, beaten until thick and lemon-colored, and beat in the sifted flour. Beat the egg whites until they are stiff but not dry. Fold them into the mixture. Fill small cake tins two-thirds full with the batter. Bake twenty to twenty-five minutes in a moderate oven — 375° F.

Frost with two tablespoonfuls of thick cream in which confectioner's sugar is stirred until it is thick enough to spread. Flavor it with vanilla or with a very little lemon extract.

Or frost them with Almond-Butter Frosting (page 76) or Boiled Frosting (page 78). They may also have a small piece removed from the centre and be filled with Lemon Filling (page 75). Cover the filling with the crusty top of the piece that you cut out and dust the whole top with powdered sugar. Properly baked Lemon Queens are level on top. Their consistency is that of a very delicate pound cake. A careless hand with the flour is fatal to them.

CHOCOLATE–PEPPERMINT CUPCAKES

This happy surprise in small cakes occurred because someone once gave Mrs. Appleyard a box of peppermints — the kind that are about the size of a half-dollar, and are sometimes white and flavored with peppermint, and sometimes other pastel shades and flavored with whatever the ingenious makers had in the house. Being — as usual — on a diet, Mrs. Appleyard could not very well eat the peppermints; the children were away, so they were no help.

She amused herself against their return by inventing these cakes. They are simply small chocolate cakes with a peppermint neatly inlaid in the top and rich chocolate frosting concealing it from the public.

Henry James has remarked that there are two different types of intellectual pleasure — the pleasure of recognition and the pleasure of discovery. Of course he took five pages to say it, but that was the idea. Chocolate-peppermint cakes embody both pleasures: the surprise of finding that something lurks in the chocolate ambush and the pleasure of recognizing that it is actually a peppermint, or a pink disk flavored with checkerberry — as the case may be.

The drawback of these cakes was soon apparent. There were favorite colors, and in the lottery of Fate the right customers did not always receive them. This problem became a family crisis. ('Is it fair for Sally to poke the cakes before she chooses?' — 'Go on — change with me Hugh. You know you like green and I've eaten hardly any of it.' — 'Oh gosh, pink again,' etc., etc.)

Of late years the peppermints have all been white.

CHOCOLATE CUPCAKES

2 sqs. Baker's chocolate	1 t. soda
¼ c. butter	2 eggs
1 c. milk	2 t. vanilla
¾ c. sugar	Pinch of salt
1¼ c. flour	

Sift the flour and measure it. Sift it three times more with the salt and soda. Grate the chocolate and melt it over hot water. Add the sugar and the beaten eggs and beat them well together. Add the sifted flour and the milk alternately in small amounts, beating them in thoroughly. Last of all, add the vanilla. If the batter seems too stiff, a little more milk may be added. Fill small, greased cupcake tins half full. Bake for twenty minutes at 375° F. These cakes should be quite level if they are baked carefully. If they rise too high in the middle, cut off small pieces before you put on the peppermints. Cover them with Chocolate Cream-Cheese Frosting (page 79).

Fortunately the tide of family receipts can flow up as well as down. This fudge cake is something that Cicely taught her mother how to make.

FUDGE CAKE

2 c. sifted flour	½ t. soda
3 t. baking powder	2 eggs, separated
½ c. butter	1¼ c. milk
1 c. sugar	1 t. vanilla
3 sqs. chocolate (melted)	Pinch of salt

Sift the flour once and measure it. Add the soda, baking powder, and salt and sift three times more. Cream the butter, add the sugar, beat till light. Add the egg yolks, well beaten, and the melted chocolate. Add the flour and milk alternately in small amounts. Beat smooth after each addition. Add the vanilla. Fold in the egg whites. Bake in three layers at 350° F. for from twenty to twenty-five minutes. Fill and frost with:

FUDGE FROSTING

2 c. sugar	2 T. butter
⅔ c. milk	2 sqs. Baker's chocolate
2 T. maple syrup	6 marshmallows
1 t. vanilla	

Grate the chocolate and cook it with the sugar and milk, stirring until the sugar is dissolved. Let it boil, watching it as a cat does a mousehole unless — Cicely says — you would like to let it boil over and gum up the burner of the oil stove for the rest of the summer. It also has a very adhesive effect on gas and electric stoves.

Cook until the syrup forms a soft ball (238° F.). Remove from the fire. Add the butter. Cool until lukewarm. Add vanilla, and beat until the frosting is ready to spread. Put part of it between the layers of the fudge cake. Cut the marshmallows into small pieces and cover the top layer with them and then with the frosting. Sprinkle a few chopped nuts over the top if you like.

As this cake will all be eaten before you know it, perhaps you had better toss off a little dark fruit cake the next day. Mrs. Appleyard bakes fruit cake in the afternoon when the oven is not needed for anything else. If the spasm strikes her late in the day, there may still be spicy and fruity smells seeping in from the kitchen during the evening.

'Go along to bed!' she has been heard to remark. 'I have to sit up with a fruit cake.'

Sitting up with a fruit cake and a thrice-read volume of John Buchan — *Mr. Standfast*, perhaps, or *The Courts of the Morning* — is Mrs. Appleyard's idea of a nice quiet evening.

A favorite fruit cake in Mrs. Appleyard's family was affectionately known as huckleberry gingerbread. Mrs. Appleyard's grandmother, Mrs. Elmore, used to keep a supply of this cake on hand in case of company. It was so spicy and rich that it was considered good enough for visiting clergymen when they came to supper — along, of course with pound cake, scalloped oysters, Parker House rolls, mince turnovers, chicken salad, six kinds of preserves, three kinds of cheese, and other delicacies of a spiritual sort. One lean and lank young minister who had eaten his way through one of Mrs. Elmore's suppers as if food were a novelty that he had only recently discovered, was asked if he wouldn't take a little something.

'Nothing at all,' replied the guest, raising a thin, ascetic hand, and then — moving it toward the place where the fruit cake rested, dark and spicy under its mantle of white frosting — 'except possibly another slice of your huckleberry gingerbread. . . .'

This is how it was made:

HUCKLEBERRY GINGERBREAD

1½ c. butter	1 t. nutmeg
1 c. milk (or ½ c. strong coffee and ½ c. brandy)	1 t. clove
	½ t. soda
6 eggs, separated	½ t. salt
3 c. sugar	1 lb. seeded raisins
½ c. dark molasses	1 lb. currants
4 c. sifted flour	¼ c. citron, thinly sliced
2 t. cinnamon	½ c. nuts (optional)

Sift the flour and measure it. Flour the fruit with half a cup of it and sift the rest three times with the dry ingredients. Add the sugar, sifted, to the creamed butter. Beat till light. Add the egg yolks, beaten thick. Add the milk or other liquids (Mrs. Appleyard uses brandy) alternately with the flour. The molasses goes in with whatever liquid you use. Add the floured fruit and fold in the egg whites, beaten stiffly.

Bake in a large round graniteware pan, lined with buttered brown paper and waxed paper, for three hours at

275° F. the first hour and 250° the rest of the time. Have a pan of water on the bottom of the oven. This keeps the bottom of the cake from cooking too quickly.

WEDDING CAKE (MRS. APPLEYARD)

When there is a wedding of one of the Appleyard daughters — either real or adopted — the family works for days slicing citron and candied peel and chopping nuts and beating eggs. The cake is baked in a five-quart milk pan and watched over for hours. Mrs. Teasdale lends her electric mixer. Patience Barlow from up the road brings down her cake-froster and begins to think up designs for initials and scrolls and flowers. In short, it becomes a community project.

The cake is eaten between rounds of 'Hull's Victory' and 'Money Musk,' accompanied by pants and puffs on the accordion, and pretty soon there is nothing left of the wedding punch but lemon peel and nothing of the cake but crumbs. *Sic transit gloria mundi.*

This, however, is not Mrs. Appleyard's philosophy. She is all ready to start in on another cake even before the confetti and the paper rose leaves are out of the lilacs. Here's the method:

1 lb. butter	1 c. orange marmalade
2 t. cinnamon	1 lb. currants
1 t. baking soda	½ lb. candied lemon peel
1 c. brandy	¼ lb. candied ginger
4 T. lemon juice	12 eggs
4 T. orange juice	4 c. flour
2 lbs. seedless raisins	½ t. each of mace, clove,
½ lb. candied orange peel	allspice

½ lb. candied cherries	1 t. vanilla
1 lb. sugar	1 T. orange curaçao
1 t. nutmeg	1 t. lemon extract
1 t. salt	1 lb. seeded raisins
1 T. apricot brandy	1 lb. citron
Grated rind of 4 lemons	½ lb. nuts

Get the fruit ready the day before the cake is to be baked. Slice the citron, the lemon peel, and the orange peel very thin and cut them into small pieces. Cut the cherries into four pieces and the ginger into small cubes. Chop the nuts — they may be butternuts, pecans, or walnuts — not too fine. Mix all these together in a large bowl and add the raisins and the currants, the grated lemon rind, the marmalade, and the vanilla and lemon extract. Pour over them the brandy, liqueurs, and fruit juices and mix them well with the fruit. Cover the bowl and let it stand in a warm place overnight. By morning the fruit should have absorbed most of the liquid.

Cream the butter and beat in the sugar. Mrs. Appleyard sometimes uses some of Mr. Appleyard's granulated maple sugar (page 82) for this, but white or light-brown sugar will do. Now beat in the eggs, one at a time. While one member of the family is doing this, another is attending to the flour. Sift it before measuring it, put it into a shallow pan for a few minutes, and set it into the oven with the door open. Stir it occasionally. When it is warm and dry, sift three cups of it with the spices, salt, and soda, and beat it slowly into the egg mixture. Dredge the rest of it — which should be quite hot — over the fruit. If the fruit has not absorbed all the liquid, drain it before dredging it with the flour. Save this liquid and add it to the batter. Now mix the fruit in well. If the batter is too stiff to stir easily, add a little more brandy or cordial.

Line the pan — or pans — with one thickness of buttered brown paper and four thicknesses of heavy waxed paper. Set the pan into another one containing hot water. Have a wire cake-cooler in the outside pan so that the water can circulate freely under the cake. During the first part of the baking, cover the cake with a double thickness of buttered brown paper. The oven should be at 250° F. The cake should rise during the first half-hour. Keep the outer pan filled with hot water until the last half-hour. The top paper may be removed then, too. A large cake — this whole mixture in one pan — will take at least five hours to bake. It may take more. Test it with a clean broom straw. When the straw comes out clean, the cake is done.

Have a cake-cooler big enough to cover the whole top of the pan. Place it over the pan and over it place a pastry board. Turn the whole thing upside down. This takes two people and enough cooperation for the whole Russian ballet. Cover the pan with cloths wrung out of cold water and some ice. It is hard to leave it alone at this stage, and it is hardly human nature not to fiddle with the pan to see if the cake has actually emerged. Don't. It won't help a bit more than it does to dig plants up by the roots to see how they are growing. After a while — and you really might as well take a rest, and goodness knows you will need it — the cake will leave the pan of its own weight, and then comes the fascinating occupation of peeling off the paper and tasting an occasional stray crumb. Better do this alone or the cake will begin to look moth-eaten.

Frost it the next day with boiled frosting (page 78). Make three times the amount given.

Keep this cake at least a week before you cut it.

Cake-baking is an undertaking needing a certain amount

of quiet and concentration. Cookies can be made in the
middle of any hurly-burly that is going on. There is a game
played on the lawn outside the kitchen at Appleyard Centre
that is like deck tennis except that it is played with the lid
of a tin biscuit can. This pastime, with its accompanying
shrieks from the gentler sex and the occasional crash of
broken glass, has often been the background for cooky-
baking. So have the voices of croquet battlers and of those
turning cartwheels, the crack of rifles aimed at tin cans, and
the grunts that go with a form of wrestling known as pig-
piling. Or, if the weather is rainy those who look forward to
dividends of broken cookies crowd into the kitchen, joggle
the elbow of the cook and keep her mind active with a peculiarly searching form of Twenty Questions. It is under
these circumstances that Mrs. Appleyard turns out a batch
of:

OATMEAL LACE COOKIES

½ lb. butter, melted	½ t. salt
2¼ c. Mother's Oats	1 egg, slightly beaten
2¼ c. light-brown sugar	1 t. vanilla, or almond
3 T. flour	if you like it

If Mrs. Appleyard is remembered by posterity, it will be
for these cookies. Here — for the first time, by special arrangement — she tells all.

'What you are trying to achieve,' says Mrs. Appleyard,
'is an irregular circle of lacy crispness brown at the edges,
golden in the middle, glazed underneath. It is no use trying
to skimp on butter or to use the quick-cooking kind of oatmeal or the dark, moist sugar that looks like snow in Boston
after three days. The right kind of sugar is light beige in

color, dry and powdery in consistency. It does not lurk in
packages but lives in a hinged bin, is removed with a generous scoop, and comes to you in an honest brown-paper bag
tied up with string. You can still get it if you make enough
fuss about it, and you can still get the kind of rolled oats that
has not had all the taste steamed out of it and then been run
through a vacuum cleaner. The best brand is Mother's
Oats and if you are lucky, you get a china cup and saucer
with rosebuds in it on the package; though sometimes — to
be sure — it's only a cereal dish.

'Never make the mistake of adding more flour because
the mixture looks too wet. Never try to bake anything else
in the oven at the same time. Don't try to get along with
less than three pans. They should be large iron dripping-
pans. The best ones have been used for years, washed but
never scoured, and have a patina like ebony. These can
sometimes be bought at auction.

'Begin by looking at the weather. It is no use trying to
bake these cookies on a hot sticky day. Make brownies or
sponge cake. The day should be cool and crisp with a few
white clouds high up in the blue. The wind should be in the
northwest. The smell of newly cut hay, the sound of a
downy woodpecker tapping on the apple tree, cowbells in
the distance, and the silky rustle of maple leaves are desirable but not absolutely essential. It is only honest to admit
that, given the right materials and the zeal, oatmeal cookies
may be made against a background of carbon monoxide,
English sparrows, squealing brakes, and the scuffing of feet
on cement sidewalks.

'Get out the big yellow bowl — or that old Bennington
one with the crack in it — and begin.

'Put the rolled oats, flour, salt, and sugar into the bowl

and stir them thoroughly together. Melt the butter. Let it get quite hot but not bubble. Stir it well into the mixture until the sugar is melted. Add the slightly beaten egg and the vanilla, and stir all together.

'Your oven should now be ready at 375° F. Each batch of cookies — there will be about six — will take about seven minutes to bake. Watch them carefully. If they are not cooked enough, they will be sticky in the middle. If they cook too long, they will be scorched around the edge. Never leave the stove. Let the telephone ring.' (Mrs. Appleyard admits that it is largely for purposes of making cookies in peace that she uses the neighborhood telephone up the road.)

'Push the batter off the end of a large spoon with a spatula. Make small lumps two inches apart. Do not smooth them down: they will attend to that themselves. Set your first pan on the top shelf of the oven. Fill the second. Move the first pan to the lower shelf and put the second pan on the top shelf. Fill the third pan. The first pan will soon be done. Take it out. Put it on the table to cool for a minute or two. Move the second pan to the lower shelf. Put the third pan on the top shelf.

'With your spatula test the edge of one of the cookies in the first pan. If it is cool enough — and not too cool — you can slide a pancake-turner under the cooky, holding the spatula in the other hand in case of need. Transfer the cookies to a large earthenware platter. Have enough platters or plates ready so that you do not have to put the cookies on top of each other.

'When you have removed all the cookies from the first pan, fill it again. Keep up this whole cycle until all the batter is baked. If you have good luck and no one comes in to ask you how to play Mah Jongg, or to ask whether any socks came home in the wash, you should have just about enough time to get one batch of cookies off the pan and the pan filled again while the next batch is baking. At the end of the time you should have about fifty cookies — minus any that were wheedled out of you and the ones you ate yourself to be sure you were doing all right.

'Be sure they are cold before you put them away. A large box with a tight cover is the Appleyard repository for them, and they are put in between layers of waxed paper. They will keep crisp as long as there are any left.' Mrs. Appleyard says she kept some once for almost two days.

BROWNIES

¼ c. butter, creamed	½ c. nut meats (chopped)
2 sqs. melted chocolate	1 c. sugar (white or brown)
½ c. flour	2 eggs, broken into the mixture
	½ t. vanilla

Mix in the order given. Spread in a shallow cake pan and bake at 350° F. for 15 minutes. If you shake a little sugar on them just before you put them into the oven, it gives them a glossy appearance that is rather handsome. If your favorite brownies are the thick kind like cake, this is not the right rule. These are more on the chewy side.

DELMONICO WAFERS

These are to the winter season what oatmeal lace cookies are to the summer. They should be made on a day when snow has just fallen and trees throw blue shadows across it;

when blue jays call across it from one frosted pine to the next, and chickadees hang upside down from elm twigs.

1 c. butter	½ c. flour
2 c. molasses	⅔ c. coconut
	1 t. soda

Boil the butter and molasses together for half an hour. Add the flour, sifted with the soda, and the coconut. Boil ten minutes, stirring constantly. Drop in small lumps into a buttered dripping-pan. Bake the wafers in a moderate oven (375° F.) until they bubble. Let them stand a minute or two. Then slip a spatula under them and lay them flat on a cold tin or platter. Or, choosing a proper stage of pliability — this can only be learned by experiment — curl them around the handle of a wooden spoon or over the thick edge of a mixing bowl. Keep the three pans going as described so lyrically in the case of oatmeal cookies (see page 69).

6

Candy, Frostings, and Cake Fillings.
A small sponge cake or a Madeleine responds happily to
being made into a surprise package. Cut out a small cyl-
inder-shaped piece. Use the top for a lid. Someone can
usually be found to eat the bottom. (Swabbing the bowl
you made the filling in is rather a popular way of disposing
of these pieces.) Fill the cavity with whatever filling you
prefer and put back the lid. Frost the top or dust it over
with powdered sugar. Almond, lemon, and orange filling
are all good.

ALMOND–CUSTARD FILLING

1 c. milk	½ t. almond extract
Yolks of 2 eggs	1 t. cornstarch
½ c. sugar	⅛ t. salt
1 c. chopped blanched almonds	

Bring milk to a boil. Add the cornstarch dissolved in a

little cold water. Beat egg yolks light with sugar. Pour hot milk over them, put the mixture into the top of the double boiler and cook till it thickens. Fill cakes or use it between the layers of cake for Washington Pie. Cover with Boiled Frosting (page 78) or Almond-Butter Frosting (page 76).

ORANGE FILLING

½ c. sugar	½ T. lemon juice
2½ T. flour	Yolks of 2 eggs
Grated rind of one orange	1 t. butter
¼ c. orange juice	A little grated lemon rind

Mrs. Appleyard prefers fillings of this kind made with flour rather than cornstarch, but it's a question of taste.

Mix sugar and flour together. Add the yolks of the eggs, well beaten, the fruit juices and rind, and the butter. Cook in the top of the double boiler, stirring occasionally until the mixture coats the back of the spoon.

LEMON FILLING

This may be made like the orange filling above, only substituting lemon for orange juice. Perhaps it is even better when it is made without **any** thickening except what is supplied by the happy harmony that exists between eggs and lemon juice.

2 oz. butter	¼ c. lemon juice
⅔ c. sugar	3 egg yolks, well beaten
Grated rind of ½ lemon	

Put the butter in the top of the double boiler. When it has melted, stir in the sugar, then the lemon juice and rind,

and, last, the beaten egg yolks. Keep stirring until the mixture thickens. Do not leave it over the fire too long or it will
separate. Take it off when it coats the back of the spoon
thickly.

ALMOND–BUTTER FROSTING

½ c. butter
1½ c. confectioner's
    sugar

½ c. blanched, toasted,
    chopped almonds
2 egg yolks

Cream the butter, add the sugar and egg yolks. Add the
almonds finely chopped. Have a few extra to chop coarsely
and sprinkle on top of the frosting.

SOUR–CREAM ALMOND FROSTING

This is the country cousin of almond-butter frosting.
Some consider the latter fit only for city slickers. Mrs. Appleyard remains neutral and simply says that if you want to
make it, you use half a cup of sour cream instead of the
butter, and half a teaspoon of almond extract. It is easier to
make than the other kind because you don't have to cream
the butter.

You may use professionally-made salted almonds, of
course, for either of these, but they are likely to be too salty.
Mrs. Appleyard likes to fix them herself. She began to do
it when she was eight years old, and it remained one of the
few household tasks that were considered suited to her
mentality.

There is something pleasantly languid about blanching
almonds. You can't hurry it. The skins simply won't come
off until they are ready. You keep stirring the almonds

around in a bowl of water with a spoon with holes in it, fishing up an occasional one and seeing whether it is ready to slip out of its corduroy overcoat. As the water cools, you put your hands in bravely. Perhaps someone is telling you a story about a leprechaun. The Boston terrier lies under the stove where the kettle will not boil over on him. Once was enough. The hairs came in white. The mark is like an arrow.

Pretty soon it is hard to tell which are your shrivelled fingertips and which are the almonds. Both are neatly ribbed. Now comes the drying of the almonds between layers of old clean damask, after which you are ready to toss them in butter. (Mrs. Appleyard has always loved that expression — there's something light-hearted about it.)

Put the nuts in a dripping-pan and give them the merest sprinkling of salt. Add a little more butter if you have any doubts about the thoroughness of the tossing process. Bake them until they are a delicate brown, stirring them occasionally in a fairly hot oven.

Naturally the child was not allowed to bake them. That took brains. Mrs. Appleyard thinks that the wonderful range that looked like a combination pipe organ and Early American settle probably produced a temperature of around 400° F. Ah — the mince turnovers that came out of one of its four ovens — the lower right hand one!

But perhaps it would be better not to start Mrs. Appleyard crying into her cup of weak tea with lemon and over her bristly health biscuit. This seems a good point at which to take up a frosting which, being of the mushy kind, is no special temptation to her. It is the young who like to bury their faces in it. They could learn to make it, too, if they would put their minds on it for seven minutes.

SEVEN–MINUTE FROSTING

¾ c. granulated sugar   White of 1 egg, unbeaten
3 T. cold water   1 t. vanilla or other flavoring

Put all the ingredients except the flavoring into the top of a double boiler and beat over boiling water for exactly seven minutes. Remove from the fire, add the vanilla. Beat until the frosting is ready to spread.

For chocolate frosting melt one and a half squares of cooking chocolate and beat it in during the last two minutes.

If the white frosting is used, decorate it with candied cherries, thinly sliced citron, nuts, or a small pool of melted semi-sweet chocolate. Ginger is all right too, or candied lemon peel. In fact the only substances that do not seem to have occurred to Mrs. Appleyard in this connection at some point are raw oysters and French fried onions.

BOILED FROSTING

1 c. sugar   1, 2, or 3 egg whites
½ c. cold water   ½ t. vanilla or almond extract

Put the sugar and water together into a saucepan. Stir until the sugar is dissolved to keep crystals from forming on the sides of the pan. Then boil without stirring. Use a candy thermometer. If you are going to use one egg white, cook the syrup until it will spin a thread that will turn up at the end — 238° F. For two egg whites the syrup must be hotter — soft-ball stage, 244° F. Still hotter for three egg whites — hard-ball stage, 254° F. Remove the syrup from the fire and let it cool a little while you are beating the egg whites stiff. Then pour it over the egg whites in a thin stream, beating steadily. It takes two people to do this unless you have either four hands or an electric mixer. Perhaps this is why many people prefer to make uncooked frosting.

UNCOOKED FROSTING

1 egg white	½ c. confectioner's sugar
	½ t. vanilla

Beat the egg white stiff, add the sugar gradually. Keep beating till the mixture is smooth and ready to spread. Beat in the flavoring.

MRS. APPLEYARD'S FUDGE FROSTING

2 c. sugar	2 sqs. Baker's cooking chocolate
⅔ c. milk	1 t. vanilla
2 T. butter	6 marshmallows
2 T. maple syrup	¼ c. chopped nuts

Grate the chocolate and put it into a saucepan with the milk, syrup, and sugar, stirring until the sugar is dissolved. Cook until a drop holds its shape in water — 238° F. Remove from the fire. Add butter. Cool by setting the pan into a pan of cold water. Add ice cubes to the water if you are in a hurry. Add the vanilla. Beat until the frosting is ready to spread. Put bits of marshmallow before you frost it. Sprinkle the top with chopped nuts.

CHOCOLATE CREAM–CHEESE FROSTING

2 c. confectioner's sugar	3 sqs. Baker's chocolate,
1 small cream cheese	melted
2 T. cream	1 t. vanilla

Mash the cream cheese and beat the cream into it, add gradually the confectioner's sugar and the melted chocolate. Beat well and stir in the vanilla. Mrs. Appleyard uses this on Chocolate-Peppermint Cupcakes (page 61). Sometimes she flavors it with three drops of peppermint extract instead of vanilla.

SALLY APPLEYARD'S FUDGE

When Mrs. Appleyard contemplates a pan of Sally's freshly made fudge, she sometimes thinks that it will be Sally's name that will be long known as that of the *cordon bleu* of Appleyard Centre. The place where the pan is hidden is the oven of a disused stove. This stove, a bandy-legged item with many arabesques in iron upon its ample surface, is not used for cooking because no one living now understands its temperament, but it stands where it has always stood because it has always stood there. Besides, like Lewis Carroll's snark, it is handy for striking a light — especially when there is cellophane to burn up. Also it has a warming oven that conceals shoe polish, rat poison, and ancient tin candlesticks. The warming oven is Chippendale in outline. The real oven is different — Duncan Phyfe, perhaps. A versatile man — its designer.

This oven door opens with a peculiar clank. Fudge, to the young Appleyards, speaks with this voice, just as to their mother it spoke with the lid of a certain box of enamelled Venetian glass. No doubt the clank of the oven is as musical to their ears as the clink of the glass box cover, stealthily lifted by her small brother's hand, was to Mrs. Appleyard's half a century ago.

Whether it clinks or clanks, this is good fudge.

⅔ c. milk, part cream	¼ lb. butter
3 sqs. Baker's chocolate	1½ c. light-brown sugar
1⅛ c. white sugar	⅛ t. salt

1 t. vanilla

Grate the chocolate. Save out about a tablespoonful of it and the same of the butter. Boil everything else — except the vanilla — together in a large saucepan. Scrape it away from the edges so that crystals will not form until the sugar has dissolved. Then boil without stirring until it will form a soft ball when dropped in cold water — 238° F. Take the pan from the fire. Drop in the extra butter and the chocolate. Let the fudge cool a few minutes. Add the vanilla and beat until it will hold its shape when it is dropped from the spoon. Pour it out quickly on a buttered pan that you may have decorated with pieces of marshmallow, candied cherries, and nuts. Crease in squares, give any small boys the pan and spoon to scrape, put the fudge furtively into its hiding-place, shut the door softly, and hope for the best.

HOREHOUND CANDY (MISS J. L. R.)

It was at least forty years ago that Mrs. Appleyard first tasted this candy. The same kind neighbor who made it then sent some over the other day. Time seems to have made her, if anything, a little more skillful at making it.

3 c. granulated sugar	½ t. cream of tartar
¼ oz. horehound	1 pt. boiling water

Cut about a quarter-inch from a package of pressed horehound herb. You buy it at the drugstore. Pour the boiling water over it and let it steep for three minutes. Strain it through fine cheesecloth over the sugar mixed with the cream of tartar. Let it come to the boil, scraping the crystals away from the sides until the sugar is dissolved. Then boil without stirring until it is brittle when tested on

a cold plate (290° F.).   Boil it in a saucepan that has a large
evaporating surface.   Crease the candy into half-inch
squares before it is cool.   Make deep creases.   Make this
candy on a bright, crisp day.   It looks like clear amber and
is excellent when you have a cough or a dry throat — or if
you haven't.

MR. APPLEYARD'S DRY MAPLE SUGAR

When the sap begins to stir in the trees Mr. Appleyard
naturally feels homesick for Vermont, and he brings up a
can of vintage syrup from the cellar.   He takes a kettle that
will hold two gallons or more and pours a half-gallon of
syrup into it.   Soon the house is full of maple fragrance.
When the children were at home this used to be a signal for
them to rush out and fill saucepans with newly fallen snow
— there always seemed to be some in those far-off times — so
that the first dipping from the kettle would be caught on the
snow and run over it in patterns of gold lace.   After they had
reached the stage where they began to think with interest
only of pickles, Mr. Appleyard would pour the rest of the
syrup into a big yellow bowl and began to stir it steadily.
It would change from dark to light amber, then to light
brown, and at last to a pale beige shade.   Mr. Appleyard
keeps working over it until it is in coarse grains.   He likes it
best with small lumps left in it, but occasionally he sifts it
through a coarse sieve and gets to work on the lumps that
are left.   This is for his wife when she is going to use it in
cooking.   The result looks something like a coarse light-
brown sugar, but it tastes of bare maple trees and crusty
snow, and sap running into the buckets, and the sun hot on
your cheek.   In fact, strangely enough, it's maple sugar.

Mr. Appleyard lists the following temperatures for the different stages of the boiling syrup.

Sugar on snow:	
Waxy	230° F.
Lacy	232° F.
Sugar stirred and poured over	
butternut meats on plate	232° F.
Sugar stirred and granulated	238° F.

7

Cheese: How to Cook It, also How to Make It.   Mrs. Appleyard likes the story about the two French peasants who, before the Revolution, were sitting under a pear tree eating pears and cheese.

One said, 'After all, my friend, there is nothing in this world to eat that is so good as fruit and cheese.'

'Hush!' said the other. 'Speak more softly — the aristocrats might hear you.'

Mrs. Appleyard is quite willing the aristocrats should have pheasant and venison if she can have cheese and fruit. Only it's got to be the right cheese. It should be made, she says, of June milk — milk that has young, juicy grass in it — grass that grows when the clouds are high up in the air, when there are fireflies lighting the mist at night under the apple trees, and the bobolinks are chasing each other through the air all day in patterns of black and white. There are wild roses in bloom and Mrs. Appleyard is making potpourri.

This cheese is not ready until October — a month that has many other good things about it. People know the others better than they do about the cheese. Buy a whole cheese. Cut out a wedge. Coat one side of the cut cheese with Parawax and cut off the other side until it is all gone — which will be a lot sooner than you think. Any pieces that are dry may be grated and used with onion soup, or in baked bread-and-cheese. This cheese with a green salad is good enough for anyone — even Mr. Appleyard, who deserves the best.

This does not mean that the Appleyards do not think wistfully sometimes of a perfect bit of real Camembert or Roquefort, that they do not appreciate Stilton or cheeses from Switzerland or Holland. They simply know they are lucky to have a sound dairy cheese where they can cut off a hunk any time. These are some of the things Mrs. Appleyard does with it:

BAKED BREAD–AND–CHEESE

6 slices of bread	½ t. salt
1 c. grated cheese	⅛ t. red pepper
1 c. milk	⅛ t. nutmeg
2 T. butter	Slice of onion

Slice home-made bread, not too thin. Cut off the crusts. Butter each slice and cover it thickly with cheese. Cut the slices into inch strips and build them up in a buttered baking-dish. Heat the milk with the onion and seasonings. Remove the onion and pour the hot milk over the bread and cheese. Sprinkle a little more cheese over the top. Bake it in a moderate oven (375° F.) for about twenty minutes, or longer if you like it very brown. Baste the bread with the milk occasionally. Serve it in the dish in which you baked it. A French casserole is a good kind of dish for it.

CHEESE CUBES

12 cubes bread, ¾ in. square	1 egg
6 drops Worcestershire sauce	½ c. grated cheese
¼ c. butter	½ t. paprika

Cream the butter, add the seasonings and the egg, lightly beaten; dip the cubes into the mixture and then roll them in the grated cheese. Put the cubes on a baking sheet and bake them at 375° F. until the cheese is melted and the cubes begin to brown. These are good served either hot or cold.

CHEESE RUSKS (to serve with salad)

1½ c. grated cheese	1 t. Worcestershire
1 t. salad oil	sauce
1 t. butter	½ t. salt
1 t. dry mustard	1 t. paprika
2 t. red wine garlic vinegar	⅛ t. soda

Mix the cheese with the oil, vinegar, and seasonings. Add the soda and beat until it is light and creamy. Spread it on rusks, or on French bread sliced thin, or on Montpelier crackers. Toast them in the oven until they begin to brown. Good with soup too.

CHEESE CLUB SANDWICHES:
OPEN-FACED STYLE

Slice of bread	A little chopped green
Slice of tomato	pepper
Thin slice of Spanish onion	2 slices of bacon
Slice of cheese	

Make as many of these as you have people. Put them to‑

gether in the order given. Bake twenty minutes at 375° F. — or until the bacon is the way you like it. Beer goes well with them.

PIMENTO CHEESE

1 lb. dairy cheese	1 small onion, sliced
6-oz. can of pimentos	1 t. salt
¾ c. cream	½ t. paprika

Put the onion into a wooden chopping-bowl and chop it fine. Add the cheese and pimentos and keep on chopping. Put the cream into a double boiler, stir in the seasonings, add the cheese mixture, and stir until it is melted and well blended. Put it into scalded jelly glasses and keep it in the ice chest till you need it. This is a good filling for toasted sandwiches. Spread one slice with butter and the other thickly with the cheese, put them together and toast them.

CHEESE BISCUITS

These look like innocent and uninteresting cookies. The plate will sometimes stay well filled until some conscientious guest who has been investigating the table says, 'These are cheese — try one.' The rest is history, and there is no hope that the family will get any for a quiet midnight snack while they are talking over the party.

½ lb. dairy cheese, grated	1 T. paprika
6 oz. butter	½ t. salt
1¼ c. flour	¾ t. baking powder

Sift the flour and measure it. Sift it with the baking powder and seasonings three times. Put the butter in a warm bowl and soften it with your hand. Work in the cheese with your hand until it and the butter are well blended. Stir in the flour with a spoon until the mixture is stiff enough to handle. Toss the dough on a floured board and knead in the rest of the flour lightly. Roll it out gently, not too thin — about twice as thick as for sugar cookies. Cut with a crimped cooky-cutter. Keep the cutter well floured. Bake the biscuits about ten minutes at 400° F. The length of time you must bake them depends upon how thin you rolled them. They should bake thoroughly but not brown.

Mrs. Appleyard generally bakes a sample to test the oven and the thickness of the biscuit and the amount of flour in the dough before she puts in a whole batch.

CHEESE PUFFS

1 c. water	½ t. paprika
½ c. butter	1 t. salt
1 c. pastry flour	¾ c. dairy cheese,
3 eggs	finely grated

Put the water and salt in a saucepan. When the water boils, dump in the flour. Stir till the mixture leaves the sides of the pan. Remove from the fire. Cool a little. Add the unbeaten eggs one at a time, beating hard after adding each one. Beat in one half-cup of the grated cheese. Line a dripping-pan with waxed paper. Put the mixture into a Swedish cooky press and squeeze it out into flower or star shapes. Sprinkle with the rest of the grated cheese. Bake in a moderate oven (375° F.) until they are thoroughly done. It will take at least thirty-five minutes. If you take them out too soon, they will fall the way cream puffs do. Be sure there are no bubbles of moisture on the outside before you take them out.

These are good with salad, either plain or filled with

CHEESE CUSTARD FILLING

3 T. butter	¾ c. grated cheese
2 egg yolks	½ t. salt
3 T. flour	½ t. paprika
½ c. thick cream	

Melt the butter, rub in the flour sifted with the seasonings. Take from the fire and add the cheese and the beaten egg yolks. Cool. Beat the cream until it starts to whip and beat it into the mixture. Keep the filling in the ice chest and fill the puffs only as they are needed. This is only for those whose digestions are those of an ostrich.

CHEESE SOUFFLÉ

½ c. butter	2 c. grated cheese
6 T. flour	1 t. salt
6 eggs, separated	1 t. paprika
2 c. milk	

Make a white sauce (page 251) of the butter, flour, milk, and seasonings. Cook until the sauce thickens. Add the cheese. Stir till the cheese melts. Cool. Add the beaten egg yolks. Fold in the stiffly beaten egg whites. Put the mixture into a buttered baking-dish. Bake in a moderate oven — 375° F. — until it is firm on top. Either set it in a pan of water or put a pan of water on the shelf below it. Baking will take about forty-five minutes. This receipt serves six. The guests must wait for the soufflé because if they don't, all they will get is either a half-cooked layer at the bottom, or some shoe leather enclosing a few weary air bubbles.... Yes, in her youth these things happened even to Mrs. Appleyard. Now the soufflé never approaches the oven until the visitors have driven through the lower gate. That means that soufflé is for those who live within the walls, not for people who come for a single meal. It is hardly worth spoiling a beautiful friendship because someone is late to lunch. Better have something that can wait — like curry — or something you must put together at the last minute anyway — like Eggs Benedict.

Less strain on the nerves because it stays up a little better is

TAPIOCA CHEESE SOUFFLÉ

1 c. milk	1 c. grated cheese
3 T. tapioca	1 t. salt
3 eggs, separated	

Scald the milk in a double boiler and cook the tapioca — which, by the way, you had better soak first for a couple of hours, unless you really prefer it like bullets — until it is clear. This will take about fifteen minutes. Add the cheese and salt. Cook until the cheese melts. Cool. Beat the egg yolks well and add them to the mixture. Beat the whites stiff and fold them in. Turn the mixture into a buttered baking-dish. Bake at 375° F. with water either under or around it for forty-five minutes or till it is firm to the touch on top. Serve at once.

WELSH RABBIT

This is quite generally and correctly regarded as the king of cheese dishes, but it must be made right. Among those who make it best is Mr. Appleyard. His usually benevolent countenance is darkened as by thunderclouds when he hears this dish described as containing flour, milk, tomato soup, or chopped olives. Yet there are handsomely bound books with luscious-looking pictures that recommend all these atrocities. Almost as annoying to Mr. Appleyard is to hear it called a 'rarebit.' It is, he says, a rabbit in the same sense that codfish is Cape Cod turkey, that a Scotch woodcook has hard-boiled eggs in it, that an English monkey is a cheese mixture, and a Bombay duck is a very dead fish that has been dried a long time.

This is how Mr. Appleyard makes a Welsh *rabbit:*

2 T. butter	2 t. Worcestershire sauce
2 lbs. mild, soft dairy cheese	2 t. dry mustard
cut in small pieces	½ t. salt
1 c. beer	¼ t. Cayenne
2 egg yolks, lightly beaten	

There is in the Appleyard treasure house a chafing-dish of antique design. Long before the Appleyards were married, the silver had begun to disappear from the bottom, rubbed off by the stirring of many spoons. It is now all gone and a fine brave blush of copper has taken its place. Mrs. Appleyard sometimes wonders when the next layer of silver will appear, and how soon after that there will be a hole that will send an entire rabbit down into the flickering blue flame of the lamp beneath. It might be any time now.

Mr. Appleyard will not use a hot-water pan underneath the top pan for two reasons. In the first place he feels that it isn't sporting. He says it's like shooting a duck sitting. In the second place, the chafing-dish was once lent, hot-water pan and all, to a church supper, and the pan that Mrs. Appleyard brought home in the redistribution of

wealth has always made the chafing-dish appear like a large
man in a small hat.

So Mr. Appleyard begins by melting the butter directly
over the flame. This helps to keep the rabbit from sticking
to the bottom of the pan. If you have ever washed one that
rabbit has been cooked in, you will appreciate the value of
this suggestion. Next he pours in the beer. When it is good
and hot he puts in the seasonings and stirs them until they
are well blended with the hot beer and butter. Now he adds
the cheese. It was Mrs. Appleyard who cut it into those
small, easily melted cubes. That is not chef's work, and she
is proud to be the kitchenmaid on these happy occasions.
Now the cheese is melting and Mr. Appleyard is working
over it gently but firmly with that strong wrist of his — the
same with which he used to deliver that reverse-twist service
that burned up the grass on the Overbrook tennis courts,
and made many an opponent wonder if he had not better
see his oculist.

During the last few minutes of the melting process — it
doesn't take long because cheese doesn't take much cooking
— he graciously allows the lady on his left to beat the egg
yolks in a small bowl with a silver fork. Mrs. Appleyard,
in the meantime, is toasting and buttering English muffins,
one to a customer and a few over.

Mr. Appleyard accepts the bowl of beaten egg yolks,
spoons into it an ample dollop of the rabbit, beats the
mixture lightly, pours it back into the chafing-dish, and
blends it in with a few powerful swirls. Now he stirs it
rather quickly — the great moment approaches.

'Now! Now!' says Mrs. Appleyard, coming in with the
hot, buttery muffins. (It is too much to expect her to do no
back-seat driving at all.)

Mr. Appleyard takes half a muffin. He dunks it into the rabbit. It emerges veiled in ambrosia and gold, dripping, succulent, ready to go on a hot plate and receive a final spoonful of rabbit. Beer foams in the tall glasses. Major Grey's Chutney circulates around the table. There is a moment of solemn hush. Then — 'This,' says Mrs. Appleyard, 'is one of your best.'

There is enough for six and everyone is happy.

GRANDMOTHER APPLEYARD'S DUTCH CHEESE

People are divided sharply into two groups, both vocal, those who like Dutch (or cottage) cheese — and those who don't. Few are indifferent. If you are one of those who enjoy it, you will like the way Mr. Appleyard's mother always made it. If you do not, you will sympathize with the small boy at Appleyard Centre who took a large mouthful of it under the impression that it was popcorn. Being a child of character, he swallowed it, and having done so remarked quietly, 'It has a dampish sour taste.'

He never joined the Appleyard Centre Dutch Cheese Club.

Grandmother Appleyard always began by scalding a five-quart milk pan and pouring into it three quarts of milk that had never been cooled or pasteurized. She let it stand in a warm — not hot — place two or three days, at the end of which it would be thick clabber, just starting to whey.

Do not try, Mrs. Appleyard says, to hurry this process. If you do, you will produce a rubber substitute as resilient as a ping-pong ball, but not nearly so edible. Probably much of the cream has been skimmed off for cooking, but if it is milk from a Guernsey cow in a Vermont pasture, more has risen. There should be several tablespoonfuls on the top of the pan.

Set the pan in the sink; fill the pan up with boiling water. Let it stand until it is cool. The whey will separate and the curd will sink to the bottom of the pan. Test the curd once in a while. When it feels just slightly rough between your thumb and finger, it is ready. If when it is cool it still feels slippery, add a little more hot water. Pour the curd into a colander. Let it drain for half an hour. If it still feels slippery, pour a little more hot water through it. Add about two tablespoonfuls of salt. This will take out the rest of the whey. If it tastes too salty, pour cold water through it and let it drain. Mrs. Appleyard likes it best when it has that deceptive popcorn look and has ivory shadows in it. The question of how dry it is to be is one of individual taste. The more hot water you put on it the drier it will be. If it seems too dry, add a little sweet cream — or some sour cream, whichever you prefer.

Good with salad, good with fruit, good with crackers, good with apple pan dowdy. Good with about anything. Oh, well — not with banana ice cream, if you are going to be fussily accurate. But *good* (if you like it).

Even those effete souls who do not care for cottage cheese sometimes respond to treatment with

MRS. APPLEYARD'S APPLE–TREE CHEESE

Perhaps another tree would do, but an apple tree with its stout curved twigs sticking out so handily, its low-hung branches, its dapple of sun and shade, is the Cream Cheese Tree, *par excellence*.

This cheese is made of cream that has thickened well and

is only just slightly sour. To make it Mrs. Appleyard brings new milk, fresh, frothing, ivory-colored, slowly to a temperature of 150° F., keeps it there for half an hour, and then pours it into a scalded milk pan. She likes to have at least four quarts. She sets the pan in a warm place for twenty-four hours. By then the cream should have risen so that most of it can be easily skimmed off without getting much milk. She then puts four thicknesses of cheesecloth over a bowl and pours the cream, which she has beaten a little with a fork, on the cheesecloth. Now she ties the cloth together at the top with a strong piece of string. Being a string-saver she has no difficulty in finding an appropriate piece. There is some that once belonged to Hugh's kite that has been helpful for many years. It was Mr. Appleyard's string first.

The cream should be thick enough so that not much will drip through the cheesecloth, but she carries the bowl along through the winter kitchen, the summer kitchen, and the woodshed. Then out into the warm July afternoon and to the Dutchess apple tree, which is reaching out a curved twig just right for a cheese-hanger. If she has chosen the right day — and usually, with the same instinct that makes goldfinches wait for thistledown to build their nests, she has — the cheese will be ready by the afternoon of the next day.

There will have been no blazing heat by day, no thunderstorms, no dank chill at night, but under the apple tree a warm green-and-gold twilight all day, a breeze just strong enough to rustle the leaves and dry the gently swinging bag, only the thinnest clouds across the stars at night. If there is a moon it shines with warmth and softness. At dawn there is silver mist down the valley, and when the sun comes out there will be cobwebs on the grass.

By late afternoon of the second day, the whey will all have drained out of the bag and the cheese will be ready. Leave it another night if it seems too soft and if there is whey still dripping from the bag. Otherwise brush the ants off the bag, take the cheese out, salt it a little, eat it with strawberries and cream, with raspberries, with raspberries and currant jelly, with apple sauce made from the apples that, in August, hang around it. You can make it in August if you choose the right day. September is too cold at night.

This cheese has a delicate sub-acid flavor and is, so Mrs. Appleyard's father used to say, the nearest thing to Devonshire cream that grows on this side of the Atlantic.

There was one interesting variant of this cheese that is not likely to be repeated. Mrs. Appleyard read somewhere that Roquefort cheese occurred because a French workman left his lunch, consisting of bread, butter, and cheese, in a cave and forgot about it. When he went back and happened on it sometime later, the cheese had become Roquefort. At the time that she learned this engaging fact — if it is one — Mrs. Appleyard had some of her cream cheese on hand. Naturally she experimented. She took about half of it and put it between two slices of buttered bread, wrapped it in waxed paper, put it in a dark corner in the cellarway, and forgot about it. She did not in fact remember it until one of her children remarked, 'I wonder what has died in the cellarway!'

Mrs. Appleyard is now in a position to state that Roquefort cannot be entered into so lightly and unadvisedly. However, the cheese was interesting and unique — something like Camembert that had met some Limburger in a bad temper. Since then Mrs. Appleyard has done her cheese-making in the wide-open spaces.

8

Desserts — if You Must Have Them.

Mrs. Appleyard's idea of a good dessert, as has been mentioned before, is some fruit and crackers and cheese. A Royal Riviera pear, for instance, and a perfect piece of Camembert will tempt her jaded appetite. Mr. Appleyard is quite happy with nuts and raisins and a glass of Madeira. Why not?

There are, however, other types of appetites; Mrs. Appleyard knows one or two things that seem to dull their sharpest edges, and feels like talking about them at this point. Ice cream, pastry, and pudding are taken up in their alphabetical place. This arrangement is just a symptom of Mrs. Appleyard's escape from being a librarian. Two of her classmates were once heard wondering why she had involved herself in such a career.

'Probably so she can classify her hats,' they finally decided.

The reference was to a little masterpiece that consisted of a bed of roses with two swallows perched among them. There was also a diamond buckle. Animal, vegetable, or mineral: it was anybody's guess. It was too hard for Mrs. Appleyard and she gave up the whole idea. However, she has never completely recovered from a tendency to file things.

Under desserts she first puts:

CREAM PUFFS

½ c. butter	1 c. boiling water
4 eggs	1 c. flour

Put the water and the butter into a saucepan. When they come to a boil, dump in the flour all at once and stir hard until it leaves the sides of the pan. Remove from the stove, and add the unbeaten eggs, one at a time, beating hard each time you add one. Like women, dogs, and walnut trees, the more they are beaten, the better. Indeed, the best ones Mrs. Appleyard ever made were some that she beat for fifteen minutes. This display of energy occurred because she asked one of her interesting children to watch the clock for her and tell her when five minutes had gone. The clock-watcher focussed on the hour hand. In the Appleyard family the rest is history.

Drop the batter by spoonfuls on a buttered baking-sheet one and a half inches apart. Shape them with the handle of the spoon — the curved metal kind — into circular or éclair shapes. Heap them up slightly in the middle. This makes eighteen small puffs or twelve large ones.

Bake them for thirty minutes at 400° F. and then reduce the heat to 350° F. They are done when there are no longer any iridescent bubbles on them. Watch them the way an eagle watches an osprey that has caught a fish. The puffs will fall if they are taken out too soon. When you think they are done, take one out. If it stays up, take out the rest; cool them, cut a slit along one side, fill them, frost them.

The Appleyards like them filled with vanilla ice cream and served with hot chocolate sauce, or crushed strawberry sauce, or with custard filling and peach sauce. They are also thought well of when filled with Lemon Filling (page 75) and frosted with Boiled Frosting (page 78).

Mrs. Teasdale has been known to fill them with creamed chicken. Mrs. Appleyard sometimes makes them mouthful size and fills them with caviar and sour cream, or with lobster or chicken salad. They are in fact a versatile form of food, well worth the danger of a little neuritis in the arm that whirrs the egg-beater.

APPLE SAUCE MARIE

The inventor of this dish saw the Dutchess apple tree with its full quota of pink-striped yellow apples. She had in her hand a package of Zo — a dry cereal popular with the Appleyards. Zo is rather like toasted crumbs of graham bread. There is a habit at Appleyard Centre of eating this cereal involved with a banana split. Mrs. Appleyard has nothing to do with this bedtime snack, except to watch in horrified fascination while the young intelligentsia split bananas, add marshmallows, peanut butter, three kinds of jam, and anything else within reach and pour cream over the whole thing. It is simply not true that she ever ate one of those collections. She did, however, sample Marie's apple sauce and found it very sustaining on a cold summer evening.

2 qts. Dutchess apple sauce	½ c. seedless raisins
2 T. butter	½ c. light-brown sugar
½ c. Zo	⅛ t. cinnamon
12 marshmallows	

Put the apple sauce into a buttered baking-dish. Stir in the raisins. Sprinkle Zo and brown sugar and cinnamon, mixed together, over the top. Dot with butter. Cover with marshmallows. Put in the oven and bake till the marshmallows brown. Serve with cream or Hard Sauce (page 222). This is a good emergency dessert if you have apple sauce on hand. It can be made with canned apple sauce.

MRS. APPLEYARD'S PANDOWDY

3 lbs. Dutchess apples, pared and quartered	3 c. light brown sugar
½ lb. butter	⅛ t. cinnamon
1 clove	Piece of thin lemon peel, 1 in. square

Melt half the butter in a large granite dish: Mrs. Appleyard uses a milk pan. Add two cups of the sugar and mix well. Add the seasonings. Put in the apples and the rest of the butter in small pieces between them. Put the dish in the oven. When the butter begins to bubble up and the apples start to cook, cover them with biscuit dough, mixed soft and dropped from the spoon in small lumps. When the biscuits have risen, sprinkle the rest of the sugar over them and dot them with a little more butter. Use either the rule for Baking-Powder Biscuit (page 34) or Sour-Cream Biscuit (page 42). Bake until the biscuits are well browned at 475° F. It will take about half an hour.

Serve with thick cream, either sweet or sour, or hard sauce.

PEACH PANDOWDY

This can be made with canned Elberta peaches, though fresh peaches from North Carolina are even better. Mrs. Appleyard has pleasant memories of the bushel baskets of peaches that used to come from there to Vermont. It was a treat just to put your head into the cellarway while they were ripening. A bushel of peaches gives you some scope, especially if they were like those miracles of sweetness. For ice cream, short cake, upside-down cake, cut up in a Sandwich-glass dish, eaten in the hand over the kitchen sink — there was nothing better.

For a pandowdy for ten people use about eighteen peaches. Peel and quarter them. Do not put in any spices but use instead three drops of almond extract. You won't taste it — it just brings out the peach flavor. Make the dough as above, using either Baking-Powder Biscuit (page 34) or Sour-Cream Biscuit (page 42).

When there are no apples yet and no peaches, in the leafy month of June when strawberries are still sulking under their leaves, when — in Vermont — leaves are about the only thing that has ripened, Mrs. Appleyard sometimes makes

PINEAPPLE PANDOWDY

She uses the same amount of butter as for the apple or peach kind, the rind and juice of one lemon, but no spices. She uses two cans of pineapple, cut into small wedges, and

dots a little orange marmalade over the top and stirs about
a tablespoonful of marmalade into the dough. She uses
either Baking-Powder Biscuit dough (page 34) or Sour-
Cream Biscuit dough (page 42).

This dish has some very faithful adherents and so, of
course, has

PINEAPPLE UPSIDE–DOWN CAKE

1 can of sliced pineapple	2 c. light-brown sugar
¾ c. butter	Small jar of maraschino cherries

Melt the butter and sugar in a large iron frying-pan.
Arrange the slices of pineapple in the pan. Put a cherry
in the centre of each slice. Add a little of the liquid from
the cherries. Set the pan into the oven and when the butter
and sugar begins to bubble, pour on the following batter:

2½ c. cake flour	½ t. salt
2½ t. baking powder	3 eggs
1½ c. sugar	1 c. milk
6. T. Melted butter	

Sift the flour with the baking powder and salt three
times. (You sifted the flour before you measured it, didn't
you? Good.) Mix the milk, sugar, butter, eggs, and vanilla
together with the egg-beater and beat them into the flour
until the batter is smooth. Pour it over the hot fruit and
bake until a clean broom straw shows that it is done (about
thirty-five minutes at 375° F.).

Turn it upside down on a hot platter that is big enough
for it. This takes courage, speed, a strong wrist, and a pancake-turner. Serve it with cream, vanilla ice cream, or
Foamy Sauce (page 227).

PEACH UPSIDE–DOWN CAKE

This is made just the same except that the batter is flavored with one quarter-teaspoonful of almond extract instead of vanilla. Halve the peaches; fourteen is the number prescribed by Mrs. Appleyard for that large frying-pan. Put a cherry in the middle of each half, and place it cut side down in the hot butter and sugar mixture. You do this with a pancake-turner. Serve the cake with thick cream, or a sauce made by crushing raspberries and sugar, or vanilla ice cream, or Foamy Sauce. It serves ten and they will probably be languid about supper. You can safely plan for soup and a green salad — with perhaps a few after-dinner mints — soda mints, for instance. . . .

Mrs. Appleyard loves to make these indigestible concoctions, but she really prefers something like

GRAPEFRUIT AND SHERBET

For this she allows half a large grapefruit for each person. She removes the seeds, takes out the fruit neatly and puts it into a bowl with the juice, and adds to it some sugar, a little white wine, some peeled sections of Temple oranges — those best of Florida oranges that are a little like a tangerine, only twice as large and six times as juicy. She allows one orange to two grapefruit. She puts the fruit back into the grapefruit shells, which have been carefully scraped out, filling them a little more than half full. She puts in only a little of the juice. Sometimes she makes sherbet of the rest of the juice herself, adding lemon juice to it, but if she feels both lethargic and thirsty — which is a lot more likely — she drinks the juice and buys the sherbet. Either way, at serving time she fills up the grapefruit halves with sherbet — orange and grapefruit or plain orange, lemon, or pineapple — decorates the tops with candied cherries and sprigs of mint. These are pleasantly cooling, especially if there was curry first.

CANDIED APPLE SAUCE

Again the Dutchess apple is the heroine of the occasion, though Yellow Transparents are delicious, too, and Gravensteins are all right if you have to pick your apples off a fruit stand instead of finding them under the tree in the thick grass or gently pulling down a loaded branch and taking only those that drop into your hand as you touch them.

1 c. sugar	A few grains of nutmeg
1 clove	2 c. water
⅛ t. cinnamon	
12 pared and cored and quartered Dutchess apples	
Thin yellow peel of ½ lemon	

Pare the apples while the syrup is heating. Add the seasonings and the lemon peel to it. When it begins to boil, begin dropping in the apple quarters and cook them until they are transparent. Stand by the stove all the time and keep paring the apples. As you take out one piece and put it into your Thousand-Eye glass dish, drop in another. Make more syrup if necessary. When all the apples are done, there should be about a cup of syrup left. If there is more — there may be if the fruit is very juicy — cook it down to a cupful and pour it over the fruit. Do this long enough ahead so that the fruit will be cold and the syrup a candy-like jelly. Serve it with Oatmeal Lace Cookies and some

Apple-Tree Cheese. Fate will not harm you — you will have dined that day.

STRAWBERRY SHORTCAKE

2 c. flour	1 c. cream, plain
¾ c. milk	or whipped
1 c. sugar	⅓ c. butter
4 t. baking powder	1 qt. strawberries
Extra butter	whole strawberries

Crush the strawberries with the sugar and set them where they will be slightly warm. Never let them get hot, as it spoils the delicate flavor. Mix and sift the flour, salt, and baking powder four times. Work in the butter with the fingertips. Mix in the milk with a knife. Toss the dough on a floured board and roll it out half an inch thick. Cut it with a good-sized biscuit-cutter. Mrs. Appleyard's antique model is square, but there is no rule about this. Excellent shortcakes have been discovered in the circular form. Bake the biscuits twelve to fifteen minutes in a hot oven — 450° F. When they are done, split them, butter them with the extra butter, which should be soft, but not melted. Put crushed fruit on the bottom half. Turn the top half upside down and place it on the bottom half. Cover it with the crushed fruit, then with the whipped cream, topping it with one of the whole berries. Since Mr. Appleyard has strong feelings about whipped cream, there are always two shortcakes on the platter from which this feminine substance has been omitted. (*Note* by Mr. Appleyard: 'We hold this truth to be self-evident: that making a dessert out of cake and strawberries and calling it *shortcake* is a felony. The injured party automatically takes custody of the children, removing them to some place — preferably in Vermont — where their innocent minds will not be corrupted. This travesty on a noble dish is an *agrarian outrage*. It is said that one of our ambassadors to the Court of St. James's taught the English that *cake* stuck together with a few berries and whipped cream was shortcake. If so, this was a fraud upon a gallant and friendly people who have the best strawberries in the world.' — S. D. A.)

PEACH SHORTCAKE

Never make peach shortcake, Mrs. Appleyard says, unless the peaches drip when you cut them. Some other use must be found for those handsome deceivers that are fuzzy inside and out. Perhaps they might be all right for pillows for hay-fever sufferers.

Pare the peaches and slice them rather thin. Cover them with sugar. Squeeze lemon juice over them. Let them stand long enough for the sugar to dissolve. Proceed as for Strawberry Shortcake (page 105).

RASPBERRY SHORTCAKE

Mash the berries with sugar. A few red currants may be added to supply a little extra juice if it is needed. Proceed as for Strawberry Shortcake.

SHORTCAKE GUILFORD

This is named in honor of the young gentleman who, on being asked by Mrs. Appleyard whether he would have peach or raspberry on his shortcake, replied, 'I would like both.'

So he got thinly sliced peaches with a squeeze of lemon juice and a little sugar between the layers, and crushed raspberries, currants, and sugar on top. Also a cloud of whipped cream and a raspberry like a rare jewel on top of that. This started what amounted to a mutiny in Appleyard Centre — they all threatened to down forks unless they got peaches and raspberries too. It's a sort of country-style Peach Melba. Mrs. Appleyard, who remembers Madame Melba, thinks she would have liked it.

MRS. TEASDALE'S POPCORN

There comes a chilly evening, and the mind turns lovingly toward popcorn. It is good any time, including dessert time. Bear-paw popcorn is good. It comes off an ear that is shaped like a bear's paw. Perhaps it is no better than what comes in cellophane, but it seems to taste better when you shuck it off yourself. Mr. Appleyard is skillful at getting the corn off the cob without getting the corn on the floor or the skin off his fingers. He rubs two ears of corn together and the kernels rain into the tin pan like hail on the porch roof. Mrs. Appleyard has never learned the knack, but she can look on and admire. The Appleyards usually pop corn over the open fire, but they admit that Mrs. Teasdale's method produces fewer unpopped and scorched grains. When they pop it for sociability, they use the popper. When they are going to use it for dessert, they imitate Mrs. Teasdale.

She puts the corn into a big saucepan with a cover that can be clamped down tight. She puts in only enough corn to cover the bottom of the pan and a generous lump of butter — about one and a half tablespoonfuls for a three-

quart pan. Then she begins to shake it over a hot fire —
the top of a coal stove, a gas burner, or an oil stove — anything that produces plenty of heat. Popcorn has to be sur-
prised into exploding. Soon comes the first faint pop and a
grain hits the top of the kettle. She keeps on shaking until
no noise of popping is heard. She lets it stand a minute or
two before she takes off the cover, because she claims that
makes it more crisp and tender than if it cools too quickly.

The Appleyards have been known to eat it for dessert
with maple syrup, chocolate sauce, molasses, or cream.
It's good with soup, too, instead of crackers — which is
Mrs. Appleyard's favorite use for it.

9

Eggs: the Good Mixers. No one has yet really decided that controversy about whether the hen or the egg came first. If it was the hen, there must surely have been a bleak period before the first eggs were laid. Mrs. Appleyard has often wondered who it was that first discovered that you could separate the yolk and the white and that when beaten, the white would turn to snow. Her opinion is that it was a woman, and she rates the invention considerably higher than bombs on wings and poison gas.

An egg is like those people who are not witty themselves but the cause of wit in others. Alone, there is nothing very exciting about it — except perhaps when it is boiled and you chip the shell, not knowing just how soft-boiled it is. But how it combines with other things...

> With hot buttered toast, with ham!
> With mushrooms, with cream, with jam!
> With chives and cheese — and to cram
> With all except cold roast lamb!

Excuse it, please... Mrs. Appleyard merely means to say that among the infinite variety of egg dishes that she could think up between now and supper, she will mention only a few, because the topic is well covered by almost everyone that ever wrote about cooking.

EGG RING WITH MUSHROOMS

4 eggs	¼ t. salt
2 c. rich milk	⅛ t. paprika

Beat the eggs well, add the milk, salt, and paprika. Butter a ring mould. Cover it, set it in a pan full of hot water. Bake it in a slow oven — 300° F. — till it is firm. It should be done in about thirty minutes, or when a knife blade stuck into the middle of the custard comes out clean.

Serve with Mushroom Sauce (page 257) in the centre.

EGGS IN RAMEKINS

A beautiful set of porcelain ramekins is one of Mrs. Appleyard's proudest possessions. She treasures them so tenderly that for six months she served devilled ham at practically every meal so that she could get enough of the vermilion jars in which her favorite brand comes. She needed them to bake eggs in, she said, when questioned about a certain monotony in her menus.

This is simple and pleasant to do as soon as you have acquired the red jars. All you need is eggs, butter, chives, cheese, cream, and salt.

Butter each jar, leaving a half-teaspoonful of butter in the bottom. Mix the chives, finely cut, the cream, grated cheese, and seasonings. Put a little of the mixture in each jar, break in the eggs, cover them with the rest of the mixture. Set the jars in a pan of hot water and bake them at 300° F. until the whites of the eggs are set. Serve thin slices of freshly made buttered toast with them. The guests may eat the toast in their fingers and try to get the egg out of the jar with the implements provided. (No one ever supplies a vacuum cleaner, unfortunately.) Or, if they are practical, they will spoon the whole thing onto the toast and go on from there.

A few tips of fresh asparagus, cooked, are good worked into this mixture.

SPAGHETTI, EGGS, AND CHEESE

Boil the spaghetti ten minutes. Hard-boil the eggs and slice them. Place slices of large ripe tomatoes, dotted with butter, under the broiler for a few minutes. Chop a large onion very fine, add it to two cups of Cheese Sauce (page 254).

Drain the spaghetti, put it on a fireproof platter. Lay the tomatoes on the spaghetti. Spread the egg slices with devilled ham and put them between the tomatoes. Cover the whole thing with the cheese sauce. Sprinkle with paprika. Put it under the broiler for a minute. Serve it right away. It was in her devilled-ham period that Mrs. Appleyard invented this — obviously: it takes two jars.

EGGS BENEDICT

It takes three people to make these, but that is no reason for not having them at home — rather the reverse.

> 6 eggs
> 3 English muffins, split, toasted, buttered
> 6 slices of baked ham, cut to fit the muffins
> Hollandaise sauce (page 255)
> A sliced truffle, or 6 mushroom caps, grilled

One of the team toasts the muffins. Another poaches the

eggs in rings the size of the muffins. The third — that large lady in the smock made out of a certain number of red bandanas; why, yes, it *is* Mrs. Appleyard — makes the Hollandaise. She has the ham ready and also the mushrooms or truffles.

Put the ham on the muffins, the eggs on the ham, the Hollandaise over the eggs, the mushrooms on top. All right — everyone may sit down now.

CURRIED EGGS

That last was pretty exhausting. Mrs. Appleyard will take up the subject of curry intensively when she feels equal to dealing with a whole chicken and a flock of relish dishes. At present all she cares to say is that when chickens are scarce, eggs are a great help. You hard-boil them and make Curry Sauce (page 163), using canned chicken soup if you have no chicken stock on hand. If your rice is well cooked (page 163) and you have plenty of relishes — especially chutney — this is a very good substitute for chicken curry.

EGGS AND SPINACH

1 box of frosted spinach, cooked	1 t. grated onion
6 eggs	½ t. salt
A few grains of nutmeg	2 T. butter
¼ t. paprika	Grated cheese

Divide the cooked spinach into six portions and put each one into a small buttered baking-dish. The Mexican kind is good for this purpose. Season the spinach with the nutmeg, salt, pepper, and onion. Make a depression in the spinach, put a lump of butter in it, and put the egg in on top of the butter. Cover the egg thickly with grated cheese and dot it with butter and sprinkle with paprika. Set the dishes into a pan of hot water and bake them in a slow oven (300° F.) until the whites of the eggs are set — about twenty minutes.

STUFFED EGGS IN ASPIC

Here's another use for that devilled ham.

Aspic is, in the professional cookbooks, a word that they use to frighten young housewives with, so that they run and hide in the delicatessen. This terror is unnecessary if they supply themselves with the kind of consommé that jellies in the can, and the more amiable sort of can-opener. These eggs are good either in a ring mould or in individual moulds. Whichever you use, begin by rinsing the moulds with cold water.

2 cans of consommé	2 oz. devilled ham
6 hard-boiled eggs	12 stuffed olives
Finely cut chives	2 T. cream
2 pimentos	

While the eggs are cooking, heat the consommé slightly and pour a little of it into the bottom of the moulds and set them in the refrigerator. Shell the eggs. Cut them in halves. Take out the yolks and mash them with the ham and the chives. Moisten them with the cream — or mayonnaise if you prefer. Fill the egg whites with this mixture. Keep what is left over in the ice chest for sandwich filling. Put the halves of the eggs together again and wrap a thin strip of pimento around them to conceal the cut place. By the time you have performed this bit of first aid, the consommé in the moulds ought to have stiffened a little. Put a slice of stuffed olive at the bottom of the mould, the egg on it and the rest of the sliced olives around it, and pour the rest of the consommé over the eggs so that they are covered and the mould is full.

If you use a ring mould, when you unmould it fill the middle with a green salad that has watercress in it, and decorate it with radish roses. If the eggs are in individual moulds, turn them out on plates and put some green salad beside them. Russian Dressing (page 243) is good with this kind of salad. It is a good deal easier to unmould six small aspics than to get a large one out of a ring without any catastrophe. Don't say Mrs. Appleyard didn't tell you.

EGGS AND BACON AND CHEESE

After all, one of the happiest affinities in the world was not between Antony and Cleopatra but between bacon and eggs.

'Butter a shirred-egg dish,' Mrs. Appleyard says, 'slide an egg into it — preferably a large brown egg, unless you are a New Yorker. It seems hard enough to be a Yorker without having to eat white eggs besides, but then everyone has his burden. There are Yorkers no doubt' — Mrs. Appleyard omits the customary adjective — 'who are not a bit interested in brown eggs, or about Vermont's being a republic in the eighteenth century, and declaring war on Germany in September, 1941.' It must be a little dull, Mrs. Appleyard thinks, to live in a place where you don't get into an argument with a total stranger on the other side of a hotel dining-room just by quoting something Ethan Allen said at Ticonderoga — but doubtless there are compensations. Mrs. Appleyard had some very good broiled kidneys in New York about twenty years ago and some excellent chicken soup some fifteen years later. Perhaps not so good as Hartwell Farm's chicken soup, but a praiseworthy effort. . . .

Let's see — wasn't she cooking some eggs?

'Having put the egg into the buttered dish,' she continues, 'lay four thin strips of bacon across it in a square, sprinkle it thickly with grated cheese, dust it with paprika and a little salt. Put the dishes into a fairly hot oven — 375° F. — and bake until the whites of the eggs are set. If you have the type of personality that demands very crisp bacon, better cook it a little beforehand.'

10

Fish: Shell and Otherwise. For people who never live somewhere near the sea, Mrs. Appleyard has a profound pity. Fortunately most of the inland dwellers do not need the pity because they do not know what they are missing. Fish that has to travel on ice for days is satisfactory to them, and that is quite all right with Mrs. Appleyard so long as she doesn't have to have any of it.

'Eastern' lobster pursues the traveller across the continent and is even offered as a great delicacy on the Pacific coast, Mrs. Appleyard discovered recently. She had to use considerable ingenuity to avoid it and to get chili con carne instead. She believes in eating the food of the country where she happens to be. The food of Kansas, for instance, is definitely not lobster, but Mrs. Appleyard had a steak in Kansas once that was a pattern by which all steaks, past and future, will be judged. Lobster she does not care to eat much farther west than Durgin-Park's.

She clings to this prejudice in spite of the malicious story about any cargo of lobsters that comes to Boston. The real fighters, so runs this myth, are sent to Los Angeles. Fairly active ones go to Denver. If they can still crawl, they are sent to Chicago, and if they are so limp that their tails barely snap when pulled, they are kept in Boston.

Mrs. Appleyard, who was brought up in the summer on an island in Frenchman's Bay, a happy paradise where a lobster car in the cove was as essential a piece of furniture as the table for twelve around which the lobster was eaten, here firmly asserts that next best to lobster out of your own lobster car is lobster out of any other Maine lobster car, and that next best to that is lobster from the Boston market.

One of the best ways to eat lobster is a way almost no one ever does eat it outside its own haunts; and that is plain boiled, just as it comes out of the kettle, with plenty of butter to dip the pink-and-white chunks into as you pry them out. No buttery crumbs, no chopped-up mushrooms, distract your attention. Oh, possibly a few hot Parker House rolls, and afterward perhaps some wild strawberries and cream and a hunk of chocolate layer cake — nothing elaborate. Mr. and Mrs. Appleyard went to a Maine island on their wedding trip and that was what they had to eat for supper every evening. With such a beginning it is no wonder that Mrs. Appleyard has enjoyed married life.

Cold boiled lobster with melted butter is good too, if you don't happen to be around when it's hot, Mrs. Appleyard says. Only you must see the lobster brought up from the shore in a basket, squirming and fighting and snapping with its green-bronze claws. Otherwise it's all right to eat it à la Newburg or even in cutlets, with Mrs. Appleyard's kind approval.

No one who has ever lived by the sea feels quite at home when fish comes out of a can. The first thing these exiles ask for on coming home is fish. When Hugh came in from the West the other day, Mr. and Mrs. Appleyard did not even wait until they got him out of the South Station, but rushed him into the oyster bar and revived him with a dozen freshly opened raw oysters. It was pleasant to see the color flow back into the boy's pale cheeks and the sparkle return to his lustreless eyes.

Oyster stew can sometimes be used in such cases with a fortunate effect. Here is how Mrs. Appleyard makes it.

OYSTER STEW

Allow at least eight oysters to a person. The more recently they are opened, the better the stew is.

1 qt. oysters	2 c. cream
4 c. milk	½ T. salt
½ c. butter	¼ t. pepper

Clean the oysters by putting them into a colander that is standing in a saucepan and pouring three-fourths of a cup of cold water through them. Strain the liquid in the pan through cheesecloth into another pan large enough to hold the stew when it is finished. Add the butter and seasonings and bring it to the boiling point. In the meantime in another saucepan, scald the milk and the cream.

As soon as the oyster liquor is boiling add the oysters and cook them gently until they begin to curl around the edges. Get the milk and cream as hot as you can without scorching it. If your nerves are of the tense sort, you can heat it in the double boiler. Many a good batch of oysters has been ruined by a suggestion of scorched hay in the milk department.

As soon as the oysters are ready, pour the hot milk over them. Have your tureen and its cover hot, pour the stew into it. Serve with it oyster crackers or — popular with the

Appleyards — pilot biscuit that have been buttered and put into the oven until the butter froths and the crackers just start to brown.

This is enough stew for four people who like stew. You could serve more people with this amount, if some of them were indifferent to its charms, but why waste it on them? The rest of the meal is not important, though perhaps by dessert time they will be ready for some pumpkin pie.

MRS. APPLEYARD'S OYSTER, MUSHROOM, AND CELERY SOUP

1 qt. of oysters	⅓ c. flour
1 bunch Pascal celery	½ t. paprika
⅛ t. nutmeg	2 c. cream
1 t. chopped parsley	1 small onion
⅛ t. pepper	½ c. butter
4 c. milk	1 t. salt
1 lb. mushrooms	2 T. white wine
Bit of bay leaf	

There is some doubt in Mrs. Appleyard's mind as to whether this prescription had better go with soup or with fish, but as it has leaped into her mind with oysters, and as it is one of those hearty soups that can be the main dish for supper or luncheon, she has decided to speak of it here.

Cook the celery until it is soft enough to put through a fine sieve. Save the juice. Chop the onion fine. Peel the mushrooms. Use only the caps, which should be cut rather fine. Save the stems and skins for soup stock for another day. Wash the oysters as for Oyster Stew (see page 118) and save the liquor.

Fry the onion slowly in the butter until it begins to soften. Add the mushrooms and cook until they are tender

— about five minutes. Remove them from the pan and rub in the flour: add a little more butter if necessary but be sure it froths before you put in any flour. When the butter and flour have cooked together gently for three minutes, work in the cream and milk slowly, and add the seasonings. When the sauce thickens, add the mushrooms, the celery purée and juice. Set the pan where it will keep warm until you are ready to finish the soup. This first part may be done some time beforehand. When you are ready to serve the meal, heat up the oyster liquor and cook the oysters in it until their edges curl. Do this in a saucepan big enough to hold all the soup. As soon as the oysters are ready pour in the first mixture. Stir thoroughly, add the white wine, and put the soup into your hot tureen. Sprinkle the chopped parsley over the top. Croutons are nice with this — or oyster crackers.

Oysters and lobsters are happy together in the same dish and are good with other fish in

MRS. APPLEYARD'S SEA FOOD

1 lb. fresh crab meat	2 c. oyster liquor
1 qt. oysters	2 c. scallop liquor
1 qt. Cape scallops	1 qt. heavy cream
Meat from a 2-lb. lobster	2 c. rich milk
1 lb. mushroom caps, quartered	½ c. white wine
	2 egg yolks, beaten
1 green pepper, cut fine	Bit of bay leaf
	¼ t. nutmeg
1 small onion, finely minced	1 T. salt
	½ t. paprika
½ c. butter	⅛ t. cayenne
½ c. flour	¼ t. pepper

Fry the minced onion in the butter, add the mushrooms

and cook until they are tender. Remove them while you blend in the flour, sifted with the seasonings, and work in the milk and the cream. Put them back and add the lobster, crab meat, and the green pepper. Now set the pan where it will keep warm until serving time. Clean the oysters and scallops by pouring two cups of cold water through them and strain the liquor.

Just as you are ready to serve the sea food, bring the strained liquor to a boil and cook the scallops and oysters in it until the edges of the oysters begin to curl. Do this in a kettle large enough to hold all the sea food. The scallops, like oysters, should not be overcooked, and by a wise arrangement of Providence they both take about three minutes. As soon as they are ready, stir in the first mixture, stirring it well. Add the wine and the egg yolks. Beat them with a fork, stir in a little of the sauce, and then stir them back into the sauce in the kettle. This distributes the eggs more evenly through the sauce than you can do in any other way.

Be sure that no real cooking goes on after the addition of the wine and the eggs, or your sauce will separate. If you have chafing-dishes with hot-water pans, they are ideal for serving sea food, but it may also be served from a large, hot soup tureen, or from covered casseroles. It does not matter so long as the dish is hot, and will keep hot for a reasonable length of time.

While you are cooking sea food, have some extra cream and rich milk on hand so that you can add it if the sauce seems too thick. There ought to be plenty of sauce. If you have to add more cream, you had better put in a little more wine, too, and some extra seasonings. Be sure to taste the sauce as you go along, Mrs. Appleyard says: that's part of the fun. She also warns you not to forget to take out the bay leaf before you serve any sauce or soup that you put it into. Her face turned slightly pink when it was called to her attention that she had never said when it went into the sea food.

'The bay leaf always goes in with the milk,' said Mrs. Appleyard, 'and I don't intend to keep harping on it. Cooks mustn't be pampered all the time or they won't learn anything.'

This seems a little late for Mrs. Appleyard to take such an attitude, but it is probably only a phase.

French bread, cut about three-fourths of an inch thick, toasted and buttered, goes well with sea food, she says. Neat triangles of bread with the crusts cut off and toasted look more ladylike, and on that ground alone are generally rejected by Mrs. Appleyard. She never feels very refined after she has made a kettle of sea food, and has an appetite like a snapping turtle's.

BAKED OYSTERS

Allow six oysters apiece for these. Buy them in their shells. Your fish man will open them for you and fasten them together again.

Shallow Pyrex dishes are good for this if you have some large enough to hold six oyster shells. They take up more room than you think. You must have a dish for each person. Fill the dishes with coarse rock salt and set them in the oven to heat. For four people take

24 oysters on the deep shell	¼ lb. butter
	½ c. French bread crumbs
2 T. onion	1 T. minced parsley

1 bean garlic
2 slices bacon
Juice of 1 lemon
6 drops Worcester-
shire sauce

2 T. white wine
½ t. salt
¼ t. black pepper
⅛ t. red pepper

Dry several thin slices of French bread in a slow oven, crumble and pound it into fine crumbs. Use crust and all. In a saucepan melt part of the butter and cook the onion, finely minced with the garlic, in it slowly until the onion is a pale straw color. Put in the lemon juice and the seasonings, and stir well. Add the wine and the bread crumbs. Add a little more wine if the mixture seems too dry, but do not get it wet and mushy. Now sink the oysters on their deep shells into the salt that you have heated in the pans. Be careful not to spill the oyster juice. Cover each oyster with the buttered crumbs. Sprinkle with parsley or with minced chives if you prefer, and put small squares of the bacon on top. Bake them ten minutes at 500° F.

Layer-cake tins will do if you have no glass dishes. When serving them, set them on dishes that are fireproof. Those dishes of salt are *hot*.

These are something like Oysters Rockefeller, but without the absinthe. Even if Mrs. Appleyard knew how to make a sauce out of absinthe and spinach she would think it only right to let concealment prey upon her damask cheek, like a termite in a beam. She really likes scalloped oysters better anyway. Why, she wonders, do cookbooks say 'escalloped'? Probably for the same reason that some people stick out their little fingers when holding a water glass. . . .

SCALLOPED OYSTERS

1 qt. oysters
½ c. oyster liquor,
  strained
2 T. cream
2 T. sherry
½ c. melted butter

1 c. Montpelier cracker
  crumbs
1 c. French bread crumbs
½ t. salt
¼ t. pepper
⅛ t. nutmeg

Roll the Montpelier crackers fine. (Oh, all right — common crackers if that's all you have.) Dry some slices of French bread in a slow oven. Pound the crust and all into crumbs. Mix with the cracker crumbs. Add the seasonings and mix well. Stir in the butter, cream, sherry, and oyster liquor. Do not get the mixture too wet. The oysters themselves supply some moisture. Butter a shallow Pyrex glass baking-dish, put a thin layer of the crumb mixture into the bottom of the dish, then half the oysters. Cover them with more of the crumb mixture, put in the rest of the oysters, cover them with the rest of the crumbs. Dot with a little more butter. Bake for thirty minutes at 400° F.

Scalloped oysters should never consist of more than two layers of oysters. If you use more layers the middle layers will still be half-raw when the top and bottom layers are properly cooked, or else the middle layers will be right and the outer ones tough. There are two sad results that wrong timing can produce: undercooking — and also too many bread crumbs and too much liquid — all tend to make a singularly unattractive form of poultice; overcooking — especially when combined with too little liquid, too little butter, and too large a proportion of cracker crumbs — may enliven the meal with a dish of sawdust containing some frizzled-up gray objects that may be either oysters or the children's old mittens.

OYSTERS AND MUSHROOMS

Scalloped oysters may be varied by making them with half oysters and half mushrooms. Use a little extra butter and fry the peeled and sliced mushroom caps in it, and also a little grated onion, until the mushrooms are tender. Prepare the crumbs as for scalloped oysters, put in half the oysters and half the mushrooms in each of the two layers, cover them with a layer of crumbs, and bake until the crumbs are brown.

HADDOCK

Life, however, cannot be all lobster and oysters. Consider the humble haddock an uninteresting fish when fried in large chunks, but one that responds cheerfully to kind treatment. It used to appear, on that island of which Mrs. Appleyard has already spoken, under the name of Turbot à la crême. During her innocent youth Mrs. Appleyard thought it was all one word and the name of a separate fish. Pronounced rapidly it is certainly a very stylish name, but the dish is still all right if you call it

SCALLOPED HADDOCK

A 5-lb. haddock, cut for chowder	½ t. white pepper
3 c. milk	1 t. thyme
1 c. cream	¾ c. butter
½ c. flour	1 t. salt
½ t. minced parsley	½ c. cracker crumbs
1 onion, finely minced	½ c. French bread crumbs
2 egg yolks	¼ c. grated cheese

Boil the haddock. There is more flavor to the haddock if

you boil the head with it and throw it away later instead of
beforehand. You need not, so far as Mrs. Appleyard is concerned, make the eyes into waistcoat buttons in the silent
night. Leave that to some aged man sitting on a gate.

Remove the bones. Flake the fish into small pieces.
Melt a half-cup of the butter in a large saucepan and fry
the onion in it until the onion is a pale straw color. Shove
the onion to one side of the saucepan and rub into the butter
the flour, sifted with the pepper and salt. Work in the milk,
add the cream, the parsley, and the thyme. Fresh thyme,
finely minced, is best, but dried will do. Beat the egg yolks
with a fork, dilute them with a large spoonful of the sauce,
and stir them into the sauce in the pan. Now butter a
large casserole, put in a layer of the sauce, a layer of the
fish, and so on. Finish with the sauce and add the crumbs,
into which you have stirred the rest of the butter melted.
Add a few more dots of butter if the crumbs seem at all
dry. Sprinkle over the grated cheese and bake at 375° F.
for from fifteen to twenty minutes or until the crumbs are
well browned.

BAKED HADDOCK

A 5-lb. haddock, cut to bake	½ t. salt
¼ lb. fat salt pork	2 t. melted butter
6 slices of bacon	1 t. minced parsley
	1 lemon, sliced

Stuffing

¾ c. cracker crumbs	¼ t. pepper
¾ c. French bread crumbs	1 onion, finely minced
⅓ c. butter	½ t. Bell's poultry seasoning
½ t. salt	1 egg, beaten

Make the stuffing first. Roll the crackers fine. Dry some

slices of French bread, and roll crust and all into fine crumbs. Stir the dry seasonings into the crumbs, then the butter, melted, the minced onion, and the beaten egg.

Brush the fish inside and out with melted butter and sprinkle it with a little salt and pepper. Put in the stuffing. If you pack it in neatly, there is no real reason for sewing. There will be a crust on the outside and by using two pancake-turners you can get the fish out of the pan whole. Perhaps you like to sew fish — in which case, go right ahead. Mrs. Appleyard prefers smocking or Italian cutwork, or even mending stockings. However, the fish is not in the pan yet. . . .

Butter an iron dripping-pan, lay the stuffed fish in it, put over it the salt pork cut in thin strips. Add a very little water — just enough to keep it from drying out during the first few minutes. Fish has more flavor if it is baked without water. Bake the fish for forty to fifty minutes — at 425° F. for ten minutes, and the rest of the time at 350° F. Baste it with the fat that runs into the pan. During the last fifteen minutes put the slices of bacon over it. Transfer it to a hot platter, pour the liquid in the pan over it, surround it with slices of lemon, and sprinkle it with the chopped parsley.

FISH CHOWDER

This rule was inherited by Mrs. Appleyard and the chowder is always eaten with gratitude to the hands that used to make it. The best kettleful that Mrs. Appleyard ever ate was cooked over an open fire built on the rounded pebbles of a beach on Frenchman's Bay. The haddock had not been out of the water more than half an hour. The salt air, the scent of the pointed firs, the smell of the burning driftwood, all seemed to be added to the chowder. Still, it is pretty good cooked on a prosaic gas stove. You can have good chowder without smoke in your eyes, but not without plenty of salt pork and onions. Without them it is just a fishy dish of potatoes and milk. Do not try to make it with cooked potatoes or without the head and the bones of the fish. Much of the flavor of the fish is in them.

CHOWDER (FOR SIX)

A 4-lb. haddock, cut for chowder, head and all	3 large onions, finely sliced
3 c. milk	6 medium potatoes
1 c. cream	1 t. salt
8 pilot crackers	¼ t. black pepper
½ lb. salt pork, diced	½ t. paprika

Slice the potatoes 'as thin as fourpence.' Mrs. Appleyard has never seen a fourpence, but she estimates the thickness as about that of a nickel. In other words, you slice them so thin that there is no danger of there being half-raw lumps of potato in your chowder. Furthermore, pork dice means dice — not hunks. Fry the dice till they are a delicate cracker brown. Dip them out with a skimmer and put them on a saucer. Fry the onion in the pork fat until it is a light straw color. Take out the onion with your skimmer and put it on the saucer with the pork. Now rinse out the frying-pan with a little hot water and pour the water into a large kettle. In this way you don't lose the onion flavor. Lay in your pieces of fish. Add the potatoes, the onions, and the pork. Rinse the saucer on which the pork was with a little more hot water and pour it into the kettle. Add the season-ings and enough more hot water to cover the fish and pota-toes. Cover the kettle and let the fish cook slowly for forty minutes, or until the fish is falling from the bones and the potatoes are done.

You are now ready to serve the chowder, so add the milk and cream. Let it come to the boil but not boil. Taste it and be sure it is seasoned to suit you. If the pork was not very salty, you may need to add more — gently, though: it's a lot easier to put in than to take out. Put two of the pilot crackers, broken in quarters, into a large hot soup tureen. It does not look right to Mrs. Appleyard in anything but blue Canton, but please yourself.

Now take the large pieces of bone out of the chowder and discard them. Drop in the rest of the broken pilot crackers. Take a large ladle and transfer the chowder to the tureen, dipping it up from the bottom. Throw away the head if you have not already done so. Unless the fish slips easily from the bones the chowder is not done. You will not be able to get all the bones out. 'Look out for bones!' is a motto that ought to be cross-stitched on a silver cardboard, and served with each plateful. Mrs. Appleyard will attend to that later. At the moment she simply urges you again to taste the chowder once more for seasoning before you send it to the table. Having been brought up in a family where one of the favorite expressions was 'This dish is poisoned with salt!' she is likely to put in too little for some tastes.

The Appleyards like a few extra pilot crackers, buttered generously and put in the oven until the butter froths and the crackers begin to brown around the edges. A little paprika sprinkled over them looks rather cheering. The Appleyards take their chowder seriously and eat enough of it so that the next course is likely to be dessert. Something about lemon meringue pie makes it seem a fitting conclusion to this meal.

BROILED SHAD ROE

When the Appleyards leave for Vermont they cannot forget that they spend most of the year near the sea. They are lucky in having some fishermen in the family, but the trout do not always bite. Most canned fish does not appeal to them, but an exception is shad roe. Shad is a fish that is not at its best even as near home as Boston. Lucky cities like Baltimore and Philadelphia deserve the best and get it. The next best, in Mrs. Appleyard's opinion, is the canned roe, done when the fish have just leaped out of the water, and plenty good enough for the Appleyards when they reach the point that even the goldfish in the pool look tempting.

Mrs. Appleyard brushes the roe with melted butter, sprinkles a very little salt and pepper on it, broils it, about three minutes on each side, basting it while it broils with the juice of a lemon mixed with two tablespoonfuls of melted butter. With it she serves plenty of bacon and garnishes the dish with quartered lemons and sprigs of parsley. Asparagus, Country Style (page 284) and Creamed Potatoes (page 305) are likely to turn up in company with shad roe.

Someone seems to have distracted Mrs. Appleyard's attention from chowder. Fish chowder, she says, turning away from a tantalizing can of shad roe in scarlet and gold, and deciding to keep it for just one more emergency, may be slammed through light-heartedly; clam chowder is a serious project. Mrs. Appleyard is still seeing red from an article that she read about chowder.

'A good chowder,' wrote the well-meaning author, 'is made by substituting milk for the ordinary tomato juice.'

Mrs. Appleyard began by punctuating this quotation with an exclamation point. Then she put another one and, as her temper rose, strung them out to the edge of the page. Finding that even that number did not express her feelings, she decided on the following understatement:

'A * * * * * [fill in adjectives at pleasure] concoction is sometimes made by substituting tomato juice for the usual milk and cream. Steps will be taken to see that no one making it is allowed to cross the Massachusetts border, the Connecticut, or Lake Champlain.'

Mrs. Appleyard would gladly have talked till next day, but she felt that the lesson must end. Here is how some very intelligent people have been making clam chowder since the days when you paid for the clams in wampum.

NEW ENGLAND CLAM CHOWDER

1 qt. Duxbury or Ipswich clams	¼ t. pepper
1 c. cold water	4 T. butter
4 c. potatoes	2 c. milk
¼ lb. fat salt pork	2 c. cream
1 t. salt	4 T. flour
½ t. paprika	8 pilot crackers
	1 lemon, sliced very thin

Put the clams into a strainer, set into a bowl. Pour a cup of cold water over them. Save the liquor. Separate the soft parts of the clams from the rest and set them aside. Put the tough parts through the meat-grinder.

Cut the pork into very small dice and cook them until they are a delicate cracker brown. Take them out with a skimmer. Fry the onion in the pork fat until it is a pale straw color. Cut the potatoes into small neat cubes and parboil them five minutes in just enough water to cover them. Drain the water off, using it to rinse out the dish in which you cooked the onions and pork. Save it. Melt a little of the butter in a kettle. Put a layer of potatoes into it, add some of the ground clams, dredge with a little of the flour, sifted with the seasonings, and put in part of the pork and the onions. Repeat this until you have used all the ground clams, potatoes, pork, onions, and two tablespoons of the flour. Add the water you drained off the potatoes and enough more hot water to cover the mixture. Cook fifteen minutes. Add the soft parts of the clams. Cook three minutes. Then add the milk and cream. Let it come to a boil, but not boil. Into the same frying-pan you used before, put the remaining butter. Rub in the rest of the flour as soon as the butter froths, and cook gently for three minutes. Blend into it the strained clam juice. Cook a few minutes longer. Add this to the chowder just before serving. It will tend to make the milk separate if it is added too soon.

Have a hot tureen ready. Put into it some of the pilot crackers, broken. Pour the chowder over them. Put the rest of the crackers on top. Add the sliced lemon. This may be left out of the chowder and passed separately if you feel there is likely to be sales resistance to it among your public. Serve a few extra pilot crackers well buttered and sprinkled with paprika and toasted in the oven for a few minutes.

BOUILLABAISSE

Bouillabaisse is just a chowder that has had the advantages of foreign travel. In Mrs. Appleyard's rag-bag mind there turn up every now and then Thackeray's lines about this famous dish.

> Green herbs, red peppers, mussels, saffron;
> Soles, onions, garlic, roach, and dace —
> All these you eat at Terré's Tavern
> In that one dish of Bouillabaisse.

Even if you can't follow the whole prescription, you can at least get the saffron from the drugstore, use a mixture ot fish and shellfish, and produce something that is distinctly good to eat. Perhaps it ought to be called fish stew, but why take the romance out of life?

NEW ENGLAND BOUILLABAISSE, MRS. APPLEYARD

A 3-lb. haddock, cut for chowder	1 T. celery, chopped
A 1-lb. halibut	3 tomatoes, chopped
1 lb. flounder fillets	1 t. parsley, minced
1 lb. fresh crab meat	1 t. thyme
A 2-lb lobster.	½ t. saffron
1 qt. oysters	2 bay leaves
1 pt. Cape scallops	1 t. salt
1 T. lemon juice	½ t. pepper
1 c. salad oil	½ t. paprika
2 large onions, chopped	Small can of pimentos
1 bunch of leeks	1 c. white wine
1 t. garlic, minced	Half a long loaf of French bread

Mrs. Appleyard assembled these things partly from the ballad, partly from an old French cookbook, partly from observation, having once eaten bouillabaisse in a French restaurant. Of course you are supposed to have mussels in it, shells and all, and if you really like the shells, you could put in some small clams to steam and open while the rest of the fish is cooking. She really likes it better without, but perhaps that's just ignorance. Anyway, this is her version and she sticks to it.

Cut up the fish into neat pieces, not too small. Save all the bones and trimmings, including the lobster shells (be sure the lobster is well cleaned), cover them with water, and cook them gently for at least half an hour. Be sure the head of the haddock and the flounder bones are in this. There should be about a quart of fish stock.

Put the oil into a large frying-pan. Fry the onions, leeks, and garlic in it until the onion is light straw color. Use the green tops of the leeks as well as the white and cut them into half-inch pieces. Add the cut-up fish and the crab meat and lobster meat. Pound up the lobster coral fine and put it in. Of course you may use some other combination of fish, but have lobster if possible.

Cook the fish five minutes, add the tomatoes, celery, lemon juice, and seasonings except the saffron and parsley. Add the fish stock and the pimentos, cut in strips, and simmer twenty-five minutes with the pan covered. Then add the oysters and scallops and cook them until the edges of the oysters curl. Add last of all the saffron, parsley, and wine.

Put the French bread, cut one and a half inches thick and toasted, into a large hot tureen or covered casserole. Pour the bouillabaisse over it. Serve the rest of the loaf of bread, some unsalted butter, radishes, olives, and raw celery with the bouillabaisse. Have some white wine to drink with it. This serves eight people. All you will want for dessert will be some fruit and cheese.

FISH MOUSSE

A 1-lb. halibut or salmon	¾ c. cream, beaten
2 eggs, beaten	¼ t. salt
¼ c. milk	¼ t. white pepper

A few grains of Cayenne

This is for a small ring mould.

Put the fish through the food-chopper. Mousse is better made with raw fish. Be sure to remove all bones and skin before you begin to chop it. Add the milk with the seasonings in it, the beaten eggs, and the cream, beaten until it begins to thicken. Butter the ring mould — or one shaped like a fish if you happened to inherit it. Put in the mixture, cover the mould with heavy wax paper, set it in a pan of hot water, and bake it until the mousse is firm. In the middle of the mould, if it is a ring, or around it, put either Mushroom Sauce (page 257), Hollandaise Sauce (page 255), or Lobster Sauce — made by simmering diced lobster in cream sauce (page 254) and, just before serving, adding one tablespoonful of white wine for each cup of sauce — Egg Sauce (page 254) or Fish Sauce made as follows:

Bones and trimmings of the fish	¼ t. salt
1 small carrot, sliced	2 c. cold water
1 onion, sliced	2 T. butter
Sprig of parsley	3 T. flour
Bit of bay leaf	1½ c. heavy cream
¼ t. pepper	Yolks of 2 eggs
	2 T. white wine

Cover the fish bones and trimmings with the water. Add the seasonings, carrot, and parsley. Cook the stock down so that there is only one cup. Melt the butter; when it bubbles, rub in the flour, cook gently for three minutes, add the fish stock and the cream. Beat the egg yolks, dilute them with an equal amount of the sauce, and pour the mixture back into the sauce, stirring it in well. Add the wine and pour it over the mousse.

SALMON AND FLOUNDER

This is a way of making your salmon go further.

Take some small chunks of salmon, wrap small fillets of flounder around them. Fasten the fillets with toothpicks, put the fish into a cheesecloth that you keep for fishy manoeuvres. Have some boiling water ready in a kettle, put in the cloth containing the fish, and poach it for from thirty-five to forty-five minutes. Never let it boil hard. Season the water with some salt and pepper.

Serve the fillets with the Fish Sauce described on page 135 or with Hollandaise Sauce (page 255) or with Lobster Sauce made as described on page 135.

Cucumbers sliced very thin, soaked in salted water, drained, and marinated in a good French dressing are nice with this. How about an old-fashioned strawberry short-cake afterward? Perhaps you prefer bread pudding — suit yourself. Mrs. Appleyard is perfectly satisfied: all the more strawberries for her.

CODFISH IN CREAM

Although there is probably good creamed codfish in Gloucester, it is in Vermont that Mrs. Appleyard first found out that it was an edible substance. That is because when Vermonters say 'cream' they mean it. So codfish in cream was considered such an exotic delicacy during the

last century that it was reserved for company. A cousin of
Mr. Appleyard's, who had left the state for the West, once
returned and made a round of visits to various relatives
who were still in the Green Mountains. He dined with
Cousin Sarah — codfish in cream; with Uncle Abdiel —
codfish in cream. The codfish was also in excellent form
at Great Aunt Susan's, and at Cousin James's, and as he
drove into the yard at Cousin Horatio's he heard a voice
from the kitchen say: 'Horatio, that looks like George's boy
that just drove in. Go over to the store and get me a codfish. I've got cream.'

There is no mystery to this dish — if you have cream.
Freshen your codfish by soaking it in cold water. Change
the water several times. When you cook it start it in cold
water, bring it to the boiling point and then put it where it
will be hot but not boil while you are making the sauce.
Make a cream sauce (page 254) and boil some eggs hard.
Flake up the fish, discarding any tough pieces, and put it
into the sauce in the top of the double boiler to keep hot
and mellow until you need it. Have plenty of sauce in proportion to the amount of fish — three cups of sauce to a
pound of fish is about the way Mr. Appleyard likes it. Slice
the hard-boiled eggs and strew them over the sauce and fish.
With it have either baked or boiled new potatoes, according
to which is best at the moment. A pound of fish serves from
four to six people, depending on where they were born.

SALT–FISH DINNER

This is an easy way to a man's heart. It seems to take
care of the same instinct that makes mud pies a favorite
occupation.

For six people:

1½ lbs. salt codfish	6 carrots
3 cups egg sauce (page 254)	6 small white turnips
½ lb. salt pork	6 beets
6 onions	6 boiled potatoes

Soak the fish in cold water overnight. Change the water three times. Before you start to cook the vegetables, put the fish in a large frying-pan, cover it with fresh water, bring it to a boil but do not boil it. Set it where it will cook gently below the boiling point until you are ready to use it. Cook each of the vegetables separately. If they are very young and small, allow several of each kind instead of the one apiece called for above. There is of course no harm in cooking some extra anyway, but this is a filling dish and second helpings are not generally needed. While the fish and the vegetables are cooking, make the egg sauce and dice the salt pork fine and try it out until the pork scraps are brown and crisp. When everything is ready put the fish in the middle of a large hot platter and arrange the vegetables around it. Serve the egg sauce in a large bowl and the pork scraps with the pork fat in a sauce boat.

It is a pretty sight to see Mr. Appleyard attack a salt-fish dinner. He takes a potato on his plate and cuts it up rather fine, and then cuts into it the fish and the various vegetables. He keeps on cutting, and works into it some pork scraps and some of the tried-out pork fat, and last of all he takes a generous amount of the egg sauce and cuts that in. The result is a superb mound that fills the plate, in which the different flavors and textures are blended into something that is different from anything that went into it, and yet has the virtues of all its parts. Be sure that the vegetables are cooked freshly and all the water cooked out of them, that the fish is tender and well drained, the pork scraps crisp, that the sauce is made with plenty of cream, that the plates are stinging hot — and everyone will be happy.

Watermelon pickle is not part of the essential ritual but it is good with this dinner, and Mr. Appleyard thinks the dessert ought to be Indian Pudding (page 235), so you'd better have johnnycake for breakfast.

11

Hors d' Oeuvres. Appetizers, Mrs. Appleyard
says, are generally eaten most by those who need them least.
This paradox, however, does not prevent their being frequently the best part of the meal. She advises anyone who
sees something really hot and tempting among the hors
d'oeuvres to eat it as rapidly as he can without scorching his
tongue, and so continue, for after all, he may be going to en-
counter frozen peas with soda in them and a feminine dessert. This strategy originated with Mr. Appleyard, who believes that a hot sausage in the hand is worth more than a
fruit salad in the bush — especially if the bush is garnished
with marshmallows.

The most popular appetizer is caviar. Shakespeare is
responsible for the idea that it is something liked only by the
sophisticated. It may be an acquired taste, but unfortunately it is acquired only too easily. Put out a lot of appetizers on a large silver platter and see which ones vanish first.
Either everyone likes caviar or those who do like it have no
self-control at all.

Mrs. Appleyard sighs for the days of imperial gray beluga, but the imitations — either red or black — are better than nothing. Perhaps the most comfortable way to eat caviar is to have a good-sized bowl of it on the table around which you are sitting. Caviar should be cold but not frozen. With it serve crusty French bread, sweet butter, sour cream, finely chopped onion, quartered lemons. Fingerbowls are a pretty good idea, and don't hurry with the next course. People sitting around eating caviar are having a good time. Take advantage of this fact if you are serving the meal yourself.

There are, however, moments when caviar served wholesale is not the thing. For these less expansive occasions Mrs. Appleyard makes

CAVIAR CANAPÉS

Thinly cut sandwich bread, not too fresh, is essential to making good canapés. In ordering a sandwich loaf, always order it the day before you are going to use it. It is possible in some shops, operated by benefactors of humanity, to get sandwich bread sliced wafer thin. This is not so thin as the most skillful cook can do with a very sharp knife, but it is a lot thinner than most of us can do in a hurry with the knife our little ones borrowed for cutting the string that tied their new skis together, Mrs. Appleyard says.

Quantities needed for twelve canapés:

4-oz. jar of caviar	¼ lb. unsalted butter, softened
Juice of ½ lemon	1 hard-boiled egg
4 large stuffed olives	1 t. grated onion

Cut out rounds of the thinly sliced bread with a cooky-cutter. Toast them lightly on one side. Spread them with softened sweet butter, then with caviar that has been mixed with a little chopped onion and a squeeze of lemon juice. Spread it thickly. Caviar spread thin is just an annoyance. Decorate it around the edge with finely chopped white of hard-boiled egg and sprinkle a little of the grated yolk over the top. A slice of a large stuffed olive in the middle looks rather cheerful and does no special harm.

CREAM PUFFS WITH CAVIAR

Make 24 very small cream puffs (see page 98).

FILLING

1 4-oz jar of caviar	4 T. sour cream
2 t. grated onion	1 t. paprika
Juice of 1 lemon	

Mix caviar with the seasonings. Split the puffs halfway through and fill them with caviar. Top them with a dash of sour cream dusted with paprika.

Either red or black caviar may be used; neither of them ever met a sturgeon, but they do their best in a hard world. In those unhappy districts where cream comes in a bottle and lives in a refrigerator, a passable substitute for sour cream may be made by mashing a small cream cheese and beating a tablespoonful or two of thick cream into it. Mrs. Appleyard does not really approve of this stratagem, but admits she has used it when hard pressed.

PLATE OF APPETIZERS NO. 1

If the rest of the meal is to be light, a plate of appetizers may be served at the table as the first course. It might include:

Half a hard-boiled egg stuffed with a paste made by mashing the yolk with one teaspoonful of devilled ham and a little mayonnaise.

A small tomato stuffed with cream cheese mixed with olive butter, and chopped chives, and moistened with a little cream. To a small cream cheese use:

1 T. olive butter	2 t. cream
1 t. chopped chives	½ t. salt

A sardine on a small oblong of toast made from wafer-thin sandwich bread, lightly toasted and spread with softened butter to which a few drops of Worcestershire sauce have been added. Sprinkle the sardine with finely minced chives.

A crisp stalk of celery stuffed with cheese. Use part Roquefort, or Argentine Blue, and part cream cheese mashed together with a little thick cream. Dust it with paprika.

A small cream puff stuffed with caviar (see page 142) or with pâté de foie gras, or with crab meat and mayonnaise, or lobster. In any case a small lettuce leaf sticking out advertises the fact that there is something good inside.

PLATE OF APPETIZERS NO. 2 (FOR SIX PEOPLE)

6 lettuce hearts	6 large stuffed ripe olives
6 celery hearts	
6 slices of tomato	3 radishes, thinly sliced
12 anchovy fillets	12 green olives stuffed, sliced
6 sardines	
6 thin slices of tongue	6 thin slices of dried beef

Arrange these on individual plates and pour over them a dressing made of:

½ t. dry mustard	1 T. oil from sardines
½ t. salt	5 T. olive oil
¼ t. pepper	1½ T. lemon juice
½ t. paprika	1 T. red-wine vinegar
2 T. chopped chives	½ t. anchovy essence
1 t. finely minced onion	

TOMATO AND CAVIAR CANAPÉS

Toast wafer-thin rounds of bread on one side. Spread the other side with soft butter. Place on it a thin slice of peeled tomato lightly spread with mayonnaise. Spread it with black caviar (née cod roe, but don't look at the label), squeeze lemon juice over it, sprinkle it with grated egg yolk.

Made with a rather generous round of bread and tomato and caviar in proportion, this is enough for a first course.

TOMATO AND ANCHOVY CANAPÉS

1 hard-boiled egg	1 small peeled tomato
2 T. tuna fish	½ green pepper, finely
6 anchovy fillets	minced

Chop all these together. Moisten with one teaspoon of mayonnaise, one teaspoon of chili sauce, and a few drops of Worcestershire sauce. Spread this mixture on six rounds of thin sandwich bread that have been buttered and put into the oven for a few minutes. Decorate the canapés with stuffed olives. Put a slice of olive cut across in the middle, and four slices cut lengthwise radiating from it. A spray of watercress wreathed around these looks rather attractive. Mrs. Appleyard considers these good but a waste of time.

TRAYS OF APPETIZERS

These are some of the things that Mrs. Appleyard likes to put on the small sticks used for spearing hot hors d'oeuvres: innocent young sausages an inch long that have been baked awhile in the oven and finished off under the broiler; large stuffed olives wrapped in bacon and broiled; oysters treated the same way; mushroom caps dotted with butter and a little salt and broiled.

It is a ticklish business to get the mushrooms broiled just right. If you cook them too much they get flabby and if you get on too much butter, your guests may avoid them. Hostesses might as well remember that if it is a choice between a man's shirt front and the rug, he will choose the rug. Perhaps you had better play safe and make

MUSHROOM AND BACON APPETIZERS

1 lb. mushrooms	½ t. salt
1 slice of onion	4 t. thick cream
4 T. butter	1 t. sherry
2 T. flour	6 slices of bacon

Chop the mushrooms and the onion fine and fry them slowly in the butter. When they are tender sprinkle the flour over them and the salt and cook a little longer. Add the cream and last of all the sherry. Spread the mixture on rounds of sandwich bread. Put a small square of bacon on top of each canapé. Cook them under the broiler until the bacon is done.

CHEESE AND CHUTNEY APPETIZERS (MRS. APPLEYARD)

¼ lb. butter	1 t. finely minced onion
½ lb. dairy cheese	6 drops Worcestershire sauce
1 cup Major Grey's chutney	

Cream the butter, add the cheese, finely grated. Chop

the onion and then in the same bowl the chutney and stir this mixture into the cheese and butter. Add the Worcestershire sauce and enough juice from the chutney so that the mixture will spread easily. Spread it on rounds of sandwich bread and put them on a baking-sheet into a very hot oven (500° F.) for about three minutes.

This amount will make about three dozen appetizers.

SARDINE AND OLIVE APPETIZERS

1 small can of sardines	3 drops Worcestershire sauce
2 T. butter	1 t. cream
1 t. lemon juice	

Mash the sardines with their own oil. Add the butter, lemon juice, Worcestershire sauce, and cream. Toast rounds of bread and spread them with the mixture and decorate them with slices of stuffed olives and hard-boiled egg if you have it.

Mrs. Appleyard feels that it is really safer to pass your appetizers than to make an arbitrary selection for the guests and serve it on a plate. Imagine, for instance, the chagrin of the hostess at finding that some of the guests toy lightly with those sacred caviar puffs and leave them half-eaten. Certainly pass them if you have one of those Chinese trays into which dishes of celadon or turquoise-colored porcelain are fitted. However, even if you haven't, it is possible to improvise an attractive tray. Mrs. Appleyard has encountered one with dishes from Woolworth's where the dishes and their contents were both full of charm.

The dishes may contain any of the things mentioned above — better keep all the hot things on one tray — and besides, shredded carrot and cabbage salad, potato salad, anchovies, stuffed olives, green and ripe, smoked sausage, artichoke bottoms, pickled mushrooms, sardines. One of them may even contain pickled beets.

Mrs. Appleyard is very unlikely to live down the fact that, when being helped from a table of such delicacies in a New York restaurant, it was noticed by her loving friends that the only thing out of the dozen presented to her notice that she did not take was the beets.

In a good many restaurants west of Chicago they bring you salad as soon as you sit down. This is a surprise to Eastern visitors who expect to begin with either soup, fruit cup, grapefruit, or oysters. There is a good deal to be said for this practice of setting salad before the hungry guest — especially from the point of view of the restaurant: it keeps the guest busy while he is waiting for the rest of his order, and perhaps makes him satisfied with a smaller portion of the main course than he would otherwise expect. There is a tendency in the East now to follow the same strategy, only they bring you relishes and Melba toast and butter. It is a pretty sight, Mrs. Appleyard thinks, to see ladies on a reducing diet virtuously choose a piece of Melba toast and cover it with butter.

If salad is going to be served first, try salad à la Max. Max was a genius who had a small restaurant in Boston — a hundred years ago, more or less, it seems to Mrs. Appleyard. This is the salad he always set before his guests, as she remembers it across the years.

He put four or five crisp leaves of native lettuce on a plate — in those innocent times iceberg lettuce was still in its native icebergs, right where it belongs — and over them he put four fillets of anchovy. In and around the anchovies he put thin slices of radishes and stuffed olives, some green and some ripe. He put a shrimp in the middle of each plate and sprinkled the whole thing with grated egg yolk. Just before he sent it to the table he poured over it a dressing made with red-wine vinegar. Mrs. Appleyard does not know exactly how it was made, but Mr. Appleyard's French dressing is a good deal like it. She says that you may add a teaspoonful of anchovy essence to it if you like. The rule for Mr. Appleyard's salad dressing is on page 239.

Of course this dressing should really be made with olive oil, but we can eat cottonseed and like it. Mr. Appleyard says you had better season it a little more heavily than you would if you were using olive oil.

Mrs. Appleyard was once turned loose at a smorgasbord where the following hors d'oeuvres were spread out. Even her excellent appetite did not allow her to sample them all, and she lists them simply as pleasant recollection of the past and a rainbow promise of the future, which she trusts will not be too distant.

1. Hot anchovy and chutney rolls. These seemed to consist of fresh bread spread with butter and chopped chutney and rolled around an anchovy fillet. The useful hors d'oeuvres sticks fastened them and they were toasted brown.

2. Small sausages on sticks.

3. Toasted cheese sandwiches.

4. Toasted mushroom sandwiches.

5. Grilled shad roe. It was cut in chunks and wrapped with bacon, skewered on toothpicks and broiled.

6. Sardines on toast with hot mustard sauce.

7. Thin slices of salami.

8. Liver paté.

9. Potato salad.

10. Dried-beef cornucopias filled with cream cheese and horse radish.

11. Thin slices of ham rolled around cream cheese mixed with chutney.

12. Caviar with chopped onion, lemon, grated egg yolk, Melba toast.

13. Celery stuffed with Roquefort cheese.

14. Rolled asparagus sandwiches.

15. Rolled watercress sandwiches.

16. Salad of raw carrot, shredded white and purple cabbage, purple onions, and watercress with French dressing.

17. Conserve of spiced fruits.

18. Tomato marmalade.

19. Watermelon pickle.

20. Chutney.

This collection seemed to be supplying something for every taste. Yet after all, Mrs. Appleyard says, is there anything better than some cold crisp celery, some jumbo-sized green olives, some very young radishes, a few sticks of raw carrot, with French bread and unsalted butter?

12

Ice Cream and Sherbet. The electric refrigerator is a great blessing to humanity, but it has something chalked up against it because of what it has done to ice cream. The whole theory of ice cream is that it is *beaten and frozen at the same time.* Nothing made in the drawer of a refrigerator is ever so good as what is cranked by hand in a White Mountain freezer, no matter how often you may take it out of the drawer and stir it. Of course it is better if you stir it than if you leave it alone to sulk, but it never has quite the cool smoothness produced by a hand freezer. Besides, there is no dash to lick. Think of the arid childhood of one who has never been handed the dash (or dasher, but never called so in this connection), a bowl, and a spoon, and who actually, in the melting sweetness, never finds a shred of peach or strawberry. . . . Let's not think of it — too sad.

Mr. Appleyard in his youth froze so much ice cream that he invented a board seat that fitted over the freezer, so that he could sit down on it and keep the freezer steady while he cranked with his right hand, and in his left held a copy of *King Solomon's Mines* by H. Rider Haggard. Mrs. Appleyard, too, has put her inventive genius to work. She thought up a cylinder with a beater inside that would fit into her refrigerator freezing compartment. This good idea occurred to her in her bath. Probably she is distantly related to Archimedes. She planned to have a small motor attached to the cylinder and a flat rubber cord that would go through the refrigerator door and not stop it from shutting. She was going to plug it into a socket near by.

No sooner said than done. All Mrs. Appleyard has to do is to think about an invention and someone else, someone who has wrestled with aluminum and motors and patent lawyers, and rubber, promptly puts it on the market. She exercises this strange power rather infrequently, because she feels that it is a serious responsibility. Within two weeks — which was certainly quick for an invention — one of the cylinders was whirring away busily in Mrs. Appleyard's refrigerator, beating up some strawberry ice cream that even Mr. Appleyard admits was just as good as any he ever made with Rider Haggard's help — or Conan Doyle's either, for that matter.

In case anyone else gets one of these Hamilton Beach Freezers, Mrs. Appleyard has a word of caution. Be sure your refrigerator freezing compartment has a space big enough to hold the cylinder. Always set your control at its coldest point. Follow the directions for using the freezer *exactly*. They were not written in any frivolous spirit. At one time Mrs. Appleyard thought she knew better. This was pure conceit: her Archimedes complex. She was wrong. She admits it. She feels sure lots of people will like to hear about this.

STRAWBERRY ICE CREAM

There should be nothing in strawberry ice cream but perfect strawberries, cream, and sugar. This does not seem like a very revolutionary statement, but as most strawberry ice cream is constructed of cornstarch, gelatine, milk, artificial coloring and flavoring, and powdered eggs, perhaps it is worth mentioning.

            2 c. thick cream
            1 qt. strawberries, picked that morning
            1 c. sugar

Mash the berries with the sugar. Put them through a fine strainer or through the potato-ricer. Don't worry if there are a few seeds and an occasional bit of strawberry pulp. What kind of ice cream is this, anyway? The amounts of cream and fruit stated above give a fine pink ice cream, but one of the charms of home-made ice cream is that it is not always exactly the same. If you have not quite two cups of cream on hand, don't worry — it will just be a slightly pinker pink.

In those happy days before the Hurricane blew down Mr. Appleyard's sugar place, Mrs. Appleyard actually used to think up ways to use up maple syrup. This was one of her inventions that turned out pretty well:

MAPLE MARRON MOUSSE

1¼ c. maple syrup   12 marrons (the kind
Yolks of 4 eggs   in vanilla syrup)
2 c. heavy cream   A few grains of salt
1 c. light cream

Beat the egg yolks till they are thick and lemon colored.

Heat the syrup and pour it over them, beating it in gradually. Cook the mixture over hot water until it coats the back of the spoon. Cool — you can hasten the cooling by setting the pan in cold water with ice cubes in it. Add the marrons, cut up into small pieces, the salt, and the cream. Freeze in a hand freezer, or in the electric freezer.

This is not too bad, frozen in the refrigerator tray, if you can burden your mind with stirring it occasionally, so that the syrup will not settle at the bottom, and so that the crystals are broken up. Of course in that case you whip the cream before you add it. Pounded-up nut brittle may be substituted for the marrons. Be sure that the refrigerator is at its coldest point when you put in the mixture.

What is sadder than chocolate ice cream without enough chocolate in it? Nothing leaps to Mrs. Appleyard's mind at the moment. It ought to be dark brown and velvety, not pallid with an occasional freckle of undissolved chocolate. It may be made simply with cream (Rule I) but it is very smooth and good made with a custard (Rule II). Mrs. Appleyard lives in a dairy country where when the cream is gone that's just all there is about it, so she makes it either way according to the state of the cream supply.

CHOCOLATE ICE CREAM NO. 1

4 c. thin cream	1 t. vanilla
1 c. sugar	A few grains of salt
3 sqs. Baker's chocolate, grated	2 T. hot water

Put the grated chocolate into the top of the double boiler, add the hot water, and when the chocolate is melted add the sugar and the salt and mix well. Scald the cream — do not let it boil — and add it to the chocolate a little at a time.

If you do this carefully with the chocolate and the cream at about the same temperature, you will not find specks of chocolate in the frozen cream. Cool, add the vanilla. Freeze.

CHOCOLATE ICE CREAM NO. 2

2 c. milk	2 t. vanilla
3 T. flour sifted with a	2 c. thick cream
few grains of salt	3 sqs. Baker's chocolate,
1 c. sugar	grated
4 egg yolks	

Put the cold milk and the grated chocolate in the top of the double boiler. When the chocolate is melted, beat with a rotary beater until smooth. Mix sugar and flour and salt and stir into them enough of the milk-and-chocolate mixture to dissolve the sugar. It must be thin enough to pour, and you next pour it back into the double boiler with the rest of the milk, cover it, and cook it ten minutes, stirring occasionally.

In between times beat the egg yolks slightly, add them to the chocolate mixture, and cook one minute. Scald the cream — be sure not to boil it — and add it to the chocolate mixture, which by now should coat the back of the spoon. Add the vanilla. If by any oversight the chocolate has lumped at all, strain the mixture, but this should not be necessary if you have followed directions. If you are going to freeze it with ice and salt, cool it first. In the electric cylinder the heat will simply help to make the good freezing contact that is essential for freezing. Did any kind friend ever tell you to touch the tip of your tongue to metal on a zero day? If so, you will understand why your cylinder freezes better if it starts hot.

POUNDED NUT GLACÉ

1 c. sugar   1 c. nuts, broken in pieces

The nuts may be pecans, almonds, walnuts, cashews, or any mixed nuts you like. Do not include peanuts in the mixture, as it will taste only of peanuts. Use them separately if you like.

Put the broken nuts into a buttered pan. Melt the sugar in a frying-pan. When it is golden brown, pour it over the nuts. This is one of the things you make on a clear, crisp day. When the glacé is cool, pound it up. It's good either frozen into a mixture — such as maple mousse — or sprinkled over plain ice cream from the drugstore. So as a matter of fact is peanut brittle that you buy in a package.

Another good dodge for turning drugstore ice cream into something rich and strange is to get it ahead of time, and pack it into your refrigerator tray with the indicator set at its coldest point for an hour. Just before you serve the ice cream, cut it into rather thick slices and roll them either in nut glacé or in powdered macaroon crumbs. Put the slices on a cold platter. Sprinkle some more crumbs over the whole thing and get it to the table with what speed you can muster at that point.

Or perhaps it would be better to make

LEMON MILK SHERBET

4 c. milk   Juice of 3 large lemons
1½ c. sugar   ½ t. grated lemon rind

This is for the freezer only and occurs in regions where you look in the ice chest and say: 'Goodness, how that milk

is piling up! What had I better do with it? No, definitely
not rice pudding. . . .'

Mix the lemon juice, rind, and the sugar. Don't let the
fact that the milk may separate slightly dismay you. It will
smooth out as it freezes. Freeze it either in the electric cylinder or in ice and salt in the hand freezer. This is about the
simplest of the frozen desserts, but it is always popular at
Appleyard Centre, where it is associated with hot days when
scythes are ringing and swallows are flying over the place
where the green oats are falling.

If you have no milk to absorb, try

LEMON WATER ICE

4 c. water	¾ c. lemon juice
2 c. sugar	½ t. grated rind

Make a syrup of the sugar and water. Cook it for fifteen
minutes. Cool it. Add the lemon juice and rind. Freeze.
Three parts of ice to one of salt is a good mixture for water
ice or sherbet.

RASPBERRY ICE

4 c. water	2 T. lemon juice
2 c. sugar	2 c. raspberry juice

Make a syrup of the sugar and water and boil it fifteen
minutes. Cool it and add the raspberry juice. It will probably take about a quart of berries to make the two cups of
juice. They should be mashed and strained through a very
fine sieve. Add the lemon juice. If the raspberries are not
juicy a few currants may be added. Freeze this either in

three parts of ice and one of salt in the hand freezer or in the electric cylinder.

FROZEN RASPBERRIES OR STRAWBERRIES

1 qt. fruit	2 egg whites or
1 c. sugar	½ c. thick cream
1 t. lemon juice	

Mash the fruit and the sugar together. Strain the fruit through a fine sieve and add the lemon juice and freeze. Taste it and sweeten it more if necessary. Ice-cream mixtures always taste sweeter before they are frozen than they do afterward. Freeze — by hand or in the electric cylinder. When the fruit is partly frozen fold in some partly whipped cream or the whites of two eggs beaten stiff, and continue the freezing.

ORANGE ICE

2 c. water	Grated rind of 2 oranges
2 c. sugar	1 t. grated lemon rind
2 c. orange juice	¼ c. lemon juice

Make a syrup of the water and sugar. Cool the syrup, add the fruit juices and grated rind, and let it stand a few minutes so that the syrup will absorb the flavor of the rind. Strain and freeze, either by hand or in the electric cylinder.

Never grate the rind of any oranges that are marked 'Color Added' — if you like candle wax in your sherbet, add it separately. Mrs. Appleyard likes Temple oranges for sherbet. They are the natural color without benefit of colored wax, and the rind has a particularly pleasant tang.

In Mrs. Appleyard's family it is felt that there is a special

harmony between orange ice and macaroon ice cream —
with macaroons in it!

MACAROON ICE CREAM

2 c. thin cream	¾ c. sugar
2 c. thick cream	2 t. vanilla or a
2 c. macaroon crumbs	little brandy

Take fresh macaroons and dry them in a very slow oven
(250° F.). Pound them, mix the crumbs — after measuring
them — with the sugar, and stir them into the cream. If you
like vanilla, use it, but Mrs. Appleyard thinks a very little
brandy brings out the flavor of the macaroons better. It
ought not to taste of the brandy. For her a teaspoonful is
plenty.

If you are actually going to embark on the project of making macaroon ice cream and orange sherbet on the same
day, make the ice cream first and pack it when frozen into
the bottom of your deepest refrigerator tray. Then get to
work on the sherbet, which freezes more quickly and needs
less ripening. Pack it in on top of the ice cream as soon as it
is frozen and let it stand awhile. Take a day off and do this
sometime. Mrs. Appleyard made some one morning while
four men were putting up a portable garage in her back
yard. They got through before she did. The garage is still
there and the ice cream vanished twenty years ago, but she
still thinks it was worth while.

PEACH ICE CREAM

Like strawberry ice cream, Mrs. Appleyard says, peach
ice cream should never be made with a custard. Neither
peaches nor strawberries are the same fruit if they have ever

been cooked, or even if there are cooked eggs and milk with them. The fresh flavor of the fruit is so delicate that it takes very little to change it. Never use any fruit that you would not like to eat plain. This does not necessarily mean the largest and handsomest fruit, but the juiciest and sweetest. Ice cream is no better than what you put into it.

Really good sliced peaches with some thick cream to pour over them are, in Mrs. Appleyard's opinion, a much better dessert than any peach ice cream that you can buy; or than anything you can make yourself out of peaches that happened to turn out either woolly or rubbery. Alas, both these substances can lurk under a skin of perfect beauty.

Mrs. Appleyard saw some peaches once in England. They were wrapped in cotton wool and cost three shillings apiece — but perhaps she had better not bring that up now. She will sing instead of Georgia, of North Carolina, of Delaware, and mention, diffidently of course, the peaches that sometimes ripen in an inconspicuous state with an unsingable name for which she has a sneaking affection. Massachusetts is its name, and she loves it in spite of its roadside fungus of hot-dog stands and signs. Yes, in spite of its politicians and its dowagers, its poison ivy and brownstone buildings, its traffic lights and those who honk their horns thereat; in spite of the fact that its baked beans are small and slippery and its winter winds as cold as raw smoked salmon, she cherishes Massachusetts.

Has it not cranberries, the pinkest apple blossoms, the loveliest lilac plumes, Chestnut Street in Salem and Salem Gibraltars, a Sacred Cod under a golden dome, and codfish balls? Listening to the best symphony orchestra in the world are there not more women with beautiful white hair than in any other space of its size in the Western Hemisphere?

Where but in Boston and Worcester are there museums with so little pompous trash among so much that is exciting and charming? In what other city than Boston can you ride in a swan boat and chuckle over Dahl's cartoon and see sunlight through tulip petals all at the same time? For the elms on its village streets, for the Charles River winding wherever you go, for the Lynn Marshes at sunset and the Custom House Tower at sunrise, for the Berkshires folding into each other in purple haze, for small girls in riding clothes and with bands on their teeth, for skinny, lumpy boys in football helmets, for Marshfield strawberries, for Bailey's candy, for the smell of S. S. Pierce's on Christmas Eve, for snowplows with storms of silver spraying over them, for cock pheasants in the autumn woods, and for — every two or three years — a good crop of *peaches*, let us all praise Massachusetts!

Mrs. Appleyard here breathed hard and returned to the subject of . . .

PEACH ICE CREAM

2 c. light cream	2 c. peach pulp and juice
2 c. heavy cream	Peach kernels
1 c. sugar	

Peel ripe, juicy peaches and crush them through a potato-ricer. Mix with the sugar and put the bowl in the ice chest for a while. In the meantime crack two of the peach stones, blanch the kernels, and let them stand in the cream. It is a question in Mrs. Appleyard's mind as to whether this has any real effect. Probably it's only a ritual. Anyway you soon remove them; very likely a drop of almond extract would do as well. Some people add a little lemon juice, but Mrs. Appleyard sticks to her story: if the peaches are good enough, they need no other flavoring.

Now freeze the mixture, either by hand or in the electric cylinder. Slice some more peaches and serve them with it. Sprinkle a little sugar over them, but they won't need much.

Mrs. Appleyard has always wished she could make spun sugar. She loves the idea of laying white wrapping paper on the floor, putting new broomsticks between two chairs — she thinks they ought to be Hepplewhite for such an elegant process, only perhaps a Sheraton back would be a better shape — and spinning sugar over the broomsticks. However, as she realizes only too well that the result would be sugar on stove, sink, table, on her favorite painting of a white mare and a black colt — which she keeps in her kitchen because she likes art where she can see it — and of course the ceiling, she has so far denied herself this pleasure. Still, the day may come, and when it does she can be counted upon to tell about it. Up to that time she thinks you had better buy spun sugar from the caterer.

13

Meat: from Roast Through Hash. Just because Mrs. Appleyard says nothing about roasting beef, lamb, or veal is no sign that she is the only one of Les Amies de Françoise Fermière that cannot put a piece of meat into the oven, and take it out again later in a fair state of preservation. Others, notably the patron saint of the order, have covered the topic so thoroughly that to read the average cookbook you would think that people had a tip of the sirloin every day or so. Mrs. Appleyard, with a humble bow, leaves them the field, and the problem of what to do with the cold lamb, and turns her attention to the other days. You might, for instance, be thinking wistfully about the time you had

CURRIED CHICKEN (S. E. D.)

A 6-lb. fowl (or two 3½-lb. roasting chickens)
1 stalk celery
1 carrot

2 onions
Sprig of parsley
½ t. pepper
1 t. salt

Have the fowl cut up at the market and simmer it for

two and a half hours with the vegetables. Add the salt and pepper the last half-hour. Take the meat out, separate it from the skin and bones, return the bones to the broth and cook them for another hour. Strain the broth and set it aside to cool. Skim off the fat.

For the sauce:

> 4 t. butter
> 4 t. flour
> 2 T. curry powder

Melt the butter (you may use some of the chicken fat if you prefer), and when it bubbles, rub in the flour and the curry powder. (If you like it very hot, add more of the powder.) Stir the chicken broth into it. The broth should be cooked down so that there are four cups of it. Let it simmer awhile until the flour is thoroughly cooked and the curry powder well blended in. Then add the chicken and set the pan where it will barely simmer while you are cooking the rice. Just before you serve the sauce, add a cup of thick cream. Mrs. Appleyard generally begins this sauce by frying minced onion, but that is not necessary unless you like, as there was onion cooked in the broth anyway. Optional also is about half a cup of strained apple sauce made from tart apples. If you use it, add it when you add the chicken.

The rice for curry is as important as the curry itself, Mrs. Appleyard says. You can spoil a good curry by serving soggy rice with it. The rice should be fluffy, and each kernel should stand apart from the others and yet it should not be really dry. Each grain should have a chance to take up all the water it really needs. To do that, it must be well washed. That, to Mrs. Appleyard, means changing the water twelve times. Probably this is more than is strictly necessary, but she would rather wash it too much than not enough.

For one cup of rice she has three quarts of water boiling violently with one tablespoonful of salt in it. She drops the washed and drained rice in so slowly that the water never stops boiling. She cooks it uncovered, until the kernels are soft, not mushy, when felt between the thumb and fore-finger — about twenty minutes. Then she puts it into a col-ander and pours hot water over it. This removes any starch that has not been washed away and makes the grains sepa-rate. After letting the rice drain a few minutes, she sets the colander into a warm oven with the door open so that the rice can warm and dry out.

When she is ready to serve the curry she has a large, hot platter ready. She takes a teacup, fills it with the rice, and turns the rice out in small mounds around the platter. Then she pours the curried chicken into the middle of the platter and serves it.

In the meantime her daughters have set nine Sandwich-glass dishes — eight small ones and one large one — on a big tray and have been busy filling them with the following things: chopped white of hard-boiled eggs, grated yolks of hard-boiled eggs, finely minced raw onion, finely chopped parsley, red tomato relish, piccalilli, shredded coconut — fresh, if possible — chopped peanuts, Major Grey's or Colonel Skinner's chutney. The large dish is for the chut-ney.

Each guest takes a mound of rice, covers it with curry, then helps himself to any combination of relishes that he likes — generally, Mrs. Appleyard notices, he takes some of each — and mixes everything together. Fried bananas are also served with this, and the dessert is something cooling — lemon sherbet, for instance.

CURRY OF LAMB

Curry of lamb is very much like chicken curry. The great point about a meat curry is that it should be made from meat cooked for the purpose and not from dry chips of roast meat that you can't think what else to do with. You need stock for the sauce, and the way to get it is out of the meat you are going to have in the curry. A less expensive curry than the chicken kind described above is made from a shoulder of lamb, cut up at the market and treated just like the chicken. The only difference is that instead of the cream that you put in the sauce you add a cup of tomato purée. Mrs. Appleyard, being languid about the purée process, uses a can of thick tomato soup for this. Be sure to get your lamb broth cool enough so that you can get all the fat off before you start to make your sauce. Almost no one really loves mutton fat.

Serve the relishes just as you would with the chicken curry, or substitute any you may prefer. A little green-apple sauce is rather good for one. Some people put tart apples into the sauce. They should be so tender that they cook down and disappear. Four apples, peeled and quartered, is about right for two cups of sauce. Mint jelly goes well with lamb curry. Have whatever you like, only it's fun to have a lot of kinds to choose from.

BEEF CURRY

This is a short cut for times when you feel both economical and hurried. Cook your rice as above. Make your stock from canned consommé or bouillon. Add a can of tomato soup, a cup of cream, two tablespoonfuls of curry powder, more if you like it very hot. Have a pound and a half of the bottom of the round ground twice. Make it into cakes and broil it. Put it on the platter with the mounds of rice around it, pour the curry sauce over it. Serve it with a lot of relishes, one of which had better be mustard pickle.

MRS. APPLEYARD'S VEAL LOAF

2 lbs. of veal and 1 lb. of lean pork
Put twice through the grinder together

½ lb. calves' liver	1 t. white pepper
½ lb. baked ham	1½ t. salt
2 truffles	1 t. Bell's poultry seasoning
6 Montpelier or Boston	⅛ t. thyme
Common crackers	4 slices of bacon
2 eggs, well beaten	1 T. flour
2 large onions	1 T. butter

The marketman will grind the veal and pork together for you. Cook the liver the day before, blanching it and simmering it till tender, and chop it very fine. Mrs. Appleyard generally uses ham cut from a ham that she has baked herself because she is likely to serve ham sliced thin along with the veal loaf, but a slice of boiled ham half an inch thick cut into dice will do.

She begins by chopping the onions very fine and then chopping the liver into them and then the veal and the pork until everything is well mixed. She rolls the crackers into fine crumbs, mixes the seasonings with them, and mixes them in. Next go in the beaten eggs, and last of all the ham cubes and the sliced truffles if you can get them. Their nutty fragrance is delicious with the veal and pork.

Now she butters a bread tin and puts in the mixture, pressing it well into the corners. She dredges the top with flour and a few very fine crumbs and covers it with the

bacon cut into small strips. She sets the pan on a rack in a
covered roaster, surrounds it with water, and bakes it for
two and a half hours at 375° F., reducing the heat if it seems
to be getting too brown, and adding more water until the
last half-hour. Be sure to chill it thoroughly before serving.

This slices beautifully. Mrs. Appleyard generally serves
with it Mushroom Sauce (page 257), sliced baked ham, and
Vegetable Salad (page 244).

VEAL–AND–HAM PIE (MRS. APPLEYARD)

Mr. Appleyard once caused a waiter in an English restaurant great pain by sending back the veal-and-ham pie with
the indestructible crust, saying — to Mrs. Appleyard — that
he preferred what he had at home. She was both pleased
and embarrassed by this tribute. Since hers can actually be
bitten into, she does think that perhaps Mr. Appleyard was
right. Veal-and-ham pie, like other things in England, is
wonderful if you get it at the right place — even better than
Mrs. Appleyard's. (This is just an attack of false modesty on
his wife's part, Mr. Appleyard says loyally. If you get a pie
that has been made since George the Fourth was king you
are lucky, and even then Mrs. Appleyard's is just as good.)
Well, leaving history out of it this is how she makes a small
one.

2 lbs. veal cutlet	1 sprig parsley
2 lbs. veal bones	Bit of bay leaf
1 lb. baked ham (page 183)	1 t. pepper
1 carrot	1 t. salt
2 onions	4 hard-boiled eggs
1 T. poultry seasoning	

Cover the veal and the bones with cold water, add the

seasonings and the onions, let it come to the boiling point slowly, and simmer for two hours. Remove the meat from the broth and cut the veal into small pieces. Cook the broth down until there is only a pint of it. Butter a baking-dish, put in the veal mixed with the ham, which may be either cut in small cubes or sliced very thin. Use only the lean part of the ham. Put in a layer of the meat, then thick slices of the hard-boiled eggs around the sides, then the rest of the meat. Add half the broth. Cover the pie with pastry; you know — *pastry* (page 212), not a tough overcoat of flour and water. Leave a hole in the crust. Bake the pie one hour at 375° F. When the crust is a good brown, take out the pie and pour the rest of the broth through the hole in the pastry, using a small funnel.

Serve it cold. The broth jellies among the pieces of meat. This is very good served with a green salad — also filling.

LAMB CHOPS DE LUXE (FOR SIX)

6 kidney chops, cut thick	¼ lb. sausage meat
6 mushroom caps	Salt
1 t. minced onion	Pepper

Have the chops cut from a large loin, double thick, and have them boned. Mix the sausage meat with the onion, fill the mushroom caps with the mixture, wrap the tails of the chops around the mushrooms and fasten them with skewers or sew them into place.

Have the broiler very hot. Sear the chops on both sides for a minute on each side — time it carefully — turning them with two pancake-turners. Lower the heat and cook the chops five minutes on each side if you like them rare, or seven minutes on each side if you like them well done.

Serve with potato balls rolled in chopped parsley and buttered and Mint Butter or Mint and Currant Sauce.

MINT BUTTER

Mint leaves
Butter
Paprika

Chop enough mint leaves to make three tablespoonfuls. Cream two tablespoonfuls butter and work in the mint leaves. Spread it on the chops just as they come out of the oven and dust them with the paprika.

MINT AND CURRANT JELLY SAUCE

2 T. mint leaves, finely minced   1 t. grated lemon rind
6-oz. glass of currant jelly   ¼ c. hot water

Heat the water, put in the jelly, lemon rind, and the mint leaves. When the jelly is melted and starts to bubble, the sauce is ready to serve. Serve it in a silver bowl with a silver ladle. Some other kind will do, but the color is nice with silver.

CLUB SANDWICHES

The Appleyards prefer their club sandwiches made with two pieces of toast to the ordinary three-decker style, which always seems to consist, somehow, chiefly of toast. The best ones, they think, are those made on the Consumers' Cooperative plan: one person makes the toast, another cooks the bacon, a third slices olives, tomatoes, and onions. A fourth gets the chicken and lettuce ready. Each person puts his own sandwich together and is soon back for another. After the first round it is a question of making your own toast and assembling the filling from what you find on various platters. After a while you get down to dark meat and cooking some more bacon, but by then it is generally too dark to see. You have beer to drink with these, if you like, and you eat them in front of an open fire. Mrs. Appleyard feels she could do with a round pretty soon.

MUSHROOM CLUB SANDWICH

For each sandwich:

2 slices of buttered toast	1 t. cream
2 strips of cooked bacon	¼ t. salt
4 large mushroom caps	1 t. butter
1 slice of broiled tomato	1 stuffed olive
Grated onion	

Peel the mushrooms. Chop the stems fine and fry them in butter with the grated onion. Add the cream. Spread the toasted side of the bread lightly with the mixture. Broil the mushroom caps, the sliced tomato, and the bacon, dotting the mushrooms and the tomatoes with butter and sprinkling them with salt and a very little pepper. Cover the mushroom toast with lettuce leaf, mayonnaise, tomato and bacon, and the mushroom caps. Decorate the top slice with lettuce, bacon, and half a stuffed olive. These can be put together on the assembly-line system too.

CHICKEN

Beef coming chiefly off cows, lamb generally leaping straight from field to frying-pan, fish, on the other hand, swimming in all too leisurely from the sea, the Appleyards, when in Appleyard Centre, eat a great deal of chicken.

Rhode Island Reds doubtless thrive splendidly in their native state, but they cannot well be better than when they have been brought up among the Green Mountains.

PAN-BROILED CHICKENS (WHITE MEAT ONLY)

Breasts of young chickens that weigh at least 3½ lbs.
Allow one wing and breast piece for each person

Large tomatoes, thickly sliced	Parsley
Sliced bacon	Salt
Wild mushrooms (*Agaricus campestris*)	Paprika
Sweet potatoes	Butter

Put some butter in a large frying-pan and brown the chicken breasts in it lightly. Transfer them to a large dripping-pan and set it into the oven. Cover the pan and cook the chicken for forty minutes at 400° F. Then take off the top pan, put the bacon over the chickens, and cook ten minutes longer.

In the meantime you have parboiled the sweet potatoes and cut them into thick slices. Spread them with butter and sprinkle them lightly with salt and pepper. Broil them till they are a good brown and arrange them around a large hot platter. The mushroom caps are to be broiled too. They take less time than the potatoes and had better be done separately unless you are sure you can manage them with the potatoes. Either broil the tomatoes with the potatoes or dip them in milk and then in seasoned flour and fry them in the same pan in which you browned the chicken. Put them on the hot platter. The chicken is almost done now, so you had better make the gravy.

GRAVY FOR PAN-BROILED CHICKENS

You are saving the livers for a purpose to be disclosed later, so you will use only the gizzards and hearts, which you have been simmering all the morning with salt, pepper, and some slices of onion. Before you began to broil the potatoes you minced the gizzard and the onion very fine. From the pan in which the chickens are cooking take three tablespoonfuls of fat. Put this into the frying-pan that has been your best friend all the morning and when it is hot, rub in three tablespoons of flour sifted with one half-tea-spoonful of salt and a little pepper. Then add the minced giblets and onions and cook gently for three minutes. Stir in the juice in which they were cooked and add one table-spoon of thick sour cream, a cup of sweet cream, and a tea-spoonful of finely minced parsley. If your cream supply is running low, use a little milk. This makes enough gravy for four people and some left over for the next day, on which Mrs. Appleyard fixes her eagle eye, because she has plans about it. Perhaps she had better tabulate the directions for the gravy, although making it is one of those affairs where you may have to vary it from day to day.

CREAM GIBLET GRAVY (FOR SIX)

Gizzards and hearts of 3 chickens	¼ t. pepper
1 onion	1 c. juice from giblets
3 T. fat from the pan	1 T. thick sour cream
3 T. flour	1 c. sweet cream
½ t. salt	1 t. minced parsley

Put the gravy in the tureen — the one with the tiny sprigs of flowers that was Mr. Appleyard's grandmother's and that has the ladle to match. Put the chicken breasts and bacon in the middle of the big hot platter with the fluted green edge — the platter that Mrs. Appleyard found in the back buttery. The tomatoes and sweet potatoes and mushrooms are already on it. Pour any juice that is left in the pan over the chickens. Garnish with parsley.

'I suppose that is all you had,' the Editor said to Mrs. Appleyard.

'Well, we did have some raspberry and currant jelly, and I happened to have pretty good luck with my mint chutney, so I just put on a little for them to taste, and Stan brought in a few peas he'd picked about half an hour before dinner, so we had those, and I put on a few new potatoes in their jackets in case anyone didn't like sweet ——'

'And dessert?'

'Oh — I hardly remember. Probably just some wild raspberries and cream and cottage cheese and some oatmeal cookies.'

'Stop! Stop!' said the Editor. 'You're making me cry....'

'Perhaps,' said Mrs. Appleyard, kindly, at this juncture, 'you would like to hear what became of the second joints and drumsticks of the chicken. Of course it was company that got the white pieces. The family had to put up with the rest.

'You had better,' she said, sandpapering a cradle about two inches long that she was making for some sinister purpose of her own, 'start this some morning when you ought to be doing something else you don't want to do, because this dish will take you all the morning. I call it

CHICKEN POCKETBOOKS

6 second joints and drum- sticks of 3½-lb. chickens	½ t. Bell's seasoning
⅓ loaf of French bread	2 mushroom caps, chopped
6 T. cream	3 chicken livers
⅔ c. giblet gravy (left over)	1 small onion
1 t. salt	½ c. sausage meat, preferably Montpelier
	4 T. butter, melted

'You take the bones out of the second joints and drumsticks.' (This sounds easy, but Mrs. Appleyard admits that she often uses three knives, the kitchen shears, and the poultry clippers. However, it must be possible for the least athletic, since she does it.) Dry the bread, cut into slices, and pound it into fine crumbs. Mix it with the cream, gravy, seasonings, and mushrooms. Mince the livers fine with the onion and the piece of sausage meat and combine the mixtures. If it seems too moist, add a few more bread crumbs. It should hold its shape.

'Stuff it into the places where the bones were, folding back the drumstick part. Either tie the whole thing up or sew it with heavy linen thread. Toothpicks come in handy in this project. Manage it without sewing if possible, because you won't enjoy unsewing it at the last minute.

'Put the pockets in a buttered pan in the oven, brush them over with melted butter, and cook them for forty minutes at 450° F. The pan should be covered. Uncover them after the forty minutes, put strips of bacon over them, and cook them until the bacon is the way you like it — ten to fifteen minutes.

'You had all the peas that were ready from the garden yesterday. Today you will have innocent young beets — and save a few and their juice to make bortsch tomorrow. There will be no gravy, so the potatoes will be creamed (page 305). There are still some oatmeal cookies left, a hiding-place having been found in one of Great-Grandmother Appleyard's covered dishes. It is still raspberry time, so the dessert is Raspberry Ice (page 156). Any complaints?'

When the chickens get big enough, Mrs. Appleyard says, they will be roasted. It would be hard indeed to roast one of Leonard Bealls's Rhode Island Reds so that it wasn't

good. You'd have to make a real business of spoiling it.
However, part of the goodness is in the stuffing. In Mrs.
Appleyard's theory of life, stuffing should not be a highly
seasoned mass of wet dough but a delicately flavored trap
for the juice of the roasting birds. This is how she goes
about it.

STUFFING — FOR THREE SMALL CHICKENS OR TWO
LARGE ONES

5 c. French bread crumbs	½ c. milk (part cream)
2 Montpelier crackers,	2 large onions, finely minced
or common crackers	2 t. Bell's seasoning
½ c. butter	1½ t. salt
2 T. sausage meat	½ t. pepper
2 eggs	

The chickens have been brushed inside with soft butter
and are covered outside with a blanket of butter and seasoned
flour. This is in addition to the butter in the stuffing.

Slice the French bread and dry it in the oven. Make it
into fine crumbs, using crust and all. Roll the crackers fine
and mix them with the bread crumbs and dry seasonings.
Add the minced onion and chop in the sausage meat. Add
the melted butter, the eggs lightly beaten, and the milk.
This stuffing may seem rather dry when you put it in, but
it will moisten during cooking. It will also swell a little, so
do not pack it in too tightly. You may add a little chopped
celery if you have it, but it is not necessary.

Make the gravy for these chickens like the gravy for Pan-
Broiled Chickens (page 171), only use the livers as well as
the gizzards.

Mrs. Appleyard's father always liked bread sauce with
roast chicken and she sometimes makes it still, to go either
with chicken, turkey, or Guinea chickens.

BREAD SAUCE

2 c. milk	½ t. salt
1 c. dried French bread crumbs	¼ t. white pepper
(inside of loaf only)	⅛ t. nutmeg
½ small onion	1 bay leaf
3 T. butter	1 sprig of parsley

Tear out the inside of the loaf, dry it in the oven, and roll it into crumbs. Be sure that it does not brown. Sift it, saving the coarser crumbs — about half a cup. Put the fine ones into the top of the double boiler with the milk, onion, and seasonings. Cook fifteen minutes. Skim out the bay leaf, onion, and parsley. Add a tablespoon of the butter.

Now fry the coarse crumbs in the rest of the butter. It should froth before you add the crumbs. Cook them until they are a light golden brown — about two minutes. Stir them all the time so that they will not burn. Put the sauce into a hot tureen, and sprinkle the bread crumbs over it.

This sauce is not like a poultice.

It is fun to cook things *sous cloche*, but if you do not have the cloches you can get nearly the same effect, Mrs. Appleyard has discovered, with covered Pyrex dishes: — that is, the same effect so far as the taste is concerned. You don't of course get quite the illusion that you are lunching at the Ritz.

When the chickens still weigh about two pounds apiece, this is a good way to use the breasts.

BREASTS OF CHICKEN UNDER GLASS (FOR SIX PEOPLE)

Breasts of 3 broilers	6 slices of very dry toast
1 qt. chicken stock	2 T. butter

6 thin slices of baked ham	½ t. salt
24 mushroom caps	¼ t. pepper
2 c. cream	½ t. paprika
1 onion, finely minced	

Cook the chicken breasts in a covered pan in the stock to which you have added the salt, pepper, and onion — for ten minutes. Use canned chicken soup if you have no stock on hand. Have ready the toast lightly buttered, cut to fit the bottoms of the baking-dishes. Butter the baking-dishes. Put in the toast and cover it with the slices of ham, cut the same size. (In emergencies Mrs. Appleyard sometimes spreads the toast with devilled ham.) Cook the broth down so that there is two cups of it. In another pan melt two tablespoons of butter. When it froths blend the flour with it and let it cook slowly for three minutes. Pour the broth on slowly, stirring it well. As it thickens, add the cream. Set the pan where it will just simmer. Put the chicken breasts on the toast and ham, surround the chicken with the peeled mushrooms. Pour some of the sauce over each of the chicken breasts. Cover the dishes tightly and set them into a moderately hot oven (475° F.) for half an hour. Serve them while the sauce is still bubbling hot.

It is easier for the guest, Mrs. Appleyard thinks, if the dishes are set on separate plates in front of the dinner plate, not on it. That is because on his own plate, before the meal has progressed very far, he will find Spoon Bread (page 49), young peas and carrots cooked together, and some of Mrs. Appleyard's currant jelly. The dessert is as likely as not to be a wreath of dark red strawberries with their hulls on and a mound of powdered sugar in the middle and a big lemon sponge cake, torn to pieces with two forks — not cut with a knife.

The next day the family will get the second joints, broiled with bacon, string beans cut very thin and left to mellow in cream and butter for half an hour before they are served, Watermelon Pickle (page 209) and, as the oven is not being used for anything else, Strawberry Shortcake (page 105).

CHICKEN PIE

Mrs. Appleyard sometimes uses chickens for this, but she thinks that young fowls really have more flavor. They should weigh at least five pounds.

For ten people:

2 5-lb. fowls	1 T. salt
3 onions, sliced	⅛ t. pepper

Begin the day before you are going to make your pies. Have the fowls cleaned and cut up, each into eight pieces. Put the meat and the onions into a large kettle. Cover the meat with cold water, bring it slowly to the boil, and cook slowly for three hours. During the last hour add the seasonings. When the meat falls from the bones, set a large colander into another kettle and pour the meat into it. Strain the broth and set it away to cool. Now pick over the meat, removing the skin and the bones. Save them, put them back into the first kettle, cover them with water, add a teaspoon of salt, and cook them for at least two hours. Strain this broth and set it away to cool. In the morning skim the fat off the two bowls of broth. If the broth has not jellied, put both lots into one kettle and cook a little longer. There should be about two quarts of the jellied chicken stock.

Now put the chicken into a large shallow baking-dish. There are some Bennington ones like old tortoiseshell that

have always been in the pantry for the last century that
Mrs. Appleyard likes, but if they are busy in some other
good work she uses a four-quart milk pan. Whichever it is,
she butters it lightly and puts in the meat.

Next she makes a sauce with the chicken stock, using

> 4 T. chicken fat
> skimmed from the stock
> 4 T. flour
> 2 qts. stock

She melts the chicken fat; when it is hot she works the
flour into it and lets it cook very gently for three minutes.
Then she stirs in the chicken stock slowly, tastes it, adds
more salt if necessary, lets it simmer for a few minutes, and
pours enough of it over the meat to cover it well. Then she
sets the pan into the oven (475° F.), and while the pie is
heating she stirs up some Sour-Milk Biscuits.

SOUR-MILK BISCUITS (FOR TEN PEOPLE)

2⅔ c. flour	¾ t. salt
½ t. soda	6 T. butter
2 t. baking powder	1 c. thick sour milk

Sift the flour with the baking powder and salt and soda
three times. Work in the butter with the fingertips, cut in
the sour milk with a knife. The mixture should be rather
stiff. Taste it to be sure you have not put in too much soda.
Add a little more milk and flour if you have. As soon as the
chicken broth is bubbling hard around the meat, drop the
dough in small lumps on top of it. Bake the pie until the
biscuits are brown — about thirty-five minutes in a hot
oven — 475°–500° F. If you have no sour milk, use the rule
for Baking-Powder Biscuits (page 34), but add extra butter
and do not roll out the dough but drop it on in lumps.

Serve Giblet Gravy with this, made as on page 172. You made it some time earlier when there was a free moment. If you were able to save any of the chicken stock for it, put it in, but it is good made with the water the giblets were cooked in. At the chicken-pie dinners in the church in Gospel Hollow they always serve with the pie white cabbage, finely shredded, mixed with salad dressing, pickled beets, mashed potato, pickles, and six kinds of pie for dessert.

Mrs. Appleyard, not requiring potato on top of pie for building up her silhouette, serves thick slices of tomatoes with French dressing. She says you don't know what a tomato is unless you have eaten them in Vermont fresh from your neighbor's garden. On the same principle — care for the hostess and her figure problem (as it is so elegantly called in the specialty shops) — you will not get six kinds of pie for dessert — or even one — but just some Dutchess apple sauce and cottage cheese with perhaps a few Brownies in case the chicken pie did not take the edge off your appetite.

Chicken is good, but life would be monotonous if you ate nothing else. In fact after two or three days of chicken Mrs. Appleyard notices that the family turns kindly eyes upon the humble dried beef. In Vermont dried beef does not mean something you get in a four-ounce jar with a fancy label. It comes off a large hunk of something that looks like petrified wood from somewhere near the Painted Desert. You buy it where you buy the Montpelier sausage and stand there while a machine of more than human skill shaves it into dark red translucent sheets that curl as they fall.

Mr. Appleyard once came home reporting that he did not approve of the new clerk who cut the beef for him.

'He saw the scales go down and took off two slices,' Mr. Appleyard reported. 'They can't have weighed more than half a picture postcard.'

Mrs. Appleyard made suitable sounds of disapproval over such ill-timed parsimony, and said, a little nervously, 'Did you say anything?'

'No,' replied her husband and favorite marketer. 'I just picked them up and ate them. . . .'

This is how Mrs. Appleyard cooked that accurately weighed half-pound of dried beef.

DRIED BEEF IN CREAM

½ lb. dried beef	1 c. sweet cream
2 T. sour cream	4 hard-boiled eggs, sliced
2 T. butter	½ t. paprika
1 c. milk	3 T. flour

Freshen the beef by pouring hot water on it, letting it stand ten minutes and draining it. Make the sauce by putting the butter into a pan, heating it till it froths, rubbing in the flour, cooking it slowly for three minutes, then adding the sour cream (lower the heat while you are doing this), the sweet cream, and the milk. Put it where it will just simmer, add the dried beef and the sliced hard-boiled eggs. There should be lots of sauce. If it gets too thick add a little more milk and cream.

Serve it with the first new potatoes that are big enough to bake, or with mashed potato. Once at a friend's house Mrs. Appleyard had it poured over French toast made by dipping stale bread in a batter of milk, eggs, and salt and browning it on both sides in a well-buttered frying-pan. That was quite an experience — she's hoping for another invitation.

If you serve the beef with baked potatoes, give the customers a chance to get their potatoes ready, mashing butter and pepper and salt into them, before you pass the dried beef.

FRIED SALT PORK WITH SOUR-CREAM GRAVY

This is a favorite Vermont dish and is made in about as many ways as there are cooks. Naturally Mr. Appleyard thinks that his mother's way was the best, and this is how she used to do it.

Boil a chunk of salt pork for an hour. Drain it, cool it a little, cut it into slices a quarter-inch thick. Dip them in milk, then in flour. Fry them rather slowly until they are a light cracker brown on both sides. Remove them from the pan and put them on a platter that is covered with brown paper to absorb any surplus fat. Cook the fat in the pan down so that there is only two tablespoonfuls or pour off some of it. Work in two tablespoonfuls of flour. Add half a cup of thick sour cream and half a cup of sweet cream. Cook very gently until the gravy has thickened. Serve the pork on a hot platter and the gravy in a hot tureen.

Baked potatoes with this, please, Mr. Appleyard says, a green vegetable — beet greens, spinach, Swiss chard — and something tart and sour for a relish — piccalilli, perhaps. Lemon Milk Sherbet (page 155) for dessert.

One of the great steps in the march of progress, Mrs. Appleyard says, was when hams began to appear already boiled and wrapped in silver paper, preferably with holly and mistletoe printed on it. Oh, well, there's no special objection to Easter lilies, but the notion that hams are especially appropriate to Easter is, in her opinion, just some-

thing thought up by the same people who have decided that
Mothers' Day is a lovely opportunity to give your mother
everything from a polo mallet to a knitted shawl. Mrs.
Appleyard has laid down the principle that she expects her
children to treat her nicely three hundred and sixty-five
days in the year and one extra on Leap Year. She looks with
no favor on the idea of being forgotten on three hundred
and sixty-four of them and remembered on the odd one with
a sense of guilt, carnations, and a hot-water bottle.

Ham, she says, is good on Easter, Mothers' Day, or Labor
Day, but on the whole she likes it best in cold weather when
she has fresh cider to pour around it.

BAKED HAM

A ham — weight after boiling 10 lbs.	3 c. cider
1 c. French bread crumbs	Whole cloves
½ c. light brown sugar (or maple sugar)	½ t. cinnamon

Skin the ham, if it has not been skinned already. If you
have boiled it yourself for the last twelve hours, let it cool a
little. Then take a knife and score the fat across diagonally
with the lines about three-fourths of an inch apart, so that it
is marked off diagonally into fine diamonds. Dry the French
bread and roll it into very fine crumbs. Mix the crumbs
with the sugar and cinnamon and rub about half of the mixture into the fat of the ham. Then press the cloves into the
points at which the scored lines cross. Sprinkle the rest of
the crumb mixture over the ham, put it on a rack in the
dripping-pan, pour the cider around it, and bake it slowly
at 375° F. until it is brown, basting it from time to time with
the cider. It should be baked for at least forty-five minutes.
Reduce the heat if it seems to be browning too quickly.

The cider should have been kept long enough in a cold place so that it has just started to fizz a little.

Pineapple juice or ginger ale may be used when cider is not available. If you are going to serve it hot, put pineapple slices around it. Baste them as the ham cooks and serve them on the platter with it. Add a little red wine if you like it.

A small shoulder is good, done the same way and served hot with pineapple, spinach, and Corn Pudding (page 51).

There is a lot of solid comfort in having a ham in the house, but ultimately it gets to the point where it seems that grinding it up would have to be its reward from a grateful public. This reminds Mrs. Appleyard that she had better make

HAM MOUSSE

2 c. cold baked ham, ground fine	1 t. dry mustard
1 T. Minute gelatine	⅛ t. cayenne
½ c. hot water	½ c. thick cream

This is for a small mould for about six people.

Dissolve the gelatine in the hot water, add the ham pounded in a mortar after you have ground it. Be sure to use only lean meat. Beat the cream stiff and add the seasonings (add a teaspoonful of horse-radish if you like it) and mix well with the meat. Dip a mould in ice water, put in the mixture. Chill thoroughly in the refrigerator for at least three hours. Remove it from the mould. Serve it with Mushroom Sauce (page 257).

HASH

A certain relative of Mrs. Appleyard's gives the following rule for hash.

'Look longingly,' he says, 'at the roast of beef while it goes through the stages of hot with Yorkshire pudding and cold with salad. When you have cut yourself off enough for a bedtime sandwich from the last chunk that is in the ice chest, put on an appealing expression and ask your hostess if she is considering *hash*. A few blandishments about how you haven't forgotten that day, etc. . . . and how hers is really etc. etc., *ad lib*. . . . come in well here.' You might also remind her that you noticed a bone from a porterhouse steak, too.'

She will then proceed as follows.

She hews the meat into gobbets. (Hash is a manly dish and calls for strong measures — and expressions.) She hurls them into a saucepan with a big onion hacked into chunks.

'Do not,' she says firmly, waving a large knife in a way calculated to produce respect for her advice, 'try to make hash by putting meat through the grinder and using odds and ends of potato, boiled, mashed, or baked. Take the long view; give such trifles to the hens or the pig and get them back later in edible form.

'Cover the meat — accompanied, of course, by its bosom friend the onion — with water and let it cook slowly till it is tender and most of the water has cooked away. Salt it during the last half-hour of cooking. When the meat is done, put on the potatoes and parboil them twenty minutes. They *must* be freshly cooked (furious wave with the knife). Cook enough so that you will have rather more potato than meat — three cups of potato to two of meat is about right. While the potatoes are cooking take out the meat and the onion from the pan. Let the broth go on cooking until there is only half a cup of it to two cups of meat. Pick over the meat carefully, removing any gristle and any large pieces of fat, and the bones. Very small pieces of fat may stay in. The meat should be so tender that it falls apart.

'Now try out the large pieces of fat in an iron frying-pan. Perhaps you saved the fat that ran down from the roast while you were cooking it, and perhaps if you were prudent you may have a cup that will have some of the dish gravy in it. It will consist of some garnet-colored juice or jelly and some creamy fat on top. Put the juice in the broth and use the fat for frying the hash. However, the tried-out kind will do very well, and failing either you may use butter. You are not, though, quite ready for the frying-pan yet.

'Chop the meat,' Mrs. Appleyard says, 'in a wooden chopping-bowl — a big one. As soon as the potatoes are ready, chop them in with the meat, not too fine. If you have two cups of meat with three cups of potatoes it will be just about the right amount for your large frying-pan — that big black one. Now add the broth that you have been cooking down.

'Heat the fat in the frying-pan. There must be plenty. It should cover the bottom of the pan and be at least a quarter of an inch deep. If there is not enough beef fat, add some butter. Put in the hash, mix it well for a minute or two over a hot fire. Then reduce the heat and let it cook slowly for about twenty minutes. You may like to do this on the bottom shelf of the oven if you do not interfere with anything else you are cooking. You may also set it on a flat gas toaster over one of the burners with the flame turned low. Whichever you do, watch it as a cat watches a robin's nest and when it is well browned around the edges, take it out.'

'That sounds easy,' Mrs. Appleyard's relative says, 'and apparently it is, if you have the muscles of Joe Louis and the dexterity of Houdini. Mrs. Appleyard begins by making a cut across the middle of the pan at right angles to the handle. She rests the pan on a platter hot enough to scorch the finish off any table not finished with linseed oil and elbow grease (Advt.), and with the pancake-turner she folds the half of the hash toward the handle over the lower half, as you would an omelet, and then teases the whole thing out onto the platter. It was a glazed, beautiful brown, like an old cherry table (one without shellac, of course), and it tasted like . . .' Finding no suitable comparison the speaker added weakly, ' . . . like hash. How singularly fortunate I was to have allied myself with such a family!' he concluded with feeling, for affection for a good pan of hash is one of the keenest emotions known to man. . . .

Mr. Appleyard sometimes likes poached eggs with hash. Mrs. Appleyard accordingly serves them, generally muttering something about painting lilies. She thinks her own brand of chutney (page 202) and some scalloped tomatoes go pretty well with it.

DUCKS WITH ORANGES IN CASSEROLE

2 young ducks	4 Temple oranges, rind
6 small carrots, sliced	and juice
2 c. peas, shelled	1 glass currant jelly
3 onions, sliced	¼ c. red wine
1 c. lima beans	1 t. salt
6 slices bacon	½ t. paprika

Have the ducklings cut in serving pieces at the market. Put a rack in your roaster. Put a cupful of water in the bottom of it, put in the vegetables. Some other combination will do, but have a variety. This is a good way to use frozen vegetables when fresh ones are hard to get.

Brown the pieces of duck in a frying-pan for a few minutes and lay them over the vegetables. Cover the roaster and cook for one hour at 375° F. Now have your individual casserole dishes ready — Mexican, French, Pyrex glass are all good. Make a brown gravy from the juice in your roaster, using two tablespoons of flour, well browned, the juice of the oranges and their grated rind, the currant jelly, and the red wine. Add the salt and pepper and paprika. Taste it and season it more highly if you wish. Put some of the vegetables into each casserole, put the pieces of duck on top. Add some of the sauce. Put on top a rosette of mashed potato sprinkled with a little more of the orange peel and some chopped parsley. Put a slice of bacon that has been partly cooked (there is enough fat from the ducks already in the dish) on top of the potato. Set the casseroles into the oven for a few minutes at 475° F., just long enough to finish cooking the bacon and to be sure that everything has blended and that the gravy is sizzling hot.

As this is the whole meal, meat and vegetables, in one dish, serve with it only some crusty rolls and some red wine. For dessert some plain lettuce salad made at the table with French dressing, toasted crackers, and cheese.

ROAST PORK

7-lb. loin of pork	*Mixed Vegetables*
1 t. poultry dressing	Peas
½ t. paprika	Carrots
4 T. flour	Wax and string beans
1 t. salt	Celery, finely cut
¼ t. cinnamon	Onions
1¾ t. cloves	

Have the loin cut so that it is easy to carve it into chops.

Sift the flour and seasonings together and rub the mixture well into the surface of the meat.

Have the oven hot — 500° F. — put the pork on a rack in the roaster and cook it for ten minutes uncovered. Then reduce the heat to 300° F. and add a little water and cook the pork for two and a half hours. Then put the vegetables around the pork and cook covered for an hour longer. If it has not browned enough, cook it uncovered for a few minutes longer while you are preparing the gravy, which you make by thickening the gravy in the pan with some well-browned flour. Put the meat and the vegetables on a hot platter and pour the gravy over them. Serve with mashed potato and green apple sauce made from early summer apples — Dutchess or yellow transparents.

For dessert: blackberries, lemon queens.

Sometimes Mrs. Appleyard varies this by cooking whatever vegetables she is going to cook separately, and the last half-hour putting around the pork a dressing made like the chicken stuffing on page 175, only moistening it with an extra egg and a little more cream. When this is brown she cuts it into squares and puts it around the pork. She makes a brown gravy with the juice and serves it separately. It is necessary to cook pork thoroughly and it is hard to cook it too long, provided you do not let it dry up. Never try to get it ready unless you have plenty of time.

POT ROAST OF BEEF

7 lbs. beef chuck	1 c. shelled new peas
6 small carrots, sliced	½ lb. beef suet
4 large onions, sliced	3 T. flour
1 c. celery, cut fine	½ t. cinnamon
½ c. young white turnips, diced	3 cloves
6 small radishes	½ t. Bell's seasoning

Pot roast, Mrs. Appleyard says, is always better the second day, so she always starts it the day before, if you understand what she means.

Have the meat tied in a neat round. Try out some of the beef suet in a large frying-pan and brown the meat on all sides in it. Now put it into a deep roaster large enough to hold the meat and the vegetables, cover it tightly, add a little water and the seasonings and cook it slowly at 250° F. for at least three hours. That's all for that day. The next day heat it up again slowly and cook it two hours longer. Add more water if necessary and turn the meat (it should have been turned at the end of the first two hours the day before, by the way). At the end of the second hour the second day, put the vegetables in. It will take another hour to cook them. Baste them and the meat well with the juice in the pan, add a little more water, but don't overdo it as there is a considerable amount of moisture in the vegetables. Do not put in the peas at first with the other vegetables but cook them separately the shortest possible time and add them and their juice — there should be very little — to the others just before you are ready to make the gravy.

This dish is of such a noble nature when it has been given a mother's care for two days that Mrs. Appleyard considers it well worth one of your best platters. She thinks it looks well on Sheffield with the grape pattern around the edge. She makes the gravy by thickening the juice in the pan with some well-browned flour, and after this has simmered she pours it over the meat and vegetables.

The radishes, she says, will never be recognized as such. They taste like very delicate young turnips, only slightly more spicy.

With the pot roast she serves mashed potato and perhaps

some asparagus, Country Style (page 284) or String Beans and Mushrooms in Cream (page 299). The dessert is sliced peaches with port-wine jelly and angel cake.

Port-wine jelly comes in a glass jar from a grocery store that she and her husband refer to simply as 'The Grocery Store' because they disagree about the pronunciation of its short and simple name. Whichever version is correct, they certainly know how to stir up a good port-wine jelly.

14

Menus: for Everyday or Holiday

LADIES' LUNCHEONS

Ladies are generally on a diet. They would faint at the sight of a baked potato but they can always eat cream.

1
Mushroom Soup (*page* 281)
Baked Eggs in Ramekins (*page* 110)
Lettuce with French Dressing (*page* 239)
Montpelier Crackers, Puffed (*page* 37)
Raspberries and Cream   Oatmeal Lace Cookies (*page* 69)

2
Mushroom Broth (Canned) with Sherry Added
Melba Toast
Eggs Benedict (*page* 111)   Green Salad (*page* 243)
Cottage Cheese (*page* 93)
Strawberries to dip in sugar   Brownies

3
Cold Consommé Cardinal
Broiled Chicken   Vegetable Salad (*page* 244)
Cantaloupe Filled with Lemon Sherbet

At Appleyard Centre the main meal is generally in the middle of the day. If, however, there are hungry mountain-climbers coming home late, it is in the evening. Those who are left at home get for lunch what they would otherwise have had for supper.

MAIN MEALS — FOR HUNGRY PEOPLE

These assume that the people who eat them swim, mow lawns, build log cabins, cook, build dams in the brook, fish, run tractors, ride hay carts, do sword dancing, and rest by wrestling, scraping furniture, and picking vegetables. They are more interested in plenty of one or two things that they like than they are in elaborate menus. Mrs. Appleyard likes to cater to these appetites. As she and some of the other members of the family are often cooking the meal, she seldom serves soup at this time because you can't serve soup, make Hollandaise, and be at the table with your friends all at once. Soup is usually served at the lighter meal — lunch or supper, whichever it is.

These are some combinations that have found favor with log cabin and fireplace builders:

1   Mrs. Appleyard's Oven-Cooked Broilers
with Pineapple and Bacon
Creamed Potatoes (*page* 305) Green Peas (*page* 291)
Raspberry Shortcake *page* 106)

2   Lamb Chops (*page* 168)   Asparagus
Hashed Brown Potatoes
Strawberries and Cream Oatmeal Lace Cookies (*page* 69)

3 Peas and Potatoes and Salt Pork Cooked in Cream (*page* 293)
Mrs. Appleyard's Graham Bread and Butter (*page* 36)
Pineapple Upside-Down Cake, Foamy Sauce
(*pages* 102 and 227)

4 Montpelier Sausage Cakes Apple Sauce
New Potatoes in Their Jackets with Butter
and Cream to Mash into Them
Young Carrots and Peas, Cooked Together (*page* 287)
Strawberry Shortcake (*page* 105)

5 Chicken Curry and Rice with Relishes (*page* 162)
Lemon Milk Sherbet Chocolate Cakes (*page* 62)

6 Baked Ham (*page* 183) Green Salad (*page* 243)
Mrs. Appleyard's Chutney (*page* 202)
Raspberries and Cream Filled Lemon Queens

7 Broiled Shad Roe (*page* 130) String Beans in Cream
Baked Potatoes
Peach Pandowdy (*page* 101) Hard Sauce (*page* 222)

8 Montpelier Dried Beef in Cream (*page* 181)
Green Peas Young Beets
New Potatoes with Chopped Chives, Butter, and Parsley
Blueberry Pudding (*page* 226) Foamy Sauce (*page* 227)

9 Pot Roast of Beef (*page* 189) with Vegetables
Rhubarb and Strawberry Conserve
Raspberry Sherbet Madeleines

10 Codfish in Cream *page* (136)
Baked Potato
Strawberries to Dip in Sugar

11 Veal Loaf (*page* 166) Mashed Potato
Corn on the Cob (*page* 287) Green Salad
Dutchess Apple Sauce (*page* 104)

12   Broiled Schrod.   Corn Pudding (*page* 51)
   Sliced Tomatoes, French Dressing   String Beans, Buttered
              Blueberry Pie   Cheese

13 Pan-Broiled Chickens, Sour-Cream Giblet Gravy (*page* 171)
          Spoon Bread (*page* 49)   Young Beets
       Apple Pandowdy   Hard Sauce (*page* 222)

14 Roast Lamb Currant, Mint, and Orange Sauce (*page* 258)
      Potatoes Browned Around the Meat   Peas in Cream
        Chocolate Ice Cream   Angel Cake (*page* 56)

Mrs. Appleyard can think of plenty more, but she de-
clined to go on any further on the ground that she was
hungry. She was, however, persuaded to speak of the Last
Day dinner.

Mr. Appleyard enjoys a table full of serious eaters. He
says it makes him feel like a patriarch. If carving serenely,
superbly, and generously is the mark of a patriarch, then
Mr. Appleyard is one. Mrs. Appleyard likes to supply him
with an audience of suitable proportions, and during this
particular summer, by judicious borrowing, the family consisted at times of twenty people. There was a good deal of
coming and going and it became a habit to remark to Mrs.
Appleyard: 'Won't you have swordfish and blueberry pudding — or chickens and peach shortcake — or whatever the
favorite objects were — tomorrow? You know it's my Last
Day.'

Probably no woman is more easily susceptible to flattery
than Mrs. Appleyard, and for a while she continued Last
Days as requested. However, even on her this occupation
began to pall and she finally — as the end of the season drew
near and departures loomed — announced that there would

be one official Last Day for everyone. They could write down on slips provided for the purpose their choices of hors d'oeuvres, soup, meat, or fish, three vegetables — one of which might be a salad — a dessert, either cake or cookies, something to drink. They could even mention things on the Emergency Shelf: nothing was sacred. And she would be alone, she said firmly, with this project.

The menu-makers left the house by ten o'clock with strict instructions to climb something high. From then on until seven-thirty Mrs. Appleyard seems to remember having been in constant motion. After comparing the various requests, she evolved, acquired the food for, and cooked the following

LAST-DAY DINNER

Caviar Canapés (Red and Black)
Cottage Cheese and Chives   Sardines on Toast
Bortsch with Sour Cream   Puffed Montpelier Crackers
Baked Broilers with Pineapple and Bacon
Raspberry and Currant Jelly
Sour-Cream Giblet Gravy (*page* 172) Candied Sweet Potatoes
Corn on the Cob   Broccoli: Hollandaise
Sliced Tomatoes: French Dressing
Dutchess Apple Sauce with Vanilla Ice Cream
Oatmeal Lace Cookies (*page* 69)
Grandmother Appleyard's Lemonade (*page* 28)

The human system is a very remarkable invention. After consuming this meal in heroic quantities and then washing the dishes while singing choruses from Gilbert and Sullivan, the young anacondas turned to and acted a few charades. Somehow Mrs. Appleyard does not remember a great deal about them.

SUPPERS

Suppers are of several types. Mrs. Appleyard's favorite kind is the one that she improvises on a cold summer evening. Mrs. Appleyard is apt to say bitterly about six times a summer, 'I have suffered more from cold than I ever did from heat in this summer resort.' When asked by someone with a logical mind why she continues to patronize it, Mrs. Appleyard replies, 'Well, I've got to get myself toughened up for winter in Boston, haven't I?'

Still, with plenty of hot soup she manages to get through the summer. She always makes enough for two helpings all around — which means that some get three.

SUPPERS FOR COLD EVENINGS

1   Onion Soup with Custard   Toast and Cheese (*page* 268)
Chocolate Pudding (*page* 234)

2   Bortsch with Sour Cream   Montpelier Crackers Toasted
Apple Pandowdy: Hard Sauce

3   Black Bean Soup with Hard-Boiled Egg and Lemon
Toasted Cheese and Bacon Sandwiches
Vegetable Salad   Chutney

4   Toasted Club Sandwiches (*page* 169)
Hot Chocolate (*page* 19)
Blackberries and Cream   Lemon Queens (*page* 60)

5   Mr. Appleyard's Welsh Rabbit (*page* 90)
Green Salad   Coffee   Fruit

On hot evenings the Appleyards drag their suppers out to a table on the lawn or to some hilltop where the sunset is easy to look at if they are not too busy eating. The menus are constructed so as to make these migrations as easy as possible for Mrs. Appleyard. Materials for making sandwiches rather than made-up sandwiches are transported. Sometimes each has his own supper strapped to him — known as Supper at the Belt. One of the various versions of Appleyard Centre lemonade goes along in a thermos pail. The most important thing is plenty of knives for spreading.

In this connection the problem arises as to whether each person has a knife or whether each thing to be spread has a knife. Mrs. Appleyard has never really solved this, but she generally brings enough extra knives so that it is not really necessary to spread sandwiches of sardines and of strawberry jam with the same knife. No set menu is suggested — as the whole point is that you make it up as you go along — but these are some of the things that seem to be easily consumed on Vermont lawns and hilltops.

Home-made graham bread.

Boston brown bread (at least a day old so it will slice well).

Sliced white bread — whatever loathsome form is being foisted upon a supine public at the moment. The bread is all the same, but it has some new seductive title each summer, such as Butter Crunch Bread or Grandmother's Sunshine Cream Loaf. Aside from the fact that neither grandmother, sunshine, nor cream enters into its composition and that you cannot crunch it, these names are accurate. It does come in the form of a loaf and the waxed paper is handy around the kitchen. Mrs. Appleyard would just as soon eat the paper as the bread. However, the younger generation finds it useful as a basis for heaping things on, so sliced bread is likely to stray into the baskets.

Mrs. Appleyard sometimes wonders what will happen to us when we have to face the facts of life and slice our own bread. She herself takes a loaf of Pepperidge Farm Bread and slices it as thin as blotting paper and rejoices that this is the only resemblance between the two substances.

One basket contains:

Cottage Cheese (*page* 93) or Apple-Tree Cheese (*page* 94)
Strawberry Jam   Peanut Butter   Devilled Ham
Pâté de Foie Gras   Sardines   Orange Marmalade
Snappy Vermont Cheese

If supper is to be on the lawn, the salad is mixed beforehand in a big wooden bowl. If the eating is going to be done away from the house, the salad goes in various glass containers. In them there are likely to be:

A jar of mixed vegetables, marinated with a little French dressing.

Mayonnaise.

Sliced tomatoes — or whole ones. (There are always some earnest admirers of Appleyard Centre tomatoes who prefer to eat them from the hand. This means plenty of paper napkins. Tomatoes and peaches, Mrs. Appleyard says, are no good unless they have to be eaten bending over.)

Lettuce — curly and bronze around the edges.

Sliced onion.

Cold meat wrapped in waxed paper: ham, tongue, chicken, or veal loaf.

Dried beef.

The dessert consists of the cold drink out of the thermos jar and whatever cake or cookies were found in the pantry with five-quart milk pans turned over them. There may be chocolate fudge cake, oatmeal cookies, Toll House cookies, brownies — it's all a matter of luck.

After these trifles have been consumed there are no scraps of waxed paper, no bread crusts, no squashed paper cups to show that anyone ever ate supper on that particular spot.

The Appleyards' friends the Teasdales often invite the whole Appleyard horde for a meal out-of-doors. Mr. Teasdale can build a stone fireplace in less time than it takes Mrs. Appleyard to make a batch of blueberry muffins. When you meet the Teasdales at their picnic place, you find that they have three or four fires going, a throne of slate stones for the grandmother of the party, hemlock logs for the children to roost upon, seats in shade or sunshine, and even a bed of hemlock boughs for anyone suffering from sacroiliac trouble. The table may be a rock or a grassy bank or some boards supported by sap buckets that have seen better days. Mr. Teasdale is roasting corn in the husks over one fire and Mrs. Teasdale is cooking Hamburgers over another. One of the Teasdale boys is doing bacon over a third and another is carefully turning sausage cakes, or inquiring whether you would like your egg sunny side up. Frankfurters have already been steamed and Bob Teasdale will grill one for you if you like. There are Frankfurter and Hamburger rolls warming in a reflecting oven near one of the fires. On the table are sliced tomatoes, sliced onions, pickles, pepper hash, butter, lettuce, mayonnaise.

There is a large lake of Mrs. Teasdale's lemonade and an angel cake a foot high, for which she apologizes on the ground that the oven wasn't just right or she only had sixteen eggs.

Anyone who cannot fix himself a succulent meal at the Teasdales' must certainly be lacking in initiative. Of what is left over campers have been known to equip themselves for a three-day trip.

15

Preserves. Mrs. Appleyard is never happier than when she is putting up something. She has an idea — of course this applies only to people like herself and not to any really virtuous housewife — that preserving is used chiefly as a defense. No woman who is making quince jelly or cucumber pickle can possibly be asked to sew on buttons or be urged to talk to the Ladies' Aid on 'The Arrangement of Flowers' or 'The Lighter Side of Chemistry.' She is so obviously busy and she has so much to show for it. There are the steaming kettles; there are all the magnificent jars and glasses with the sunshine glowing through them. Such a tangible achievement is a valid excuse for skulking at home even after everything is sealed with Parawax. There is something pleasant about having a duty to a large watermelon or a crate of strawberries. And when you come back to the country next year and find that the ravening hordes actually missed a few jars of this and that, it is like finding a pearl in an oyster. At least Mrs. Appleyard supposes that finding pearls is at times a rewarding occupation: the only ones she ever found were boiled.

Among the treasures that she sometimes finds on hand when June comes rolling round again there may be a jar of chutney that she made when the apples were ripe last year. This is what went into it:

APPLE–MINT CHUTNEY

12 Dutchess apples, cored, pared, and quartered	½ c. seedless raisins
4 ripe tomatoes — big ones	⅓ c. chopped mint leaves
3 large green peppers	3 cloves
2 lemons, sliced very thin	3 c. cider vinegar
1 orange, sliced	2 t. dry mustard
3 onions, chopped	2 t. salt
½ lb. preserved ginger	½ t. cinnamon
1½ c. seeded raisins	1 t. ginger
	4 lbs. brown sugar

Begin by chopping the mint very fine; add the onions and chop fine; then add the peppers, split and cleaned of seeds, and chopped medium fine, next the apples, and last of all the tomatoes, leaving them chopped fairly coarse. Add the sliced lemon and orange cut into quarters. Scald the vinegar with the sugar, syrup, and spices, pour over the fruit. Add the raisins and the preserved ginger very finely shaved into slices. Stir well. Cook half an hour the first day and let it stand overnight. The next morning reheat the chutney and cook it fifteen minutes. The third day cook it till the syrup is thick. It will probably take about twenty minutes after it begins to cook.

Watch it carefully, stirring to make sure it does not stick to the bottom of the kettle. Pour it into scalded jars. Para-

wax them and try to keep the chutney if you can. This
amount makes about twelve pint jars.

Earlier in the summer Mrs. Appleyard makes a combination of rhubarb and strawberries that is all gone by the time
the chutney is ready.

RHUBARB AND STRAWBERRY CONSERVE

12 c. rhubarb cut fine	1 c. red currants
12 c. small strawberries	Thin yellow rind of 1 lemon
1 can sliced pineapple	Juice of 1 lemon
(no juice)	16 c. sugar

Put everything together in large granite pans — those
milk pans Mrs. Appleyard keeps talking about. Bake the
fruit in a moderate oven — 375° F. — for one hour. Then
put the fruit into a large kettle and cook it until the juice
jellies on a cold saucer. This amount fills twelve pint jars.

An accident, such as might happen in any home — if
Mrs. Appleyard happened to be in it — produced an interesting variant on this conserve and also a word for the Appleyard family dictionary. There were not quite enough
strawberries for the full twelve cups, it was discovered after
Mrs. Appleyard had been out and pulled up the rhubarb
from behind the springhouse and had cut it into juicy green
and pink cubes. Remembering that she had seen a bowl
of crushed strawberries in the ice chest, she got it out and
with a sweeping dramatic gesture poured it over the rhubarb and strawberries. Now, the flavor of onion is a delicious one, but not usually associated with strawberries.
The bowl, in point of fact, contained about a quart of
bortsch with plenty of onions in it.

No one needs to think that our heroine was dismayed by

this happening. She simply added a half-teaspoon of cloves, a teaspoon of cinnamon, a little nutmeg, two more lemons thinly sliced and quartered, and proceeded as above. The conserve was a peculiarly handsome color and of a flavor that — luckily, perchance — defied immediate analysis. Some brave spirits preferred it to the established variety even after they knew what was in it.

It was natural, after this episode, for the verb 'to bortsch' to establish itself in the family dictionary. It is defined as 'to add some unexpected ingredient to a mixture, as "to bortsch the conserve."' (You can bortsch a dinner party, too, Mrs. Appleyard says — but not always with such happy effect.)

So far she has never put any onion into her brandied fruit and she is not planning to do so. Brandy is not generally considered a sedative, but Brandied Fruit is a peaceful sort of preserving that Mrs. Appleyard finds a restful change after some of her activities. It goes on all summer and lasts all winter — if you make enough.

BRANDIED FRUIT

Take as many quart jars as you think you will need. You will use about half a pint of brandy for each one, so let your supply of brandy be your guide. Mrs. Appleyard uses California brandy. She puts into each jar the different kinds of fruit as they come along and adds, each time, about half as much sugar as fruit. She begins with strawberries, both wild and cultivated, adds fresh ripe pineapple, finely diced (canned will do), red raspberries, red and white currants, black raspberries, sliced peaches, and blackberries. She covers the first lot of fruit and sugar with the brandy and from time to time adds a little more brandy as she puts in fruit and sugar. The result is a fine dark reddish-purple syrup with fruit floating in it. She uses it to put on ice cream or for pudding sauce.

Some cooks insist on making cottage pudding. Mrs. Appleyard has never had much sympathy for this habit, but she thinks you might take part of the curse off it by using this sauce.

BRANDIED HARD SAUCE

½ c. butter   ½ c. brandied fruit
1 c. powdered sugar   1 egg, well beaten

Cream the butter, add the sugar gradually, stir in the brandied fruit and the egg well beaten. Beat all together with a wire whisk. You can control the consistency by the amount of the fruit juice that you add, according to whether you prefer a thick or a thin sauce. This makes a rather thin one.

POTPOURRI

You can't eat it, even on cottage pudding, but if you have roses, it is fun to make it. Rugosa roses have very fragrant petals and their petals keep their bright color in the potpourri for a long time.

Gather the roses in the middle of a clear morning when the dew is off them. If you have rose geranium, lemon verbena, or syringa blossoms, add those too, but be sure there are three or four times as many rose leaves as of the other sorts. Put the petals to dry in the shed chamber, spread out on newspapers. What — no shed chamber? Well, that's hardly Mrs. Appleyard's fault, is it? Anyway choose a dry place where they will be out of your way.

To two quarts of dried petals use:

2 oz. allspice	8 drops oil of rose
2 oz. stick cinnamon	¼ pint brandy
½ oz. whole cloves	Thin peel of 1 orange
1 oz. orris root	Salt
2 oz. dried lavender flowers	

Put the dried rose petals into a large bowl. Sprinkle them lightly with salt. Do this for several days until you have enough petals. Stir it up every time you add a fresh lot. At the end of about a week, mix the spices with the petals and let them stand covered for a day. Then add the orris and put the potpourri into your jars, placing a little of the orange peel and the brandy in each. What Mrs. Appleyard made in 1937 is still fragrant. It is nice to scatter in the drawers where you keep your sheets.

Also easy to make and more appealing to the practical members of the family is Tomato Conserve. This can be made with either fresh or canned tomatoes. Three large cans of tomatoes about equal four quarts of whole tomatoes. Mrs. Appleyard thinks that unless you have tomatoes that come from your own or your neighbor's garden the canned tomatoes are about as good for this purpose. Their color is often better than that of ordinary tomatoes that you buy in the city. The bright color is one of the attractive things about this conserve. Cook it in a shallow pan so that the liquid will evaporate rapidly and it will keep its color.

MRS. APPLEYARD'S TOMATO CONSERVE

4 qts. ripe tomatoes (measured whole)	½ oz. stick cinnamon
3 oranges	1 c. seedless raisins
3 lemons	sugar
	2 t. salt

Peel the tomatoes by holding them by a fork over the gas flame until the skins pop and sizzle. Peel off the skin, slice the tomatoes. Cut them up and pour off about a quart of their juice and keep it to drink chilled or to use in soup.

Measure the tomatoes and add an equal amount of sugar or maple syrup. Slice the lemons and oranges paper thin. A sandwich-slicer is a great help for this, but you can do it by hand if you have patience and a sharp knife. Cut the slices into quarters — a kitchen shears comes in handy at this point. If you heat the sugar in the oven, it will dissolve more readily than if you have it cold. If you use syrup heat it a little first before pouring it over the tomatoes. Tie the spices in bags and put them into the kettles — you had better use two so that the conserve will cook quickly — with the tomatoes, lemons, oranges, and raisins. When the juice of the tomatoes begins to bubble add the heated sugar or syrup. Cook, stirring often from the bottom, until the juice begins to crinkle when tested on a cold saucer. Put the conserve into sterilized jars. Serve it with cold meat, meat loaf, fish, or curry.

RED–PEPPER RELISH (TO SERVE WITH CURRY)

12 red peppers	1 lemon, sliced thin
6 green peppers	1 qt. cider vinegar
6 tomatoes	2 c. sugar (or maple syrup)
3 large onions	1½ T. salt

Split the peppers and take out the seeds. Mrs. Appleyard left some in once, with surprising results. She also once cut a large batch of them by hand very fine. It took most of the skin off her hands. She is glad someone else is a bride now.

Chop the peppers in a large wooden bowl. Cover them

with boiling water, let them stand ten minutes, drain, pour over some more water, let them stand five minutes, and drain again. Add the onion chopped fine, peel the tomatoes, by holding them over the gas flame until they pop and taking off their rubber overcoats. Chop them in with the peppers, not too fine. Add the lemon sliced thin and quartered.

Heat the vinegar, sugar or syrup, and salt and let them boil five minutes. Then add the chopped pepper mixture. Bring it to the boil again and cook ten minutes. Let it stand overnight. In the morning cook ten minutes longer, stirring carefully. Put it into sterilized glass jars. Good with meat or fish as well as with curry.

PICCALILLI (TO SERVE WITH CURRY)

Frost comes early in Vermont and always leaves some green tomatoes that were hastily picked off the vines some evening when the sun went down in a windless sky behind Mount Hunger, and the moon came up over Spruce as sharp-edged as a new axe, and the crickets chirped so slowly you thought they had stopped for the winter.

The next day is the day to make Piccalilli.

½ peck green tomatoes	2 t. stick cinnamon, broken
3 green peppers	1½ t. allspice
3 large onions	½ t. mustard
1 sweet red pepper	1 c. sugar
1 bunch celery	3 t. salt
1 t. whole cloves	Vinegar

Chop the onions fine. Split the peppers and take out the seeds and chop the peppers with the onion. Add the celery and keep chopping, not too fine, and last of all the tomatoes and chop all together. Put the mixture into a kettle, add the salt, and let it stand overnight. In the morning pour off the juice. Add the spices in a bag and cover the chopped vegetables with cider vinegar. Cook slowly until the peppers are tender. Taste it and add more salt if you like. Good with hamburg or hot dogs.

Watermelon, Mrs. Appleyard says, is good for two purposes — to look at and to make into watermelon pickle. Anyone who does not mind eating water flavored with water is welcome to the pink part, she says. It is to her the most deceptive of all foods. Nothing is so delectable-looking, and nothing but a green pear — in her opinion — is so tasteless. Let her have the cool green rind and everyone will be happy.

WATERMELON PICKLE

4 lbs watermelon rind	3 lemons, juice and thin yellow peel
4 lbs. sugar	1 t. whole cloves
1 qt. vinegar	¼ c. salt
1 qt. water	4 t. stick cinnamon, broken

Cut the pale green part of the watermelon rind away from the hard green outside rind. If it is inconvenient for you to weigh it (it almost never *is* convenient for Mrs. Appleyard to weigh anything but herself, and the whole idea depresses her), it is fairly safe to figure that four quarts — cut up — amounts to about the same thing. A pint's a pound the world around, isn't it? It's true of water and logically should be true of watermelon. Anyway Mrs. Appleyard proceeds on that theory.

Make a brine of the water and salt and cover the rind with it and let it stand overnight. If there is not enough brine to cover all the rind, make some more of the same strength. The rind must be all covered: it is the brine that makes the pickle crisp instead of flabby and mushy.

The next morning drain off the brine, pour some more cold water over the melon, drain it again, add enough more clear water to cover it, and cook it till its tender. Sometimes it seems as if this were going on all summer, but cheer up, the end is in sight. Let it stand once more overnight, drain it again in the morning, and cut it into small cubes. Peel the lemons so thin that you get none of the white part of the rind. Squeeze their juice over the lemon rind, spices tied in a bag, vinegar, and sugar. Heat this up and when it is just starting to boil, add the melon cubes. Cook over a hot fire until the melon cubes are transparent. Take out the spices, put the rind into sterilized glass jars, pour the syrup over it.

If there is not enough syrup, make some more out of vinegar and sugar or heat some maple syrup. Whichever you do, put back the spice bags into it again. Be sure you divide the rind and syrup that it was cooked in so that no jar contains only the second lot of syrup. If you have to add a second batch, be sure to cook it down enough. Better put some more lemon peel in it too.

Probably — although it is hard to judge just how much syrup you need — being obliged to make a second lot is just something that happens to Mrs. Appleyard.

16

Pastry: Mostly Pies. Almost everyone who likes pie at all has strong opinions about piecrust. Mrs. Appleyard supposes it is all in how you were brought up. Probably there are perfectly worthy, honorable people to whom a pallid, white pie looks attractive. Mrs. Appleyard was educated in a circle of pie-eaters that liked the crust brown, and flaky, and crisp at the edges. There was in fact at one time a demand for pies baked in an oblong tin, because there arose in it a peculiarly fine opportunity for crusty pieces at the corners. This fad died out because if you cut the pie in six pieces, two of them were not corner pieces. There were enough opportunities for family competition without this situation, so the circular tin came back into style. It was fortunate for our language that the original form of tin was preserved. Otherwise the word "pie-shaped," meaning, of course, shaped like a wedge, would have lost its true significance.

Mrs. Appleyard's family cherished pie in various forms,

but not for breakfast. There must always have been some slight radical tendency in the family, some flaunting of tradition. Even in Emerson's day Mrs. Appleyard's ancestors contented themselves with a breakfast consisting of fruit, cereal, coffee, chops or steak, omelet and bacon if you preferred it, toast, honey, and three kinds of hot bread.

Mr. Emerson, so tradition runs, when asked if he ate pie for breakfast, replied with grave sweetness: 'Why, what is pie for?' It was also this well-loved sage who — on being offered some cherries in between meals — replied: 'What — set the whole fearful and wonderful machinery of my digestion at work upon a single cherry! No, I thank you.'

What kind of pie he had had for breakfast that morning is not recorded.

Not for breakfast, but for dinner and supper and an occasional setting of the digestive machinery to work in between meals were the pies and turnovers that Mrs. Appleyard's grandmother made. This is how she made her pastry. (Don't read this if you belong to the school of thought that admires blondes among pies.)

4 c. flour	½ t. salt
1 c. butter	Extra flour for rolling
1 c. lard	out
1 c. ice water	Extra butter for enrich-
⅛ t. soda	ing crust later

Sift the flour, measure it. Sift it three times with the baking soda and salt. Have the lard and butter very cold. Put them into a wooden chopping-bowl with the flour and chop them with a cold chopping-knife until they are in small lumps the size of your little finger tip. Put an ice-cube in a cup, fill the cup up with water and when your ice is melted, add the water, half a cupful at a time, blending it in with your chopper. Chop a little more, mixing the whole thing together.

Flour your pastry board and roll out the paste with a floured rolling-pin. Be gentle: pastry hates to be thumped. Roll it out about three-fourths of an inch thick. Cut it in thirds with a cold spatula. Do not touch it with your hands. With the spatula and a chilled pancake-turner pile the outside pieces over the one in the middle. Turn your board ninety degrees and repeat the process, cutting the pastry in thirds each time, rolling it out gently to the original thickness and putting the outside pieces over the middle one. Keep turning the board ninety degrees and do this four times, always as gently as if you were handling a week-old baby.

Have a cold platter ready with a cold, damp napkin on it, wrung out of ice water. Put the pastry on it and wrap the ends around it. Always make the pastry long enough before you want to use it so that you can chill it for several hours. It is even better to make it the day before you plan to use it.

When you roll it out for your pies, put a few extra dots of cold butter on it, because with the flour you have used on your board and rolling-pin you will find that it will stand some enrichment.

Bake in a hot oven — 450°–500° F. at first so that the chilled spaces that you made by your turning and cutting will suddenly expand, and so that your shortening will blend with your flour before the fat melts and gets oily. If it does melt, your pastry will be tough. When the crust begins to brown, you can reduce the heat a little. Pies with a double crust and a fruit filling need longer cooking than pies with a single crust and custard filling. They all need careful watching.

MINCE-PIE MEAT

3 lbs. round of beef
Tart apples, twice as much as meat, measured after they
    are pared and quartered and after the meat is cooked
    and chopped

1½ lbs. suet	¼ t. clove
1 gal. sweet cider	1 T. cinnamon
1 lb. citron	2 t. allspice
½ lb. candied orange peel	4 grated nutmegs
2 lbs. seedless raisins	2 T. lemon extract
1 lb. seeded raisins	4 lemons — rind and juice
3 lbs. currants	3 c. brandy
2 T. salt	Stock from meat

Begin the day before you plan to make your pies. Put the
beef on in cold water, let it come to the boil, and keep it
simmering until it is tender. It will take five hours probably. Be sure not to let the water cook away. Cool the
meat, remove any gristle, and chop the meat fine by hand in
a wooden chopping-bowl. Measure it.

Now pare, core, and quarter tart apples, and chop them
fine. Fix enough so that you have twice as much apple as
meat (the apple will cook down so there will not be too
much). Chop the suet fine and mix it with the meat and
apples. In the meantime you have put your sweet cider on
to boil with the citron and the candied peel cut in pieces.
When it has cooked down to two quarts, moisten the meat
mixture with one quart of it and let the other go on cooking
with the citron and peel until they are tender. Take them
out, chop them fine, and add them to the meat. Add also
at this time the raisins, currants, and spices, the lemon
extract, juice of the lemons and their grated rind.

Then add the liquor that the meat was cooked in and

simmer the whole thing for two hours over a slow fire. During the last hour add gradually the rest of the cider and the brandy. Cook a little longer if the mixture seems too moist.

Mrs. Appleyard's grandmother used to make turnovers with this mincemeat and keep them in a certain crock in the china closet. There was a spicy smell about the place that lasted winter and summer. Huckleberry gingerbread probably kept the good work going during the summer months. The turnovers were intended for children on their way home from school. They had a healing effect on scholars who had been wrestling with the more spiteful forms of mathematics and coming off second best. Even the division of fractions, the Theory of Limits, and circles with dotted lines skew-angling about them seemed better after a mince turnover or two.

The turnovers were also all right filled with dried-apple sauce. Mrs. Appleyard does not know, she says, just how the apple sauce was made, but she does know that the apples were not bleached with sulphur. They hung on strings from the kitchen ceiling and turned a nice pigskin brown. Anyone who wanted sulphur in those days took it where it belonged — in a large spoon with molasses in the springtime.

One of Mrs. Appleyard's saddest memories is connected with these dried-apple turnovers. There was a picnic on an island in Frenchman's Bay about a mile from Great Porcupine, where Mrs. Appleyard's grandmother, Mrs. Elmore, had a summer place. Mrs. Elmore was in many ways wiser than her granddaughter is ever likely to become, and one way was that when the rest of the family went on picnics she stayed at home. Thus she preserved the serenity that was one of her great charms. Her only defect — if she had one — was that she was likely to provide the picnickers with more food than they really needed. And she did not want any of it brought home. It must all be consumed on some other island, or on some pointed-fir-covered point on the mainland, in a becalmed catboat, on a sandy beach part way to Grand Manan, or on their own Shag Ledge with the tide coming in. It was a matter of indifference to her under just what conditions of sun, fog, wind, or tide they ate it — so long as they ate it all.

On this particular picnic when the bacon, broiled by setting up a salty driftwood board in front of a driftwood fire and pinning the bacon to the board, was all gone and they had eaten all the buttered toast with the marks of forked alder twigs through it and many more things that Mrs. Appleyard preferred not to mention, she said, because she was hungry enough anyway, the apple turnovers were produced.

Try as the picnickers might they could not eat them all. To be sure, Mrs. Appleyard would willingly have immolated herself, but for reasons of a statistical nature, accurately recited to her, she was denied the opportunity of making the supreme sacrifice. Some were even coarse enough to refer to her age — it was eight — and mention that they had to go home in the boat with her.

So the turnovers — there were two of them — were placed a little way below high-water mark; neatly they were placed on a shingle, sadly the shingle was laid on the smooth pebbles of gray and white and dull orange and porphyry color. Below the seaweed wreath at the tide mark with the driftwood like a deer's antlers sticking out of it lay the shingle with its precious freight.

The tide was coming in fast, and as the boat shoved off with that still hungry, skinny eight-year-old, Susan Markham, in the bow, the waves began to lap gently around the edges of the brown crinkly crust, and pretty soon one wave larger than the rest lifted the shingle. . . .

'Oh, well, I too have lived in Arcadia,' says Mrs. Appleyard. ' Perhaps I'd better talk about pumpkin pie now.'

The best pumpkins for pie, she says, are the small ones. They have less string and more sweetness than the jack-o'-lantern style. Cut them in halves, take out the seeds and string, cut them into large pieces and steam them until they are tender. Separate the pulp from the shell and put the pulp through a fine strainer.

Mrs. Appleyard has often gone all through this process, and she has on other occasions opened a can of pumpkin. Mr. Appleyard disapproved of anything but the home-grown product — never having tried anything else. He is, however, a man of reason, so when his mother and his wife conspired against him and made two pies — one of canned pumpkin and one of fresh — and he, poor innocent, voted for the canned one as being a trifle the more utterly delicate of the two, he simply beamed upon the plotters when they confessed, and had another piece of each pie. He has never since been so crude as to inquire which kind Mrs. Appleyard was devoting to his nourishment this time, and if he can't tell, no one can.

However you acquired your cooked pumpkin, either by steaming and straining it yourself or by opening a can, you have really only just begun. You take a large iron frying-pan, butter it lightly, put in the pumpkin, and cook it down until it is dry and brown. This cooking, plenty of cream, a delicate accuracy in seasoning, rich flaky crust, are the essential things in turning out a good pumpkin pie. The cooking in the frying-pan is well worth the trouble of standing over it and stirring it constantly. It will scorch if it is not stirred often, and what you are trying to do is to dry the moisture out of it and just slightly caramelize the natural sugar that is in the pumpkin. If this is done right, turning the whole mass over so that it all comes in contact with the hot pan from time to time, it brings out the flavor and sweetness of the pumpkin. Drying out the pumpkin in the oven is *not* a substitute for cooking it in the pan on top of the stove. In the oven it is likely that the pumpkin will simply dry on the outside and still be moist inside. Keep turning it over as the steam puffs out of it. It will take about twenty minutes and at the end of that time it should be a rich golden brown all through instead of orange, and thick and smooth instead of watery. There should be about one and a half cups if you are planning to make two large pies.

PUMPKIN PIE (B. H. K.)

1½ c. cooked and browned pumpkin		1 t. cinnamon
		½ t. ginger
2 T. flour		⅛ t. mace
2 eggs		3 c. rich milk
1 t. salt	1 c. sugar	1 c. cream

Put the pumpkin in a bowl, sprinkle it with the flour, and stir in the flour thoroughly. Butter the bottom of a saucepan and scald the milk in it. Add the cream and the seasonings. Pour it over the pumpkin mixture and add the eggs — well beaten. Get pie shells ready, built up around the edge, and nicely fluted or crimped (for pastry see page 212). Do not have the pie shells too full of the mixture; three quarters of an inch deep is about right. If your tins are only of medium size this will be enough for another small pie tomorrow. Bake only what you are going to eat within twenty-four hours. Both pastry and filling will keep in the ice chest until you need them. Cut cheesecloth into inch strips or use one-inch strips of gauze, moisten it a little and put it around the edge of your pies. This will keep them from browning too fast at first.

Bake the pies in a fairly hot oven — 450° F. for forty-five minutes, reducing the heat to 325° F. if they seem to be cooking too fast. They are done when they will just shake in the middle when moved.

To leave out some Vermont cheese when you serve the pie is a serious offense in the Appleyard family.

If you want to make squash pie, go right ahead, but don't expect any help from Mrs. Appleyard, who would rather speak about Lemon Meringue.

It is not true that Mrs. Appleyard has the digestion of an anaconda. Her constitution is really an organism of peculiar delicacy; for instance, she is allergic to cornstarch. Anyone who wishes to make lemon pie — or anything else, such as that pudding that tastes like slate pencils — had better carry on his researches somewhere else.

LEMON PIE WITHOUT CORNSTARCH (B. H. K.)

5 eggs	3 T. water
1 heaping c. sugar	Grated rind of 1 lemon
½ c. lemon juice	

Separate the eggs. Beat the yolks slightly, add the sugar, lemon juice, finely grated rind, and water. Beat all together. Have a large pie shell ready with one crust, built up and fluted around the edge, pricked all over, baked ten minutes. Fill it, put a strip of gauze around the edge so that it will not brown too quickly. Bake it for ten minutes at 450° F., then reduce the heat and bake for twenty minutes longer at 325° F. Remove it from the oven, cool it, and cover it with a meringue made, while the filling is baking, as follows:

MERINGUE NO. 1

Whites of 5 eggs
1 heaping c. powdered sugar
2½ T. lemon juice

Put the whites of eggs in a bowl and beat till the mixture will hold its shape. Add the lemon juice, a drop at a time, and keep beating. This will take about half an hour.

If you have a feeling of lethargy or have not an electric mixer, both of which drawbacks are generally keeping Mrs. Appleyard in a relaxed state, better do it this way:

MERINGUE NO. 2

Whites of 5 eggs
1 t. lemon extract
1 c. powdered sugar

Beat the egg whites stiff. Add a quarter of the sugar gradually, and beat hard; then another quarter, keep on beating. Fold in all the rest at once and add the flavoring — vanilla, if you prefer. Heap it on the pie and return pie to the oven for a few minutes until the meringue starts to brown.

These directions are for a large pie and a lot of meringue. The Appleyards consider a small pie something made simply to annoy.

Apple pie depends, strangely enough, on the apples of which it is made. They should be tart and juicy. Dutchess, Yellow Transparents, Gravensteins, Mackintosh Reds all make good pie and all slightly different. There are so many possible faults in apple pie that it is depressing to mention them all, but perhaps the two worst, assuming that your crust is good, are apples still partly raw because they were hard and dry to start with, and too much spice. An apple pie should taste of *Apple*. A very little lemon juice or rind, the merest hint of cinnamon or nutmeg do bring out the flavor of the apples, but they are dangerous substances, to be used, like arsenic, in small medicinal doses.

APPLE PIE

6 apples with a tang	1 c. sugar
$\frac{1}{4}$ t. lemon juice or $\frac{1}{8}$ t.	$1\frac{1}{4}$ t. cinnamon
lemon rind	$\frac{1}{8}$ t. nutmeg
1 t. butter	

Better not put the spices in at all if you cannot trust yourself not to scatter them about. If you use them, mix them thoroughly with the sugar so that they will be evenly distributed through the fruit. Line your pie plate with well-chilled pastry (page 212). Work a little more butter into the top crust than into the bottom crust. Never grease a pie plate: good pastry does its own greasing. Set the plate and the top crust back into the refrigerator while you are getting the apples ready. Pare the apples, core them, slice them very thin. Be sure to fix plenty. Put them into the pie plate on the lower crust, shaking the spiced sugar over each layer. Dot the top layer with the butter and sprinkle it with the lemon juice. Cover the apples with the top crust. Gash it in three places to let the steam escape. Bake the pie for forty minutes. Have the oven at 450° F. for the first ten minutes and then reduce the heat to 425° F. for the remaining half-hour.

Apple-tree Cheese (page 94) is good with this, and so is vanilla ice cream, if you like your pie à la mode. The Appleyard children do. One of them ordered beef à la mode at a restaurant once and asked when it came, 'But where's the ice cream that goes with it?' Mr. Appleyard, however, says there is nothing better with apple pie than a piece of a well-ripened Vermont June cheese, and his wife is inclined to agree with him.

Double the amount of apples baked in a large earthenware dish with one crust is a good way to make your first apple pie, and you can graduate to the two-crust style later. This is a fine way to use the later apples when the early ones have gone. Be sure to slice them thin. Baldwins are good in a deep-dish pie. This may be spiced a little more than a pie made of early apples, but don't overdo it. It will probably take fifty minutes to bake a large pie. Begin with the oven at 450° F., and after the first ten minutes reduce the heat to 400° F.

Because of her youngest child's tastes Mrs. Appleyard generally serves vanilla ice cream with this, but some of the others like Hard Sauce and get it when their turn to be pampered comes.

HARD SAUCE

½ c. butter   ¼ t. nutmeg
1 c. powdered sugar   1 T. powdered maple sugar
½ t. vanilla

Cream the butter. Work the sugar in gradually. Add

the vanilla. Do not get the sauce too stiff — you may like to leave out part of the sugar. Sprinkle it with the nutmeg and powdered maple sugar (page 82). You are not really likely to have any unless you know Mr. Appleyard intimately. It's not a bad idea to learn to make it, though. Of course you can take a cake of maple sugar and grate it if you would rather.

The annual expedition to the top of Catamountain to get blueberries results in a certain monotony in the Appleyard menus. Blueberry pudding, blueberry pie, blueberry muffins all have their adherents among the pickers. Mrs. Appleyard makes them all: pie for dinner, muffins for supper, and pudding the next day.

Pie is the most sensitive of the three, so it is made with the freshest and best berries. In blueberry pie there should be *nothing but blueberries and sugar.* The suggestion that there should be flour dredged over the berries is one that is so shocking to Mrs. Appleyard that she can hardly think that it can be meant to be taken seriously. She has also heard of the macabre notion of adding a few green grapes 'to improve the flavor.' Where could blueberries have been picked that need improving in any such way? Not in Vermont, nor yet in New Hampshire, Mrs. Appleyard is sure; and Maine, too, is innocent of any such crop. If grapes, Mrs. Appleyard inquires, why not a few spoonfuls of cornstarch, some gooseberries, and a little almond extract?

At this point the Editor, realizing that talk of this sort was not doing Mrs. Appleyard's blood pressure a bit of good, tactfully led her back to her Queen Anne chair and the subject of pie.

'Blueberries,' she continued more calmly, 'should have on them a bloom that is like the sky above Catamountain, over a skin as dark as the mountain itself when seen just before a thunderstorm, some August afternoon. Pick the stems and leaves out of the berries. Take out any that are mashed. Handle them as little as possible. If there are a few that are still a reddish purple or even slightly green, leave them in. They'll do instead of those green grapes to add a little tartness. Line the biggest Bennington pie dish with pastry (page 212). To fill this particular dish you will need two and one-half cups of berries and one cup of sugar.

'Mix them well together, being careful not to crush the berries. Perhaps it is not necessary to mention that the berries should not be washed, but stranger things have happened — there were those grapes.

'Have the top crust a little more enriched with butter than the lower one. Put in the berries and sugar and cover them with the top crust. Make three gashes in it and be sure that the edges of the under and upper crusts meet neatly everywhere. Brush the lower crust with water very lightly before putting on the upper one and press the two crusts gently together with the back of a fork. Bind the edge of the pie with a strip of gauze. This will help to keep the juice in and stop the edge from browning too quickly. The only possible excuse for putting in flour is to keep the pies from leaking. It is not necessary if you bind the edges. Have the oven at 450° F. for ten minutes and then reduce the heat to 425° F. and bake the pie for thirty to thirty-five minutes longer.

Be sure your pie is well browned. There are few lovelier color combinations for interior decoration, Mrs. Appleyard says, than the golden brown of piecrust and the rich purple of blueberry juice.

'Green grapes indeed!'

Mrs. Appleyard goes off muttering, but turns back to say over her shoulder: 'And now, children, you had better all brush your teeth. I can't have you looking like chow dogs. . . .'

17

Puddings, and Sauces for Them

STEAMED BLUEBERRY PUDDING

This is Mr. Appleyard's favorite dessert, as it was his father's, and we hope that the Appleyard boys will choose wives who will take this hereditary task seriously. Few words have ever pleased Mrs. Appleyard more than some from her husband in praise of her blueberry pudding. This is how he likes it:

2 c. flour	1¼ c. blueberries
1 c. milk	½ t. salt
4 t. baking powder	2 T. butter

Sift the flour and measure it. Sift it three times more with the baking powder and salt. Work in the butter with the fingertips. Add milk and berries — which you have jounced up and down with a little of the flour — alternately. Put the batter into a buttered tin that has a tight

cover. A quart coffee can, the kind that is higher than it is
wide, is a good shape and size. Vacuum-packed cans are
no good. An old Chase & Sanborn can is a great treasure.
Mrs. Appleyard's whole career as a wife and mother was
almost wrecked once because the tin she used got thrown
away by some non-New Englander. However, she found
another one at an auction, and cherishes it with the fond
devotion of a motorist for his spare tire.

Steam the pudding one and a half hours. Steaming is
easy if you have the mould (née coffee can), a kettle with a
tight cover, a rack to set the mould on, and something
heavy — Mrs. Appleyard uses an antique stovelid retired
from active service for this — to put on top of the can containing the pudding so that it will not tip over. If the pudding stands upright and if the water never stops boiling,
there is no reason why your pudding should not fill the
mould and be fluffy inside and a delicate biscuit tan outside
with rich purple spots through it.

Do not fill your mould more than two thirds full. Be sure
that the water comes halfway up around the can and that
it does not cook away. You will have noticed that the pudding is made with a biscuit dough — not a cake batter.
The richness is in the sauce.

FOAMY SAUCE

½ c. butter	1 c. powdered sugar
2 eggs	1 t. vanilla

Cream the butter. Add gradually the sugar, the eggs well
beaten, and the vanilla. Cook in the top of the double
boiler, beating with a wire whisk or an egg-beater, until the
mixture thickens. It takes only a few minutes. Mrs. Apple-

yard has the butter and sugar ready in the top of the boiler and finishes the sauce while the table is being cleared.

This is supposed to be enough to go with one can of pudding. It does indeed supply enough for a liberal coating of six thick slices (try saying that fast) into which the pudding is cut. (Not over three quarters of an inch thick, says Mr. Appleyard.) However, on glancing through Mrs. Appleyard's book of rules — that battle-scarred volume — the Editor noticed a remark, deeply underscored, which was deciphered to read 'Never enough.'

ALMOND RING (E. M.)

Whites of 4 eggs	½ t. almond extract
1⅔ c. ground, blanched almonds	4 macaroons
1 c. sugar	

Make the macaroons into fine crumbs. Butter a ring mould and dust the crumbs over it. Beat the eggs to a stiff froth, fold in the sugar and the almonds alternately. Put the mixture into the mould. Bake in a moderate oven — 375°–400° F. — for half an hour. Serve the ring either hot or cold. Strawberries, slightly crushed with sugar, and some vanilla ice cream are good with it if it is served cold. Chocolate sauce is nice with it if it is served hot.

CHOCOLATE SAUCE

2 sqs. Baker's chocolate	½ c. light brown or maple sugar
1½ t. butter	½ c. boiling water
1 c. white sugar	½ t. vanilla

Melt the chocolate, add the butter. Pour on gradually, stirring well, the boiling water. Bring to the boiling point add the sugar, and cook fifteen minutes. Cool slightly and add the vanilla.

This sauce is good on cream puffs, pudding, or ice cream.

Mrs. Appleyard's rule for plum pudding was given to her by a friend from South Carolina at whose house everything to eat ought to have been recorded in shorthand on the spot. Unfortunately being then young and frivolous, Mrs. Appleyard missed her opportunity. She regrets that she never learned how to cook those soft-shell crabs, that hominy in her hands never has quite its full charm, that her stewed tomatoes just miss some subtle flavor, that she never could have greeted with quite the same aplomb the episode of the turkey.

Mrs. Rodman was one of those who can always inspire good cooking in others, even when the material seems unpromising. The material at hand when the turkey was roasted was a willing but inexperienced little Swedish girl named Sigrid. She was round and slow, with earnest blue eyes. It was a mistake to think that she was stupid and Mrs. Rodman did not think so, but it was also a mistake for her to try to move faster than her own rhythm dictated. It was unfortunate that, filled with zeal and pride over its splendid appearance, she tried to hurry the Christmas turkey into the dining-room.

It was an enormous turkey. It had, Mrs. Appleyard seems to remember, oyster stuffing inside it. Chains of brown sausages were draped over its noble breast. Parsley and celery wreathed it artistically. It was on a silver platter so large that Sigrid's plump arms could hardly go around it, and her platinum head with its neat braids came just high enough above the crackly brown turkey for you to see the pride in her blue eyes and the pink flush that baking the sizzling bird had given her.

Sigrid's pride lasted only just through the swinging door and around the Chinese screen. She herself had waxed the floor to the polish of an old mirror. Turning the corner by the screen at unusual speed was too much for her. Her feet went out. The platter rolled one way, the turkey another. Parsley, celery, sausages flew through the air.

Mrs. Appleyard remembers that Mrs. Rodman always looked the way a French marquise ought to look — only probably one never did. She may have recently taken off her cooking-apron, but she never brought the kitchen into the dining-room. This neutrality toward a meal after it was ready she carried out in the case of the skidding turkey.

Into the silence that fell upon the eleven people around the mahogany came her voice, saying kindly but crisply, 'Pick up the turkey, Sigrid, and bring the other one.'

Of course there was no other turkey, but when the first one emerged from the kitchen once more, it looked as handsome as ever. Its roll on the immaculate waxed floor had done it no harm. Sigrid's face was saved. The guests, according to their own discretion, had either the satisfaction of thinking that there really were two turkeys or of enjoying the joke.

When Mrs. Rodman was asked later why she knew that Sigrid would respond in the emergency, she replied, 'I've cooked with her.'

It is still, Mrs. Appleyard thinks, a good way to know another person.

After the turkey came the plum pudding. It arrived safely in blue flames with a spray of holly stuck in the top, and this was the way it was made.

PLUM PUDDING (A. C. R.)

1 lb. beef suet, ground fine
½ lb. citron, diced
½ lb. raisins
¼ lb. candied cherries
½ lb. currants
½ lb. almonds, blanched and ground
2 c. French bread crumbs
½ nutmeg grated
½ t. salt

1 t. each of cloves, cin-
   namon, and allspice
Juice of 1 lemon
2 T. rose water
2 T. rum
1 c. sherry
10 eggs
2 c. sugar
1 c. flour

Dry the French bread — inside of the loaf only — and make it into very fine crumbs. Mix it with the chopped suet, almonds, citron, raisins, currants, and cherries. Sprinkle the spices and salt over the fruit and mix well. Pour the rose water, lemon juice, sherry, and rum over them. Stir. Cover the bowl and let it stand overnight. The next day beat the yolks of the eggs well and add them to the sugar. Beat the whites stiff but not dry and fold them into the yolks. Add this mixture to the fruit mixture. Scatter the flour over the whole thing and fold it in.

This will make about eight pounds. Use coffee cans, large baking-powder cans, anything with a tight cover to steam the pudding in. Butter them well. Fill them not more than two thirds full. Set them on a rack in a large kettle with a tight cover. Steam them for five or six hours.

Mrs. Rodman used to make these puddings and send them to her friends for Christmas — a pleasant custom. In serving hers Mrs. Appleyard used to steam it long enough to heat it through, stick holly into it, pour brandy around it, and bring it in lighted. She never did so without thinking of her friend saying, 'Sigrid, pick up the turkey....'

In fact she has told the story often enough so that it is entered in her children's under-the-dinner-table notebook under Food and Wine Anecdotes, No. 87.

There are various kinds of sauce that are good with plum pudding. Hard Sauce (page 222) is good. So is Foamy Sauce (page 227). Mrs. Appleyard sometimes makes hard sauce and puts a little of her Brandied Fruit (page 204) with it, but as there is perhaps already enough brandy in the pudding for some tastes, she sometimes makes

VELVET–PUDDING SAUCE

½ c. butter creamed	1 egg, well beaten
1 c. powdered sugar	½ t. vanilla

This is very easy to make as it is not cooked.

Cream the butter, add the sugar gradually and then the beaten egg. Add the vanilla. This can be fixed, except for the egg and the flavoring beforehand. It takes only a minute to beat in the egg.

If you like rice pudding — Mrs. Appleyard can't see why anyone does — this kind has at least the advantage of being creamy and delicately flavored.

RICE PUDDING (S. W. E.)

2½ T. rice (level measurement)	1 qt. milk
3 T. sugar	¼ c. seedless raisins
¼ t. lemon extract or	½ t. salt
¼ t. vanilla	

Wash the rice in several changes of water. Butter a thick pottery baking-dish. Put in the milk and stir into it the rice, sugar, raisins, and flavoring. Bake it for at least two hours in a slow oven — 300° F. During the first hour, stir it three times. There will be skin over the top and you must slide your spoon carefully under it at the side and stir the contents without breaking the skin. Reduce the heat if the skin is browning too fast.

Purists, those who like rice pudding, often prefer it without the raisins. Mrs. Appleyard sees no point in taking sides in this argument. There is a tradition in her family that she always wept at the sight of rice pudding — large silent tears trickled down her upturned nose and made her look somehow more than ever like the King Charles spaniel that she was said to resemble.

She has learned since not to shed tears, but that is as far as she plans to get. Still, she has acquired a taste for horehound candy, cottage cheese, and spinach — all substances to which the average child is hostile. Perhaps she will graduate to gruel, rice pudding, and rennet. Nothing is impossible. She may even learn to cherish tripe — that dishonest dish that looks like a waffle, feels like a raw eel, and tastes like an umbrella.

Mrs. Appleyard shudders, and turns to her own chocolate pudding. It happened one day at Appleyard Centre that, owing to world conditions or something, there was discovered in the pantry a third of a chocolate cake and half a stale coconut frosted cake. This circumstance is something like the likelihood of Mars, Jupiter, and Venus all hanging in the west in a straight line in a primrose-and-blue sky with rose-colored clouds above them — yet both things have happened in Mrs. Appleyard's lifetime, and may again. Anyway, sponge cake would do and you would just add more chocolate and some coconut. You have to be a little daring in this world every now and then.

CHOCOLATE PUDDING (MRS. APPLEYARD)

One-third of an 8-inch chocolate
cake with chocolate frosting
Half an 8-inch coconut cake
2 c. milk
1 t. vanilla
½ c. sugar

2 sqs. chocolate
¼ t. salt
2 T. Zo or Grapenuts
2 eggs
2 T. light-brown or maple
sugar

There should be about three cups of cake crumbs when you have rolled them fine. Heat the milk, add the sugar and the chocolate, grated. Stir till well mixed, add the vanilla and the salt, and pour the mixture over the cake crumbs. Beat two eggs light and beat them well into the mixture. Butter a baking-dish, put in the mixture, sprinkle the top with the Zo and brown sugar mixed together. Bake for half an hour at 400° F. The top should be crisp and crusty. Serve it hot with Hard Sauce or Foamy Sauce, or cold with thick cream.

The best Indian pudding that either Mr. or Mrs. Appleyard ever ate was in a little Vermont inn not far from the Connecticut. Mr. Appleyard would not rest until he found out how it was made. He turned on his full charm and the waitress guaranteed to wheedle the rule from the cook.

When she came back, she said, with blushes and giggles, that the cook did not want to tell. She was of the opinion — as Vermonters usually are when asked for a receipt — that it was not fit to eat anyway, that she didn't think she'd had extra good luck with it, and that if Mr. Appleyard knew how it was made, he'd never eat her cooking again.

These preliminaries being disposed of, the secret was then revealed: there happened to be some cold johnnycake left

from breakfast and the pudding was made from that. Mr.
Appleyard thinks that the fact that the corn meal in the
jonnnycake had already been cooked and that the johnnycake had plenty of eggs and sour cream in it helped to make
the pudding especially good. This was how it was done:

INDIAN PUDDING (CONNECTICUT RIVER VALLEY)

Square of cold johnny cake 6 by 8 inches.
Spider Corn Cake (see page 50) may be used

1 qt. of milk	½ t. salt
½ c. molasses	½ t. nutmeg
2 eggs	½ t. cinnamon

Crumble the johnnycake very fine. Pour the milk over
it and soak it well. Add the molasses and seasonings, mix
well, and let it stand on the back of the stove for a while.
Beat two eggs and add them. Taste it and add more
molasses if you like. Put it into a buttered baking-dish,
earthenware, and bake it for one and a half hours at 350° F.
Stir it three times the first hour, slipping the spoon in at
the side and taking care not to break the skin.

Serve with thick cream and powdered maple sugar
(page 82) or vanilla ice cream.   What a surprise it would
be to an Iroquois to find vanilla ice cream on his pudding!...

18

Salad, and Salad Dressings. Assuming
that whatever vegetables go into a salad are in good con-
dition — and why make salad at all if they are not? — Mrs.
Appleyard thinks that the dressing is more important than
the precise combination in the salad bowl. Therefore she
begins with some different dressings. What you put them
on is really your own affair, she says. Coming from her this
is unusually liberal treatment.

Ideally all salad dressing made with oil should be made
with olive oil, but probably for the next few years we are not
going to see much of it. Mrs. Appleyard, who has cooked
and eaten through one war, thinks that there are worse fates
than cottonseed oil in your salad dressing. We all eat a
good deal of it in commercial salad dressing without notic-
ing it much, she says. If you have olive oil on hand, treasure
it for your French dressing and begin by using part olive oil
and part Wesson oil. Gradually increase the proportion of
the Wesson oil and you will hardly know when the olive oil
is gone. Some people even get so that they prefer cotton-

seed oil. In using it, season the dressing a little more highly than you would for olive oil, use the very best vinegar, always have some chives on hand, and you'll get by somehow.

A good many of us are going to have to practice forgotten economies and ingenuities. We have also got to stay at home more because we are not going to have cars at our disposal when it occurs to us that it would be fun to drive out to Ye Olde Blacksmythe and Plumbinge Shoppe for lunch. As long as we have got to give up this pastime — the tantalizing, sticky rolls, the agonizing choice between lobster and chicken, the ball of ice cream set like a rare jewel in its small paper frill, the brightly colored vegetables that all taste alike — and stay in that half-familiar house quaintly known as home, perhaps we might as well spend some time making our own mayonnaise. That isn't a bad place to start our new life. By all means do it if you are lucky enough to have an electric mixer.

If you make it by hand, use a bowl with a rounded bottom. Use a French whip or a rotary beater. Have the bowl, beater, and eggs, well chilled.

MAYONNAISE DRESSING

2 raw egg yolks	1 t. salt
3 T. vinegar or lemon juice	¼ t. pepper
2 c. salad oil	½ t. paprika
1 t. powdered sugar	1 t. dry mustard

Mix the dry ingredients together, add them to the egg yolks, beat well, and add the vinegar or lemon juice (use some of each if you prefer) and beat some more. Then add the oil gradually, drop by drop at first, later in larger quantities, beating all the time. If the dressing begins to curdle, start over again with a third egg yolk, beat a little of the remaining oil into it and then work in the curdled dressing. Remember that mayonnaise should be kept in a cool place but not in the very cold part of the refrigerator. It separates if it gets too cold. A good cool cellarway like the one at Appleyard Centre is an ideal place to keep mayonnaise. As this is not yet standard equipment for city apartments, perhaps it is better to make mayonnaise in quantities that will be quickly consumed.

Remember too that mayonnaise separates if you mix it with the salad too long ahead of time, and that mayonnaise to which cream is added will be thinner than plain mayonnaise.

When you get the trick of it there is a quick way of making mayonnaise that is much easier than the version given above. The difficulty about this way is that you have to exercise judgment about the amount of oil used, and that is something you have to learn by trying.

QUICK MAYONNAISE (M. W.)

1 whole egg, unbeaten	1 t. powdered sugar
1 T. vinegar	¼ t. pepper
1 T. salad oil	½ t. paprika
1 t. salt	Extra salad oil — at
1 t. dry mustard	least a cup

Mix the seasonings together and put them into a chilled bowl with the egg, vinegar, and one tablespoonful of salad oil. Beat them together thoroughly with the egg-beater. When the mixture is thick and well blended, splash in the rest of the oil, beating all the time, and put in all the mixture will hold. If it separates, start over again with another egg, beat in a little of the oil, and add the rest of the dressing. If you like tarragon vinegar, use it in this. You can make it yourself by pouring some mild cider vinegar over a few fresh tarragon leaves. One plant in your garden will produce enough tarragon leaves for a whole year's supply of vinegar and some to give away. Mrs. Appleyard buys sweet cider in the fall — the kind without any preservative — and leaves some of it in a warm place.

It obligingly turns to vinegar, and Mr. Appleyard is very handy about straining it through cheesecloth. This gives you a supply of vinegar for no trouble and fifty cents a gallon. Mrs. Appleyard makes some into tarragon vinegar, uses some plain in mayonnaise or anything that calls for it, and uses the rest in pickles of different kinds. The time soon arrives when she wishes she had made more.

For French dressing, however, she buys red-wine vinegar and puts one or two beans of garlic in the bottle. That is one reason why people ask Mr. Appleyard how he makes his French dressing.

It has been often wisely said that there is no such thing as a little garlic. Either you have garlic or you don't have garlic. Mr. Appleyard says that a bean of garlic in a quart of vinegar really produces something that may be honestly described as a little garlic. It's there but you don't know it: all you know is that the dressing has some zip to it.

This is how Mr. Appleyard makes French dressing for a bowl of native lettuce:

FRENCH DRESSING (MR. APPLEYARD)

1 T. garlic red-wine vinegar	½ t. salt
½ t. dry mustard	A few grains of cayenne
¼ t. black pepper	3 T. salad oil
½ t. paprika	

Mr. Appleyard begins by putting all the dry seasonings into a large wooden spoon (blessings be upon the head of the giver of that salad spoon and fork a quarter of a century ago) and mixing them together with the fork over the blue Canton soup plate in which he is going to mix the dressing. He really likes to have this plate set into a larger one with ice in it, but he doesn't make too much fuss about it. Next he pours into the spoon over the mixed seasonings a tablespoonful of garlic red-wine vinegar and goes on mixing with the fork. This may begin to splash out into the plate a little, and it does not matter because he needs room for the oil in the spoon, and pretty soon he fills up the spoon with the oil, still mixing all the time, of course. By now the seasonings are well blended and he dumps the whole spoonful into the plate and fills up the spoon again with oil until he has used three tablespoonfuls, adds it to the vinegar mixture, and stirs hard. After a little while he takes a small piece of bread crust, dips it into the dressing and tastes it, looking wise.

Mrs. Appleyard accuses him of doing this because he likes the taste, but it is true that he does sometimes make some minute addition to the seasoning — his private preference being for more mustard than he has found others like — and he has been known to add a drop or two of Worcestershire sauce.

The salad — plain lettuce with some chopped chives sprinkled over it or some combination of greens — is now ready in a bowl that is big enough to mix it in. He pours in the dressing with a handsome flourish, and turns over the greens with the fork and spoon gently so that each leaf is coated with the dressing. It is a waste of good dressing, he says, to pour it into the bowl without this thorough mixing.

If you hurry it, the dressing goes to the bottom of the bowl and the salad is still just a collection of rabbit food and the dressing is ultimately poured into the sink, where its only effect is that the sink is hard to clean.

If there is more than the usual amount of lettuce, Mr. Appleyard starts all over again on a second batch of dressing. He says you can't mix it thoroughly enough with large quantities and get the seasonings really blended with the oil and vinegar.

VARIATIONS OF FRENCH DRESSING

Roquefort Dressing. Add 1 T. crumbled Roquefort cheese after you add the oil. Argentine or Wisconsin blue cheese may be used instead of Roquefort, and Gold N' Rich cheese, crumbled, is also good.

Anchovy Dressing. Omit ¼ t. of the salt and add 1 T. anchovy paste before you add the oil. This is good for a salad of lettuce hearts garnished with strips of anchovy fillets. If there is oil with the anchovies, use it in the dressing.

Olive Dressing. 1 T. ripe olives chopped, 1 T. green stuffed olives, chopped, half a green pepper — minced, 1 hard-boiled egg — white chopped, yolk grated), 1 T. chopped chives. Make a double quantity of the French dressing. Put all the other ingredients into a jar, pour the dressing over them, cover the jar tightly and shake it hard. Good with a salad of lettuce and tomatoes. Give the jar another good shaking before you pour the dressing over the salad.

Chutney Dressing. 2 T. of Major Grey's chutney, minced fine. Mix well with the dressing and serve it with plain lettuce, mixing it in well. Serve toasted cheese sandwiches with this.

SOUR-CREAM DRESSING (FOR POTATO SALAD)

½ c. thick sour cream	½ t. paprika
½ t. salt	¼ T. pepper
½ t. powdered sugar	1 T. chopped chives
1 T. lemon juice	1 T. minced parsley

Mix all together and beat well. Use tarragon vinegar in place of the lemon juice if you prefer. The sugar may be omitted from any of these rules: it merely serves to bring out the flavor a little and is not strictly necessary if you are on short rations of it. These amounts are so small, however, that it seems as if the saving might better be done on a larger scale.

LEMON MAYONNAISE (FOR FRUIT SALAD)

Make regular mayonnaise (page 237) with lemon juice. Take off the thin yellow peel of one lemon, let it stand in a half-cup of thick cream for half an hour. Remove the lemon, whip the cream, and add it to the mayonnaise.

CREAM DRESSING (FOR SHREDDED CABBAGE)

¼ c. thick sour cream	1 t. powdered sugar
1 whole egg, beaten	½ t. salt
¼ c. mild vinegar	¼ t. pepper
1 t. mustard	½ t. paprika

Mix the vinegar and the dry seasonings. Beat the egg and beat the cream into it. Just before serving beat the two mixtures together and mix them thoroughly with the shredded cabbage. Some grated carrot and a little grated onion combine well with the cabbage.

RUSSIAN DRESSING

1 c. mayonnaise (page 237)	1 T. chopped chives
2 T. chili sauce	1 t. chopped green pepper
1 t. Worcestershire sauce	½ t. paprika

Probably this dressing is no more Russian than Mrs. Appleyard, but anyway it's good on a salad of raw cauliflower and tomato, and also good to serve in a bowl with raw cauliflower broken up to dunk in it.

Mix everything up together and stir it into the Mayonnaise.

SALAD MATERIALS

Combination 1. Lettuce, chicory, asparagus tips, tomatoes. Serve with French dressing into which you have mixed 1 t. pickled beets, finely chopped, 1 t. minced parsley, 1 t. chopped onion.

Combination 2. Lettuce and watercress with finely chopped herbs — fresh tarragon, chives, parsley, chervil, thyme, a very little sage. French dressing.

Combination 3. Curly bronze lettuce, romaine, plain lettuce, sliced cucumbers, radishes. Olive Dressing (page 241). With this serve toasted Montpelier crackers and Frozen Cheese made by blending ½ lb. cottage cheese, ¼ lb. Roquefort or Argentine blue cheese, 2 t. minced chives, ½ t. Worcestershire sauce, ½ t. salt, ½ t. paprika, and ¼ c. cream. Chill the mixture in the refrigerator tray for an hour. Cut it in cubes and toss it in with the salad.

Combination 4. Shredded iceberg lettuce, shredded white cabbage, romaine, chicory, sliced tomatoes, small cubes of tongue or chicken, and ham, crisp chopped bacon, sliced stuffed olives. French dressing.

All these are good and so are many others. So is the Vegetable Salad that is served on the lawn at Appleyard Centre on warm evenings.

APPLEYARD CENTRE VEGETABLE SALAD

Mrs. Appleyard brings out the big oblong wooden salad bowl — it was once used for working butter. It has seen hard times, but lately it has enjoyed life. Mrs. Appleyard, with sandpaper, broken glass, and steel wool — none of which ingredients appear in the salad — has brought it back to something fairly close to its old smoothness. Not caring for the flavor of linseed and turpentine in her salad, Mrs. Appleyard uses French dressing to finish her salad bowls. This makes a better furniture polish than those without an analytical mind might think. The vinegar bleaches the wood, the dry seasonings act as a slight abrasive, the oil protects it from absorbing liquids that might stain it. A bowl finished this way should never be scoured. Just rinse it out, rub it hard, and put it in the sun to dry.

Mrs. Appleyard has told elsewhere [1] how she finishes table-tops with linseed oil and powdered pumice. She did not however at that time tell the Editor that, after starting a table with linseed oil and getting the grain well filled up with the hardened oil, you can keep it shining simply by rubbing in anything that comes handy — a dash of salad dressing, a little Hollandaise, and especially cream. You can generally identify anyone who has ever spent a summer at Appleyard Centre by an absent-minded habit of rubbing cream into any table at which he is sitting. This is one of those local customs — like that practiced automatically by

[1] *Mrs. Appleyard's Year.* Houghton Mifflin Company, 1941.

Harvard students who have eaten at their native tables, of wiping the silver on the napkin before use — that sometimes draws a raised eyebrow from the hostess. It is distinctly not politic to try to rub cream into a damask or lace tablecloth. . . .

There is also, Mrs. Appleyard has read somewhere, the possibility of finishing a table with orange juice. There is something attractive about this idea, but Mrs. Appleyard's first attempt can hardly be rated as a success. You were supposed to rub the juice in with the peel. She did, but it seems that there is more in it than meets the nose. The only point on which she has no doubts is that grapefruit or orange juice spattered on a table makes little lacquered spots that have to be washed off with warm water. Perhaps, therefore, if you had enough orange juice, you could really lacquer a table with it. Mrs. Appleyard, however, prefers to drink it and, for a heat-, water-, and alcohol-proof finish, to depend on that old reliable bottle of two parts boiled linseed and one part turpentine, the finest powdered pumice, plenty of rags, and shoulder power. In spite of old saws about elbow grease, it is with your shoulders and back that you do most of the rubbing.

This isn't the way to get the salad bowl filled, is it?

The ingredients are usually: cauliflower, carrots, beets, tomatoes, celery, green peas, green and wax beans, onions, curly lettuce, sliced hard-boiled eggs.

In the middle of the bowl Mrs. Appleyard puts a small but perfect head of cauliflower, cooked. Next a ring of tiny new beets, cooked. Then a ring of very small carrots, cooked and diced. The next row is getting pretty big, so it will probably consist of small heaps of different kinds of vegetables: crisp raw celery, bright green peas, the yellow and the green beans, cut fine and cooked, some cubes of cooked potato mixed with chopped chives and parsley. Next come slices of ripe tomatoes, peeled and cut thick, and last of all is a border of green and bronze lettuce.

All these vegetables are first marinated in some French dressing that has in it several teaspoonfuls of onion, minced so fine that you hardly know it is there. This supplies most of the flavor, but to please the eye there is Quick Mayonnaise (page 238) to which some sour cream has been added dotted here and there among the vegetables. Mrs. Appleyard obligingly answered the following questionnaire on vegetable salad.

'How much does this bowl you mention — I believe you referred to it as a butter boat — hold, Mrs. Appleyard?'

'Oh, I don't know. A couple of gallons, I suppose.'

'How long does it take to fill it?'

'Well, including picking the vegetables, about a day, I think.'

'You consider that a good way to spend your time?'

'I do.'

'What did you do with what was left over?'

'I don't know.'

'You don't know? Now really, Mrs. Appleyard, our radio audience isn't going to believe that — just try to think. No coaching, please. . . .'

'There never was any.'

'Do you know any other kinds of vegetable salad?'

'What am I — a Quiz Kid? Of course I do. . . .'

VEGETABLE SALAD 2

This time Mrs. Appleyard takes another wooden bowl, a big round one, and sets into the middle of it a glass dish of

mayonnaise. She surrounds it with the following vegetables that have been marinated in a French dressing with
plenty of minced onion in it: cooked beets, asparagus tips,
peas, raw carrot and cucumber cut into matchstick pieces,
finely cut celery, purple onions — sliced, red tomatoes —
sliced, yellow tomatoes — peeled and left whole. Chicory
and watercress go around the edge.

VEGETABLE SALAD 3

This kind is all mixed together. It has raw cauliflower,
separated into flowerets, raw carrot, cooked beets, cooked
potato, string beans, peas, chopped onion, white cabbage —
finely shredded, green pepper — minced, cubes of baked
ham and tongue.

It is first marinated in French dressing, then has mayonnaise mixed with it. It goes into a big yellow pottery bowl
with curly lettuce around it. There is of course no end to
the different combinations of vegetables that you may use.
One charm about these salads is that they are never twice
exactly alike. They are distinctly country salads, meant for
hearty appetites and depending for their goodness on the
vegetables' being perfect of their kind.

POTATO SALAD

6 potatoes, baked or boiled in their jackets	1 T. finely minced onion
¼ t. pepper	
½ t. salt	1 T. finely minced parsley
2 T. cider vinegar	

As soon as the potatoes are cooked — Mrs. Appleyard
thinks the baked ones have the best flavor — dice or slice

them into a mixing-bowl. Sprinkle over them the vinegar
mixed with the seasonings and the onion. Cover the bowl.
When the potato is cool, set the bowl into the refrigerator.
When you are ready to serve the salad, stir into it some
Sour-Cream Dressing (page 242) and the minced parsley,
mixing it all gently together. This has much more flavor
than salad made out of any left-over potatoes that you happen to stumble over when you are looking for those egg
whites you know you had left from the Hollandaise yesterday.

CABBAGE AND RAW CARROT SALAD

White cabbage	Onion
Raw carrots	Mayonnaise

Grate white cabbage and raw carrot until your elbow
gives out. Grate a little raw onion and mix the whole thing
together with mayonnaise or part mayonnaise and part
sour-cream dressing.

This is especially good with sausage, roast pork, or pork
chops.

VEGETABLE SALAD DE LUXE

1 c. cubes of cooked carrot	1 onion, minced
1 c. cubed potato	2 hard-boiled eggs
1 c. cooked peas	2 T. red caviar
1 c. cooked lima beans	Smoked salmon
1 c. beets, cooked and cubed	Anchovy fillets
1 c. raw celery, cut fine	Watercress
2 T. minced parsley	Lettuce

Put the vegetables in separate bowls and marinate them
with French dressing and add a little of the chopped onion

to each bowl. In the middle of a large deep platter put a silver bowl or a glass dish of Russian Dressing (page 243). Arrange the lettuce and watercress around the edge of the platter and then make wedge-shaped sections of the vegetables around the bowl of dressing, alternating the bright colored ones with the green and white ones. Divide the sections with lines of minced parsley. Garnish two of the sections with smoked salmon, two with anchovy fillets (or sardines, if you like them better), one with chopped egg white, one with grated egg yolk. Dot a little of the red caviar here and there. This is a good salad to serve with Baked Ham (page 183).

SPRING SALAD WITH CHOPPED BACON

Watercress	Cucumber, thinly sliced
Chicory	Tomatoes (little hothouse ones,
Lettuce	sliced)
Radishes, sliced	Bacon, fried crisp and
Purple onion	crumbled

Put all the salad materials into a large bowl. Scatter the bacon through them. Make the French dressing at the table, pour it over the salad, mixing it gently and thoroughly so that every bit of it is coated with the dressing.

Boston Brown Bread (page 40) sliced thin and buttered and made into sandwiches is good with this.

19

Sauces. If you are going to make sauces for meat, fish, or vegetables, there are certain things that are convenient to have on hand. Among them are:

Worcestershire sauce (always pronounced Worcester)
Dried onion flakes (when you want only a suggestion of onion or run out of onions)
Bay leaves (ten cents' worth will last for years)
Dried parsley (in case fresh is not available)
Tarragon vinegar
Cloves of garlic
Garlic red-wine vinegar
Pepper, ground: white, black, cayenne
Whole black peppercorns
Paprika
Spices, ground: cloves, nutmeg, allspice, mace
Whole cloves, stick cinnamon, whole nutmegs
Curry powder
Celery salt
Dry mustard

Canned tomato soup or tomato paste
Canned consommé
Canned chicken broth
Currant jelly
Lemons
Fresh or dried sage, thyme, marjoram
Bell's poultry seasoning

This magnificent list makes it seem as if Mrs. Appleyard bathed everything in sauce. As a matter of fact, she is generally eating plain cold lamb and wishing there were some mint-sauce left from yesterday. Still, when she is in a mood to make sauce she likes to have the seasonings needed, and they last a long time after you have once bought them. Whole books have been written about sauces — and a lot of nonsense incidentally. There is supposed to be some dark mystery about them that keeps ordinary people from dealing with anything more exciting than brown gravy. Yet a lot of people who are not exactly Doctors of Philosophy manage to make them, and you certainly can make the ones that Mrs. Appleyard mentions if you will remember the simple principle that unless you use the best materials it is a lot better not to have any sauce at all.

WHITE SAUCE

Mrs. Appleyard sometimes thinks there ought to be a law against white sauce.

'Go out into our fair land,' she says, 'so beautiful for fields of amber grain, and eat your lunch where you happen to stop. You will get the impression that a lot of the amber grain has gone into the making of paperhanger's paste and then, by some strange industrial accident, been transferred to dishes prankishly listed as creamed potatoes, creamed carrots, creamed fish, and so on.

'I have even,' she says, 'in a city that I hesitate to name, having received much kind hospitality there, encountered the same substance, only colored a bilious yellow and travelling under the name of Hollandaise....'

Here Mrs. Appleyard began to pace the floor, uttering low imprecations, but was calmed down by the application of a few puff-paste cheese straws, and went on to say with only a moderate amount of bitterness that Hollandaise sauce should contain eggs and butter, and that cream sauce should be made with cream. (This woman is certainly a fearless, original thinker.)

Cream sauce, she said, should not be a mixture of skim milk and half-cooked flour. If you feel cream is too expensive, put on a little butter and let it go at that. Never try to make a white sauce with less butter than flour: always use at least equal amounts, and use rich milk with the cream left in it and add a little more cream.

So many dishes — soups, sauces, soufflés, scalloped dishes — depend on white sauce as their basis that you should know how to make it well and quickly, even if you do not use it often on vegetables. Your rule may call for thin, medium, or thick white sauce. Use these proportions:

THIN WHITE SAUCE

1 T. flour	1 T. butter
½ c. cream	½ c. milk
¼ t. salt	⅛ t. pepper

MEDIUM WHITE SAUCE

2 T. flour	2 T. butter
½ c. cream	½ c. milk
¼ t. salt	⅛ t. pepper

THICK WHITE SAUCE

3–4 T. flour	3–4 T. butter
½ c. cream	½ c. milk
¼ t. salt	⅛ t. pepper

Melt the butter. When it bubbles and froths, rub in the flour sifted with the seasonings. Reduce the heat and cook this roux of butter and flour very slowly for three minutes — this is how to get the taste of raw flour out of your sauce. Stir it carefully and be sure it does not get darker than a deep rich ivory color. Now stir in the cold milk, a little at first, and rub it to a smooth paste with the back of the spoon. Be sure you get out all the lumps at this stage unless you like to meet them later. When this paste is perfectly smooth, add the rest of the milk and then the cream. Cook it slowly for another ten minutes below boiling point — a double boiler is a good place for this. Taste it and add more seasoning if you like.

Into each life some rain must fall, and it happens to almost everyone sooner or later that the white sauce has lumps in it. Perhaps the telephone rings or that delightful gentleman with the brushes-of-more-than-human-intelligence comes to the door. You relax your grip on the sauce just at the crucial moment and chaos results. Don't worry too much. Strain it through a fine sieve, rubbing all you can of the flour through, and no one will ever know — especially if you remember to wash the strainer.

Mrs. Appleyard generally makes white sauce in an iron frying-pan. She likes the sauce to cover a large area as it cooks. She thinks it is easier to cook raw flour thoroughly and slowly this way.

CREAM SAUCE

Use all cream instead of milk and make like thin white sauce. Add whatever you are creaming — chicken, eggs, a vegetable — add the seasoning you like — a little onion, some paprika for Mrs. Appleyard — and let the sauce and whatever you have added to it mellow and blend for twenty minutes in the double boiler while you are doing something else.

CHEESE SAUCE

Add ½ c. grated cheese, ½ t. grated onion, ⅛ t. mustard, and ½ t. paprika to medium white sauce.

EGG SAUCE

Add 1 hard-boiled egg and ¼ t. grated onion to medium white sauce. Remove the onion when you serve the sauce.

OYSTER SAUCE

Heat ½ pint of oysters in their own juice for each cup of thick white sauce. Cook them until their edges curl. Cook a slice of onion with them. Add them to the sauce. When you serve it, sprinkle some paprika over it and remove the onion. Good to serve with boiled fowl.

ONION SAUCE

Mince three large onions fine for each cup of medium white sauce. Cook them with butter until they are tender. Add enough more butter to make two tablespoons and work in the butter, milk, and cream. Add about a teaspoon of minced parsley. Good with fish.

CHICKEN CREAM SAUCE

To 1 c. cream sauce add 1 c. chicken stock. Canned chicken broth will do. Add some slices of onion. Beat two egg yolks. Spoon some of the sauce over them, mix well, and put the mixture back into the sauce. Cook in the top of the double boiler. Add a pinch of nutmeg. When serving, remove the onion and add some minced parsley.

HOLLANDAISE SAUCE

This is generally considered hard to make, but Mrs. Appleyard says that if you follow the directions it is really less trouble than almost any other sauce.

½ c. butter	1 T. lemon juice
¼ t. salt	Slight grating of lemon rind
Yolks of 2 eggs	Pinch of cayenne

Use only the very best butter. Divide it into three pieces. Put the egg yolks, unbeaten, the salt, pepper, lemon juice, and rind into the top of the double boiler over hot, not boiling, water. Begin beating with a wire whisk and add the first piece of butter. Keep beating and as the butter melts, add the second piece. The sauce will start to thicken and you keep on beating and as the second piece of butter disappears, you add the third piece. Here's your danger point. Just as this last piece of butter melts — keep on beating all the time — remove the sauce from over the hot water. If you leave it even a second too long it will separate Don't have hysterics if it does, because it can be brought back by beating in about a teaspoonful of cream. Be sure the cream is well chilled. Put the sauce into a warm — not hot — bowl.

There is no such thing as keeping Hollandaise sauce hot. It must be served *at once*. This is the only difficulty about it. Making it simply means that you must plan an extra five minutes just before you are going to send the asparagus — or what ever you serve it with — to the table.

This rule makes a thick sauce. It may be thinned by adding two teaspoonfuls of cream and one of hot water mixed together so that they are not too hot.

Always make plenty of Hollandaise and never spurn any that is left over. You can work it into salad dressing, or sandwiches, or into some other sauce. Just use your ingenuity.

BÉARNAISE SAUCE

This is very much like Hollandaise. Use white-wine vinegar instead of lemon juice. Cook a tablespoonful of chopped shallots or young onions and a teaspoon of tarragon leaves first in the vinegar. Start with enough vinegar to cover the leaves and cook it down to a tablespoonful. Strain it and go on from there as you did with the Hollandaise and at the end add a teaspoonful of minced parsley. Mrs. Appleyard remembers pleasantly some thick lamb chops with this sauce on them. Good with steak, too — but then, what isn't?

HOLLANDAISE TOMATO SAUCE

You can make a rather handsomely colored sauce, good with white fish, by adding two tablespoonfuls of thick tomato soup to Hollandaise. Have the soup warm — not hot — and beat it in just before the last of the butter melts. (Mrs. Appleyard thinks Hollandaise is better plain.)

MUSHROOM SAUCE (MRS. APPLEYARD)

1 lb. mushrooms, peeled, caps only	1 c. light cream
4 T. butter	1 T. sherry
2 t. flour	Bit of bay leaf
½ small onion minced	½ t. salt
1 c. heavy cream	¼ t. pepper
	⅛ t. nutmeg

Save the mushroom skins and stems for soup (page 281). Cut the peeled caps into quarters. Fry them gently in the butter with the onion till they are tender — about five minutes. Take them out and put them into the top of the double boiler. Now rub in the flour as you would for white sauce, adding more butter if necessary. There should be at least two tablespoonfuls in the pan. Be sure the roux is thoroughly blended and let it cook very slowly for three minutes. Now add the thin cream, slowly at first to make a thin smooth paste free from lumps, and then more rapidly. Add the seasonings — or sift them in first with the flour — and add the heavy cream and the bay leaf. Let the sauce cook gently — but do not let it boil — for five minutes and then pour it over the mushrooms in the double boiler. This sauce will be all the better if you make it ahead of time and leave it to blend in the double boiler. Add the sherry just before you serve it. Good with fish, ham, or chicken mousse.

CURRANT-JELLY SAUCE (MRS. APPLEYARD)

1 8-oz. glass of red-currant jelly	Thin peel of 1 orange
½ c. consommé	Juice of 1 orange
Thin yellow peel of 1 lemon	1 t. lemon juice

Mix the consommé, the peel, and the lemon and orange juice. When it starts to boil, add the currant jelly and let it melt. Set it aside where it will keep hot. Remove the peel and have it very hot when you serve it.

Mrs. Appleyard sometimes solves her cold-lamb problem by heating it up — cut in thick slices — in this sauce. It is supposed to taste like venison and does taste at least as much like venison as it does like cold lamb, and that's something anyway.

Variations of this are:

Currant Bitter-Orange Sauce. Instead of the orange and lemon juice and peel add two tablespoonfuls of orange marmalade. Good with duck.

Currant Mint Sauce. Add two tablespoonfuls of finely minced fresh mint leaves. Good with roast lamb.

Currant Raisin Sauce.

1 8-oz. glass of currant jelly	1 c. seedless raisins
1 c. consommé	3 cloves
1 lemon, sliced thin	⅛ t. cinnamon
2 T. orange marmalade	

Cook the raisins in the consommé until they are tender. Add the rest of the ingredients and serve when the jelly is melted and the sauce is very hot. A smoked shoulder is much cheered up when served hot with this — good with pork or tongue, too.

SPANISH SAUCE FOR OMELET

1 tomato	6 mushrooms
1 green pepper, seeded	4 T. butter
1 small onion	½ t. salt
2 sprigs parsley	½ t. paprika
1 stalk celery	⅛ t. cayenne

Chop everything together. Add the seasonings. Simmer

in the butter until the pepper is tender. Put half the sauce inside the omelet and the rest on top with grated cheese sprinkled over it.

TOMATO-CHEESE SAUCE

2 T. butter	½ t. mustard
2 T. flour	½ c. grated cheese
1 c. cream	½ t. salt
1 t. minced onion	¼ t. pepper
2 c. thick tomato soup	6 drops Worcestershire sauce

Fry the onion in the butter, make a roux of the butter and the flour, sifted with the pepper and salt. When it is thoroughly cooked add the cream slowly. Add the cheese. Stir until it melts and add the tomato, mustard, and Worcestershire sauce. Beat thoroughly. Serve it with spaghetti or rice.

BROWN GRAVY

The success of brown gravy depends on the thorough browning of the flour — which does not mean burning. The fat that you use generally comes from a roast and is brown enough anyway. Use two tablespoons of flour to two of fat. Cook the roux well before you add either a cup of consommé or a cup of boiling water in which you have dissolved a soup cube. Taste it and add more seasoning if you like. A few drops of Worcestershire sauce or a little kitchen bouquet help it.

Strain it, if there are any lumps, and then — as far as Mrs. Appleyard is concerned — throw it away, and eat the gravy that runs out of the roast into the well of the platter when Mr. Appleyard has sharpened his knife and made the first cut. It is a pleasant sight, Mrs. Appleyard always thinks, to see his skillful and benevolent carving. Perhaps that is why the dish gravy tastes so good.

20

Soup. Let's be honest about soup, Mrs. Appleyard says.

Most cookbooks are written as if the readers spent their time dallying with large shins of beef, cooking them three days with herbs, and spices, and vegetables, straining, skimming, clearing with egg, throwing away the vegetables — and then being just ready to start making soup. Yet among the facts of life is the homely truth that the chief gesture now used in soup-making is the circular motion by which you guide a cutting edge around a can.

The reason why there are twice as many soup cans as any other kind of can in people's ash barrels is that there are certain kinds of canned soup that are better than anything the average cook can turn out, even after one of those epic struggles with a shin of beef. Canned consommé is stronger, clearer, and better than home-made consommé. Canned black-bean soup is smoother and better flavored than most amateur attempts. Consommé cardinal is more beautifully colored and clearer than anything you can do with white of egg and cheesecloth. Canned tomato soup tastes better than tomato soup made out of anything except the very best tomatoes from your own garden. There are plenty of other good kinds of soup, too, and if your time and patience are worth anything to you, it may be actually more economical to use canned soup than to make your own. By the time you have paid for the materials and the fuel, you may even be out of pocket when your work is over.

However, Mrs. Appleyard does not recommend that one kind of canned soup should follow another just as they come from the can. She regards them rather as a basis for experiment. She frequently combines them, almost always changes the seasoning somewhat, and very often adds to them other stock that she saves, or juice drained from vegetables, or small quantities of vegetables themselves. She seldom serves canned cream soups without adding real cream to them, because somehow when it comes time to add the cream the manufacturers get absent-minded.

There are certain soups that have not yet been canned so that they equal the home-made variety.

Canned chicken broth is useful in cooking where you need a small amount of chicken stock in a hurry, but don't expect it to be quite the same as the chicken soup from Hartwell Farm in Lincoln, Massachusetts, where they use seven or eight chickens to a gallon of soup. This soup is so good that people drive for miles to get it and refuse to believe that there is not some great mystery about the way it is made. Yet there is nothing more to it than this — according to the proprietors of the old weathered farmhouse that has been standing under the huge elm since before the Revolution.

HARTWELL FARM CHICKEN SOUP

To make a gallon of soup they cut up seven or eight plump young fowls, put them into a big aluminum kettle, and cover them with two gallons of water. They think perhaps the water from Sandy Pond in Lincoln may have something to do with the goodness of the soup and also of their coffee. There is certainly, they say, a difference in any cooking you have to do with water that is heavily chlorinated. Sandy Pond water is without the pungent flavor of chlorine.

The chickens go on cooking slowly until they are tender — two or three hours — and until the liquid has cooked down to about five quarts. They take the chickens out and lay them on platters to cool. The meat is to be used in salad or one of their other special dishes. When the stock has jellied around the chickens, the cooks scrape off all the jellied stock that is on the platter and put it back into the soup kettle with the stock. They season the liquid, allowing half a teaspoonful of salt and one quarter of a teaspoonful of pepper to each quart. Next they make a paste of some flour with some of the soup — it takes one cup of flour for a gallon of soup. They strain this back into the soup so that there will be no lumps in it and simmer the soup for seven or eight minutes.

Now the soup is strained into a big aluminum container that has a spigot at the bottom, to keep it hot until it is needed. It is allowed to stand a little while before any of it is drawn off so that any fat that has not blended with the flour can rise to the top. They think one reason why the soup is so good is that it is drawn off from under this floating seal of fat. There is about two inches of it in their big cylindrical container on a gallon of soup. The fat is drawn off and discarded before another lot of soup is put into the container.

The soup is served in earthenware tureens, so hot that you can hardly eat it, and when you have had three plates of it, the waitress comes around and asks you if you would like some more!

Now, the equipment and the number of chickens are not exactly the usual thing for home soup-making, but Mrs. Appleyard has made soup at home by a method quite similar and almost as good. She cooks the young fowls — two usually — cut up and covered with water until the meat falls from the bones. It takes about three quarts of water to cover them and the soup cooks down to about two. The meat she uses for salad or creamed chicken. She puts the jelly on the platter on which the chicken is placed to cool back into the kettle. She also puts back the bones and the skin of the chickens after she has removed the meat from them, and lets them cook a little longer. At this point — there is now about a quart and a half of stock — her practice has been to depart from the Hartwell Farm method because she has no shining kettle with a spigot at the bottom.

Mrs. Appleyard strains the soup into a bowl and sets it away to cool overnight. The next morning she carefully skims off the fat. The soup will be so stiffly jellied that it is easy to separate the fat from it. She takes four tablespoonfuls of the fat and makes a roux of it with an equal amount of flour. When the flour and fat have cooked together for three minutes, she adds a little of the chicken stock warmed enough to melt it, but not hot, works it in, and then adds the rest. She lets it cook gently for a few minutes, tastes it.

and adds a little salt, just enough to bring out the chicken flavor. Half a teaspoonful is enough for her, but you may like more — that's your problem. The soup is improved by slow cooking after you add the flour: the top of the double boiler is a good place.

This is a good soup, though not quite so good as the Hartwell Farm version. Perhaps it's that Sandy Pond water (Appleyard Centre water is pretty good too). Or it may be those big tureens like bean pots, or the enormous fireplaces with the big logs blazing in them, or that aluminum tank, or the generous way everything is served, or the whole way in which you are made welcome. Anyway the lesson is: if you want chicken soup, put some chicken in it. It's all right to cook the bones of roast chicken, turkey, or duck for stock, but remember that the poor exhausted creatures have already given you their juice in the meat and in the gravy you made with the juice in the pan. It is unreasonable to expect them to provide a strong soup besides. By all means get what stock you can out of them — it will be useful in many ways, but don't expect miracles.

Returning to those brilliantly labelled cans that certainly should be on your emergency shelf, Mrs. Appleyard is far from spurning them, but she likes to improve on Nature. These are some of the things she does:

Black-Bean Soup is always served with its traditional accompaniment of sliced hard-boiled eggs and lemon. She allows one lemon and two eggs to each can. She also adds a tablespoonful of sherry just before she serves it. If the situation arises where an extra guest drops in at the last moment and it is necessary to spread out the soup a bit, she dilutes it, not with water but with consommé and more sherry.

Mock Turtle is improved, she thinks, by the addition of sherry and sliced lemon.

Consommé is helped by sherry, lemon, and a little very finely minced parsley. Consommé is also changed into something new and different by adding a tablespoonful of chili sauce for each cup. Let it simmer a few minutes and then strain it into cups with slices of lemon in them.

Chicken Soup is a good deal more exciting if you add some heavy cream and a little curry powder to it and shake a little paprika over the top of each cup.

Pea Soup is mixed with tomato soup to make *Purée Mongole*. Add a very little curry powder, and if you are feeling energetic, some carrots, leeks, and white turnip, finely diced and cooked gently in butter until tender. Half a cup of the vegetables is plenty for a quart of soup.

Pea soup responds gratefully to a little finely chopped mint sprinkled over it. It's always tactful to find out if anyone is allergic to mint in soup before you do it. Almost everyone likes fresh mint in drinks, but those who don't like it with soup or meat are very firm in their prejudice.

Tomato Soup is good thinned with consommé instead of with water or milk. It is also good with cream added to it — half a cup of cream and half a cup of milk to one can of condensed soup — and served with croutons and a few roasted peanuts scattered over each cup.

Mushroom Broth — the best canned mushroom soup — is much helped by the addition of sherry.

Concentrated Celery Soup and Asparagus Soup are both better if you dilute them with chicken broth than with water or milk, and if you add some cream or a little white wine. Almost any canned cream soup is helped by a little white wine, a teaspoonful to the cup. You hardly taste the wine, but the soup is more interesting than without it.

These are all familiar ideas about soup — Mrs. Apple-yard just mentions them in case they have slipped your mind.

There are some other things that she does that take slightly more thought. There is, for instance, a soup that she invented one cold evening when there wasn't enough of anything for some unexpected and hungry company. She calls it Mexican Tomato Bisque. The only reason for dragging Mexico into it was that some of her children had just visited it and had had such a wonderful time that the word Mexican became a handy word of praise. Also Mexicans do put whole beans in soup sometimes; also the returned travellers liked the soup.

MEXICAN TOMATO BISQUE

2 cans Campbell's tomato soup	2 c. hot baked beans
1 c. rich milk	½ t. red pepper
1 c. cream	Pinch of soda

Dissolve the soda in the milk, add the cream and stir it slowly into the soup. Heat it to the boiling point but do not boil it. Put a tablespoonful of the baked beans into each plate or soup bowl — brown Mexican pottery is nice for this — and pour the soup over the beans. Serve the soup with Thin Scalded Johnnycake (page 47). This is enough like tortillas for Mrs. Appleyard, who does not see herself getting up at dawn to grind the corn, even if when she sees herself in a shop window she does sometimes wonder if she is a fresco by Diego de Rivera. Brown Bread (page 40), cold-sliced and buttered and made into sandwiches or buttered and put into the oven until the butter melts, is good with this too.

ONION SOUP (MRS. APPLEYARD)

Allow for each person:

1 large onion	1 T. butter
1 can Campbell's consommé	1 bouillon cube
2 T. grated cheese	A few drops of Kitchen
2 slices French bread,	Bouquet
½ inch thick	1 T. red wine

Slice the onions and fry them gently in the butter. They should not be cooked too soft at this stage — a delicate straw color is the right tint for them. Stir them well so that they do not brown. Now add the soup and a can of water for each can of soup. Don't worry about its being too weak — the water is going to cook out again. Add the soup cube and the Kitchen Bouquet and let the soup simmer for a while. Toast the bread lightly on both sides. Put the soup into a large earthenware casserole, add the wine, put the slices of toast on top of the soup. Cover them thickly with the grated cheese. Set the casserole in the oven and cook for half an hour or until the cheese is well browned.

Serve it from the casserole at the table into pottery bowls. With a substantial dessert this is a good supper.

ONION SOUP DE LUXE (MRS. APPLEYARD)

Mr. and Mrs. Appleyard had this once in a French restaurant, and as Mr. Appleyard expressed great approval of it his wife went rapidly home and invented how to make it. The soup is made just like that described above up to the point where it goes into the casserole. When it has simmered long enough so that the onions are tender and the

soup has cooked down to its original strength, add the
wine

Earlier in the day you made the following:

CONSOMMÉ CUSTARD (FOR FOUR PEOPLE)

1 egg	4 T. cream
Yolk of another egg	1 t. salt
2 T. consommé	¼ t. pepper

Beat all the ingredients together. Have a small buttered
mould ready — a baking-powder tin makes a good one.
Fill it two-thirds full with the custard, put it on a rack in a
baking-pan and surround it with boiling water. Bake it ten
minutes in a moderate oven — 350° F. — or until it is set.

When serving the soup (use your best soup plates for this,
as it is for company) put a slice of toasted French bread in
the plate. Cover the bread with a slice of the custard. Pour
the soup over it, being sure that everyone gets some onions,
and sprinkle grated cheese over the custard. Pass some more
cheese and some more of the toasted bread with the soup.

BORTSCH

The chief difficulty about this soup is spelling it. Mrs.
Appleyard chose this version because it seemed the hardest.
She loves to see five consonants together: it makes her feel
intelligent. This is a soup that is pleasant to have because
you can vary it according to what you have on hand. The
only absolutely essential thing is the beet juice. In fact,
Mrs. Appleyard makes it because she can't bear to throw
the beet juice away. She uses either fresh or canned beets.
Beets are an accommodating vegetable: they do not resent
canning as peas and beans and spinach do. Try to get Mrs.

Appleyard to serve canned string beans and see what happens to you. . . . Fresh beets are superior, but there is not that wide gulf between the best brand of canned miniature beets that there is in the case of beans.

For ten people she uses

1 pt. beet juice	2 cans thick vegetable soup
2 cans consommé or strong soup stock	1 c. tomato juice
	2 c. water
6 small beets, finely chopped	3 large onions, sliced
	3 T. butter
½ c. shredded cabbage	1 c. sour cream

She begins by frying the onion and the cabbage in the butter, using a large iron frying-pan and adding more butter if necessary. She cooks them, stirring constantly until the onions are a light straw color. Then she adds the consommé, water, tomato juice, the chopped beets, and the vegetable soup. If she has small quantities of other vegetables on hand such as cooked carrots, peas, string beans, or celery, she adds them, and also any water drained off them while they were cooking. If she has a little jellied chicken stock, she adds that too. She lets the whole thing simmer for forty minutes. When she serves it she passes the sour cream and those who like it take some and stir it into the soup. The soup itself is a fine dark red. The cream changes it into an equally enticing shade of pink.

Sandwiches of Boston Brown Bread (page 40), either buttered or filled with a mixture of cream cheese and horse radish, go well with this. With Bortsch and a hearty dessert — Apple Pandowdy (page 100), for instance — even sixteen-year-old boys with hollow legs seem to think they have had enough for supper.

OYSTER AND CELERY SOUP (FOR FOUR)

This is another short cut that is made possible by canned soup.

1 can celery soup (condensed)	1 T. white wine
	Bit of bay leaf
1 c. cream	Slice of onion
1 c. oysters	⅛ t. nutmeg
½ c. oyster liquor	1 T. butter
½ t. celery salt	4 large mushroom caps

Scald the cream with the bay leaf and onion and strain it over the celery soup, to which you have added a half-cup of hot water. Set this where it will simmer. Heat the oyster liquor and cook the oysters in it till their edges curl while you are also cooking the mushroom caps in butter. This is a good plan because it keeps you mentally active. Add the oysters to the soup. Add the wine to it also and the nutmeg. Put the mushroom caps into heated soup plates and pour the soup over them.

VICHYSSOISE

Canned chicken broth comes in handy when you make this, although Mrs. Appleyard prefers home-made chicken stock.

4 leeks (white stalks only)	1 sprig of parsley, chopped fine
½ c. butter	1 T. chives, chopped
1 stalk celery	1 c. cream
4 raw potatoes, sliced very thin	1 t. salt
2 c. chicken broth	¼ t. pepper
2 c. water	⅛ t. nutmeg

Mince the leeks and the celery fine and cook them slowly

in the butter for ten minutes. Do not let them brown. Stir them all the time. Add the sliced potatoes, the chicken stock, and the water and seasonings. Cook slowly for half an hour. Now either add the cream and the chopped chives and serve it hot with croutons, or strain it through a fine sieve, stir in the cream, pour the soup into cups, chill it, and serve it very cold with the chopped chives scattered over the top just before serving. Mrs. Appleyard thinks it looks especially beguiling in those scarlet jars that the devilled ham came in of which she has spoken before. Better have some extra ones, because someone will want two.

If you have no thick cream on hand you can make the soup richer by adding two egg yolks when you are ready to serve it, if it is to be eaten hot, and after you have strained it if you are going to chill it. Beat the egg yolks slightly, spoon two tablespoonfuls of the hot soup into them, beat it into them, and stir the mixture back into the soup. Never cook the soup after you have done this or it will separate.

You may use sorrel instead of parsley in the soup. Almost anyone who neglects a garden conscientiously is rewarded by having sorrel spring up in it. Half a cupful of the leaves are chopped and added to the leeks with the stock and strained out again before you chill the soup and add the cream and eggs.

When amateurs plant vegetable gardens lots of seeds and vegetables are wasted. It's astounding what one small package of lettuce or spinach seed will do. Mrs. Appleyard has been confronted by a wilderness of green leaves for years, and although she can hardly say that she has really subdued the lettuce jungle, she does manage to use a good

deal of it. Here is a way that you might not think of —
something to do when you are tired of salad, but still have
an active conscience toward your garden and the crops you
raised up in it.

Suppose you have also a roast chicken that still has a
little meat on it, a problem child among chickens. There
isn't enough to cream but there is too much just to abandon
it to those who raid the refrigerator for sandwich materials.
Perhaps there is also a chunk of ham too small to do anyone
much good, the day is too chilly to make cold cuts and salad
attractive, your garden has no corn or peas in it, but more
spinach, lettuce, and Swiss chard than you know what to
do with; no one has caught any trout or perch; the meat
cart won't be around till tomorrow. In short it is one of
those days!

Confronted with this combination of circumstances Mrs.
Appleyard makes

GREEN SOUP

She begins the day by putting on the chicken carcass to
boil. A little stuffing clings to it. She cuts the meat off,
puts the remnants of stuffing with it, breaks up the bones,
covers them with cold water in a large kettle, sets them
to simmer over a low flame, puts on a broad-brimmed
hat and a pair of dingy gloves, and goes out into the
garden. There she inspects the green-leaf situation and
begins to pick things into a basket that will hold about a
peck. Curly lettuce she puts into it and the plain green
kind. She picks Swiss chard and spinach, a few sorrel
leaves, some beet tops and turnip tops. There will be young
beets and turnips on the end that are still almost too small

to see, but they will all go into the soup. If she can find half a dozen young onions she will pull them up, and a few leeks too. Next she will visit her daughter's herb garden and help herself to a sprig of thyme, one of lemon thyme, a few sage leaves, a sprig of summer savory, parsley, chives, a leaf or two of chervil, the same of tarragon. She wishes she had some watercress and vows to get someone to plant some next year down by the brook.

When she gets home with her basket and her bouquet of herbs, the soup has begun to boil and she turns the heat down so that it will simmer, and begins to pick over the vegetables. The beets and turnips have to be cleaned carefully, and any dirt washed out of the whole collection, but naturally they were carefully picked so it is not much trouble. She probably has a white cabbage on hand and she takes a few of the outside leaves of that. If there is celery, she cuts off some of the tops, and if she has a stalk of broccoli, she uses that. If she found no young onions, she slices up some old ones.

By the time she has made her collection and talked to the neighbors about this and that, and picked over the greens, it is time to start chopping. She takes the biggest wooden chopping-bowl, strips the leaves from the tough stems such as the thyme, puts all the washed greens and the herbs together in the bowl, and starts chopping. She puts in the young onions or leeks if she has them, but if not she begins by chopping up three sliced onions and then chops the greens in with them. She chops the greens for about five minutes and then adds them to the chicken broth — from which she has removed the bones — and lets it cook hard while she is cutting the chicken meat and the ham into neat cubes. She adds these to the soup and lets it go on cooking. If she has no ham she may add some bacon, cut in cubes and tried out a little, or some salt pork. She sometimes adds them anyway even if she has the ham.

At this point she is quite likely to decide that there is not enough broth, and if so she adds a couple of cans of chicken soup to the kettle. She tastes it and adds salt and pepper. Dinner time is now approaching — don't think for a moment that she has not made two blueberry pies and a batch of Dutch cheese and some Corn Muffins (page 45) in the pauses — and it is time to thicken the soup. She does this by making a roux of four tablespoonfuls of butter and the same of flour, cooking them three minutes slowly together, blending some of the broth with the roux, cooking it a few minutes longer and then returning it to the kettle. She cooks it very slowly now, watching it carefully to be sure it does not scorch. If the family are standing around looking hungry — and as they have been smelling the soup all the morning it's rather likely that they are — she adds a few sliced pimentos out of a can, stirs everything well together and puts it into a big hot brown bowl. If she thinks there is anyone around whose native refinement would suffer, she may put the soup through a fine strainer before adding the meat and the pimento, but she herself prefers it with all its native ruggedness.

Veal and pork bones may be added with the chicken bones, and small pieces of veal may be added with the meat. Duck and turkey may be used too. In fact this is a very versatile soup and Mrs. Appleyard feels as if she could hardly wait till summer. She has already found in the seed catalogue some watercress that sounds as if, given favorable conditions, it might grow about the size of a lilac bush. She is certainly going to have some around her lily pool. She thinks it would provide a nice shelter for the frogs — unless of course it cut off too much sunlight from the lilies. She thinks she could keep it down fairly well by making plenty of soup.

ASPARAGUS SOUP (FOR FOUR)

If you cook your asparagus country style (page 284), you will have some very good strong asparagus liquor left over. Here is a chance for a good soup.

1 c. asparagus liquor	½ t. salt
1 c. milk	¼ t. pepper
1 c. cream	⅛ t. nutmeg
1 c. chicken soup	1 egg yolk
4 T. butter	2 T. asparagus tips
4 T. flour	1 t. white wine
1 small onion, sliced	

Make a white sauce of the butter, flour, seasonings, milk, and cream (method on page 251). Put the sauce into the top of the double boiler. Cook the onion in the asparagus liquor and strain it into the sauce. Just before you are ready to serve the soup, beat the egg yolk slightly, add a table-spoonful of the soup to it, mix well, and return it to the soup. Put a few asparagus tips into each cup and fill them with soup.

CREAM OF SPINACH SOUP

2 c. spinach purée	1 egg
1 qt. chicken stock	Slice of onion
2 T. butter	½ t. salt
2 T. flour	⅛ t. nutmeg
1 c. cream	

Wash the spinach thoroughly, cook it as quickly as possible with only the water that clings to it. Put it through a fine sieve. Melt the butter; when it froths, rub in the flour sifted with the seasonings and cook slowly for three minutes. Add the soup stock and put it into the top of the double boiler. Add the spinach and let it cook uncovered for twenty minutes. It should be quite thick. Add the cream. Just before you serve it add the beaten egg yolk, first beating into it some of the soup. The soup when done should be of the consistency of thick cream. Serve it in cups with Cheese Biscuits (page 87).

CREAM OF SQUASH SOUP

Make this just like Cream of Spinach Soup, above, substituting squash for the spinach. This is a beautiful color as well as good to eat. You may use part milk in either of these if you have not enough chicken stock.

CONSOMMÉ CARDINAL WITH PEARLS

Among the best of the canned soups and one of the hardest to make well at home is the beautifully clear red consommé that is known as consommé cardinal. It jellies by itself in the refrigerator and is delicious on a hot evening simply served with a slice of lemon. It is also good hot, and Mrs. Appleyard likes this way of serving it.

For six people:

4 cans consommé cardinal	6 slices of lemon
6 T. pearl tapioca	1 c. cold water
4 T. sherry	2 c. boiling water

Soak the tapioca in cold water for at least two hours.

It must be the old-fashioned kind like small bullets. Drain, add it to the boiling water, cook in a double boiler until the tapioca is transparent. This will take about half an hour. Be sure the tapioca is really clear. Nothing is worse than half-cooked tapioca. Add the soup and the sherry and let it cook a few minutes longer. Add more consommé if it seems too thick. Serve it hot in your very best soup plates with a slice of lemon in each one.

LOBSTER SOUP

3 small lobsters	3 c. cream
A 3-lb. haddock	⅛ t. nutmeg
3 c. milk	2 egg yolks
1 small onion, sliced	½ T. butter, extra
6 T. butter	6 toasted and buttered
6 T. flour	rusks
2 t. salt	2 T. sherry
½ t. paprika	2 T. cream, extra

Have the haddock cut for chowder and cook it all, including the head, until the fish slips from the bones. Remove the fish from the bones and save it for scalloped fish the next day. Return the bones to the broth, add the onion and seasonings, the lobster shells and claws, and the pounded-up lobster coral. Let this cook for at least an hour. It should cook down so you have about two cups of strong fish stock The haddock simply serves to enrich it and bring out the lobster flavor.

Cut the lobster meat up neatly but not too fine. Now make a white sauce (page 251) with the butter, flour, milk, and cream. Put it into the top of the double boiler to keep hot and add the lobster. When you are ready to serve the soup, put a toasted rusk into each soup plate, stir the strained fish bouillon into the white sauce, add the sherry and the extra cream. Then add the beaten egg yolks, first diluting them with some of the soup and then stirring them into the soup. Slip in the extra bit of butter — it should be cold and hard. Stir the sauce until the butter melts. Put some of the lobster meat on each rusk, pour the soup over the rusk boats with their cargo of lobster, and serve.

Serve with Soufflé Crackers (page 37) which have been thickly sprinkled with soft crumbled cheese and paprika the last few minutes of their cooking time.

Canned soups, as Mrs. Appleyard has been admitting cheerfully and perhaps too often, are a great help. We may however have to cut down on their use, or even get along without them. Luckily there are good soups that you can make without them and without much trouble. Some of the best soup Mrs. Appleyard ever remembers eating was served in a Southern family where they kept a soup kettle going. Into it they put bones and trimmings of meat, juice from cooked vegetables, and the vegetables themselves if there were any left over. There was always onion in it and generally tomato, but its virtue was largely in its never being twice the same.

It is simple to make soup this way if you have a range where it can simmer gently without attention, but it is possible to manage with other types of heat. With modern refrigerators vegetables and their juices can be saved until there are bones with which to cook them, or vice versa. If you have plenty of onions you can make good soup, can or no can, so let no lamb or beef bone escape you until it has given its all.

Don't forget either the soups without stock such as

POTATO AND ONION SOUP

6 potatoes	2 T. flour
3 large onions	1 T. salt
3 c. milk	¼ t. pepper
1 c. cream	Chopped peanuts
4 T. butter	

Pare the potatoes and slice them thin. Slice the onions thin. Cook them in water, covered, until they are tender and the water has nearly all cooked away. Make a white sauce of the butter, flour, seasonings, and milk. Put the onions and potatoes into the top of the double boiler, pour the white sauce over them, mix well, add the cream. If you do not like the pieces of onion and potato in the soup, rub it through a fine strainer. In either case sprinkle the chopped peanuts over each plateful before you send it to the table.

CREAM OF LEEK SOUP

1 bunch of leeks	1 t. salt
3 c. milk	¼ t. pepper
1 c. cream	½ t. paprika
6 t. butter	Yolk of 1 egg
6 T. flour	Grated cheese
1 t. minced parsley	

Slice the leeks thin, using the green and white parts both. Fry them slowly in the butter. Remove the leeks to the top of the double boiler and make a white sauce of the butter in the pan and the flour, seasonings, and milk. Pour it over the leeks, stir in the cream, and cook forty minutes in the double boiler. Just before serving time add the egg yolk, first beating it slightly and diluting it with some of the soup, and then stirring the mixture into the soup. Serve the soup with the parsley and paprika sprinkled over each plateful and pass the grated cheese with it. Sandwiches made by buttering bread and spreading it with devilled ham and then toasting the sandwiches lightly are good with this.

MUSHROOM SOUP

Skin and stems of 2 lbs.	2 T. flour
mushrooms	½ small onion, sliced
Caps of 6 mushrooms	1 bay leaf
2 c. milk	⅛ t. nutmeg
1 c. cream	1 t. salt
4 T. butter	1 T. sherry

This must be started the day before you serve it. Chop the stems of the mushrooms fine, add the skins, the salt, bay leaf, and onion, cover with cold water, and simmer for at least an hour — two is better. This should give you a cup of strong mushroom broth. Add a bouillon cube and a little Worcestershire sauce if it is not strong enough.

Make a white sauce of the butter, flour, and milk, add the cream and the mushroom stock. Put the soup in the double boiler and cook it forty minutes. If it seems too thick, dilute it with a little cream or rich milk. If it is thinner than you like, thicken it with an egg yolk, first blending the beaten yolk with a tablespoonful of the soup, and stirring it in well. Add the sherry and serve at once. Into each plate or cup put one of the mushroom caps, either broiled or fried in a little butter.

21

Vegetables: Including Spaghetti. Mrs.
Appleyard's proudest moment was when her friend Mrs.
Teasdale said to her, 'I learned a great deal about cook-
ing vegetables from you.'

Mrs. Teasdale and Mrs. Appleyard once spent a summer
cooking co-operatively. They ate their breakfasts and suppers alone — if you call alone eating supper with your husband, four children, three kittens, two turtles, and any visitors of strong nerves — but took turns cooking dinner for
the combined families.

There was a great deal of merit in this plan. Each of the
cordons bleus had a day off every other day, and when there
was anything left from a meal, which happened seldom, it
was the other cook that had to exercise her ingenuity upon
it. There was excitement for everyone in this plan, especially for the families, because of course the cooks naturally
tried violently to outdo each other all summer, with interesting results. It certainly speaks very well for everyone that

with this threat to digestion the competitors still remain friends. Their families must have been tough.

Mrs. Teasdale may have learned about vegetables, but it was Mrs. Appleyard who learned about chicken salad in cream puffs, and how to roast corn and pop it, and some valuable facts about walnut wafers.

Mrs. Appleyard's vegetable cookery has nothing very mysterious about it. She is simply firm in the notion that the juice of vegetables with its minerals and vitamines ought to be in the vegetables, or in soup or stew the next day, and not down any sink. She cooks vegetables in the smallest possible amount of water and as quickly as they can be cooked. She watches them carefully to be sure that the water does not cook away before they are cooked and to be sure that it does cook into them just before they are sent to the table. If by chance there is any water left, she saves it and dilutes canned soup with it instead of using plain water, or adds it to the meat she is using for stew.

She does not put soda into vegetables because she has had it well beaten into her head that soda kills the vitamines and she knows it takes all the taste away, except of course the taste of soda, to which anyone is welcome who wants it. She considers it a poor business deal to swap delicate flavor and vitamines for a shade of green that never was very becoming to her anyway. And besides, she says, if you pick vegetables just before you cook them and cook them quickly without much water, you keep most of the color.

In following the policy of cooking water into vegetables she has scorched her quota of beets, it is true, and there has been an occasional batch of carrots that had rather more caramelized carrot-sugar at the bottom of the pan than was really necessary. However, her average is fairly good — as witness Mrs. Teasdale's tribute. (Of course what she learned may just have been not to try to paint a blue jay on your living-room walls while you were cooking beets, but Mrs. Appleyard prefers to swallow compliments like oysters — whole and with trust.)

She says she thinks it isn't necessary for her to go through the entire list of vegetables in the cookbook, from asparagus to zucchini. There was a certain sadness in her voice as she remarked: 'People who have always thrown the water from vegetables down the sink and seasoned them with soda when they weren't poisoning them with salt are going to do it just the same even if I tell them not to thirty-nine times. If they are going to learn, they'll learn without my screaming and flying up the lace curtains. If I had any.

ASPARAGUS, COUNTRY STYLE

Those handsome stalks of asparagus that always remind Mrs. Appleyard of a tenor playing Faust in green tights, the ones that come from the West and are so expensive — not the tenor, stupid, the asparagus — in the spring are naturally cooked whole and placed handsomely on a Minton platter. Mrs. Appleyard is not talking about these, but about the kind that come in your own garden or from a roadside stand in the apple-blossom country, which is also asparagus country. Some places seem to have all the luck! The stalks will not be all the same size and they twist around at strange angles. Trying to tie them into a neat bunch is hard as well as silly, so this is how you cook them:

Start your water to heat and go out and cut the asparagus. Break off the tough ends. Any part of it that won't break easily is too tough to cook, so throw it away. Now with the kitchen shears cut the stems into pieces about three quarters of an inch long. Leave the tips an inch long and put them into a separate pile. Salt the water, which by now should be boiling hard, drop in the cut stems and cook them fifteen minutes. Then put in the tips and cook them ten minutes longer. By that time the tips should be tender and the water almost cooked away. If the tips are done and there is still water not cooked away, either:

(1) Drain the asparagus into a hot dish and put some soft butter on it, saving the juice for soup (page 276), or

(2) Drain the asparagus into a hot dish containing some buttered toast, cook the rest of the juice down rapidly until there is only two tablespoonfuls, take it from the fire, add butter to it, and pour it over the asparagus, or

(3) Instead of the butter in either of these methods, pour Hollandaise over it and send it to the table — quick like a mouse, or

(4) Keep the asparagus cooking until you are sure there is only a spoonful of water (this means standing over it and shaking the pan), then add thick cream, put it into the top of the double boiler and let it stand long enough to soak up some of the cream. Pour it over hot buttered toast.

Any of these ways will make you utter kind words in memory of the man who planted the asparagus bed ten years ago. Asparagus once started is as hard to kill as a dandelion. For all Mrs. Appleyard knows, the same bed from which Samuel Pepys used to get his may still be growing. An asparagus bed is a much better monument than a granite tomb and not half so expensive. Really, she has almost talked herself into planting one.

There are two pitfalls to be avoided in this way of cooking asparagus: you may forget to put the tips in soon enough;

you may let the water cook out. If you do the latter, open all the doors and windows and wish you had decided on raw celery. If you do the first, go on and cook it some more. Mrs. Appleyard has committed both these crimes. The first is not really serious unless it leads to the second — which unluckily it is likely to do — just as one murder leads to another in the mystery stories. Fortunately the consequences are not necessarily fatal: you open a can of beets and like them.

CARROTS

There was a time when carrots used to be considered as something you gave a horse to make his coat shine. The horse very sensibly ate his carrots and never told anyone that a young carrot is better raw than any other way — wanted to keep them all himself, probably. Human beings at last learned to cut carrots into sticks and serve them with radishes, celery, olives, and young onions with French bread and unsalted butter, either as an appetizer or instead of a salad.

There is almost as much difference between young carrots that you yourself pull out of the warm earth while the water is boiling and the carrots you buy, as there is between asparagus you pick and asparagus you buy. The sugar in them hasn't had time to change into whatever it is it changes into. They are still sweet and they need very little cooking.

Cut them into rather thin slices. Cook them in the smallest possible amount of water and cook every drop of water out of them. Either add thick cream and let them stand in it awhile in the top of the double boiler or add soft butter and serve at once. If the carrots are getting large

you may add a very little light-brown sugar and some butter to them just as the last of the water cooks away.

CARROTS AND PEAS

There are a few days in the summer when the carrots are
very young and innocent and the supply of peas is getting
rather low, when Mrs. Appleyard cooks carrots and peas
together. She starts the carrots first. When they are nearly
done, she drops in the peas. She stands right over them
as they cook. In five minutes' time the water should be all
cooked out and the peas tender and a lovely emerald green
among the orange and gold of the carrots. Add either butter or thick cream, whichever you prefer. Mrs. Appleyard
likes butter. Vegetables cooked this way need very little
salt. Add it after they are about half cooked.

CORN

No corn is better than what Mr. Teasdale cooks over a
fire in his outdoor fireplace. The corn is Golden Bantam
and it is cooked in the husks. Mr. Teasdale keeps turning
it over on the grate over the fire with a forked stick. He
knows by instinct when it is done so that the milk is still in
the kernels and the skin has just begun to brown. A pretty
good guide is if the silk tassel has scorched away and the
husk at the tassel end is getting black. It depends on the
fire. If there is a good bed of coals, it takes about fifteen
minutes.

Plenty of butter, plenty of salt, corn just off the stalks, a
crisp September evening, and there you are.

However, even lacking Mr. Teasdale's practiced hand

and smoke-proof eyes, you can still have some good corn if you cook it soon enough after you pick it. Mrs. Appleyard sometimes roasts it in the oven in the husks, turning it often. The oven must be as hot as you can get it. Unless you can give it your whole attention — which you can't if you are broiling swordfish, making Hollandaise, and baking blueberry muffins at the same time — she thinks it is better to boil it.

She starts the water in a big kettle and a tight lid while she is picking and husking the corn. She puts in only about a third of the water that the kettle will hold and she makes everyone she can lay hands on husk corn for her. When the corn is ready and the water is boiling hard, she packs the kettle full of corn and clamps down the lid. She watches it carefully to check the time when the water begins to boil again. This will vary with the amount of corn. After the kettle is steaming hard again, five minutes is long enough to cook the corn. For a big kettle of corn, picked on a cool evening the whole thing may take fifteen minutes. Have ready a hot platter with a clean damask napkin on it and don't let anyone be late to supper.

CELERY

Cut celery into small pieces. Don't be afraid to use the green part: it has more vitamines than the white part and just as much flavor. Cook in salted boiling water to cover it and either cook out all the water or save it for soup. Add either some soft butter or some thick cream. If you use the cream put celery, cream, and some paprika into the top of the double boiler and let them get well blended. Just as a personal favor to Mrs. Appleyard don't half-cook celery and cover it with paperhanger's paste. If you're saving up for a mink coat, better eat your celery raw.

BRAISED CELERY

This doesn't happen often. When it does, it's an event.

2 bunches Pascal celery	1 sprig of parsley, minced
2 cans consommé	1 leek, sliced fine
2 c. water	1 bean of garlic, minced
1 t. salt	1 t. whole peppercorns
½ t. paprika	1 sprig fresh thyme
⅛ lb. salt pork, diced	(or ⅛ t. dried thyme)
1 carrot, sliced	1 T. butter
1 onion, sliced	

Put the diced pork into a large dripping-pan and try it out a little. Add the butter, carrot, onion, leek, parsley, and seasonings except the salt and paprika. Cook this mixture (it is Mrs. Appleyard's version of what the French call a *mirepoix*) until the onion is just beginning to brown. Lay over the *mirepoix* the celery, washed, with the leaves cut off. Leave on just enough root to hold the branches together. Season it with the salt and paprika. Pour over it the water and consommé and let it boil hard for five minutes. Then set the pan into the oven — 400° F. — for forty minutes. Cover the celery with a sheet of buttered brown paper. When you serve it, take out the celery and put it in a hot dish, strain some of the juice over it, and save the rest and the *mirepoix* to use in soup the next day.

This is good to serve with meat loaf and may be cooked in the same oven. Better have creamed potatoes — which you can also cook mostly in the oven (page 305) — and Tomato Sauce (page 259) with the loaf.

When you serve the humbler vegetables, it helps if you make them look attractive. This way of serving spinach happens because your own garden always seems to grow enough spinach but never enough peas. Serve it sometime with ham or tongue.

SPINACH: COUNTRY STYLE

½ peck young spinach	2 hard-boiled eggs
16 very small beets	4 T. butter
16 young carrots	1 T. light-brown sugar
Slice of onion	1 T. chopped parsley
2 t. salt	

Begin by cooking the beets with a half-teaspoonful of the salt until they are tender. While they are cooking start the carrots with the onion, and another half-teaspoonful of the salt. When they are almost done, start the spinach, well washed, and cook it with only the water that clings to it with the rest of the salt. Chop it fine as it cooks. It will take only a few minutes and you stand right over it all the time, because you are not trying to produce something that looks like weary old seaweed, but something green and cheerful as a background to the other vegetables.

You are also — Mrs. Appleyard thinks she'd better break the news to you now — serving Inside-Out Potatoes (page 306) at this meal, so you have already baked them, starting them when you did the beets, and they have already been mashed and put back into their shells and are at present browning in the oven.

All right! By the time the spinach is nearly done the water should be cooked out of the carrots. Add to them two tablespoonfuls of the butter and the sugar, and set them where they will just simmer gently. Your eggs are cooked and cooled (if you were Mrs. Appleyard you probably put them in with the beets and fished them out some time ago, but you may use your own judgment on this point).

Everything is getting done at once now and Mrs. Appleyard is going to 'dish up.' The ham is already sliced and it is on the table. So is the chutney. Now the potatoes are a delicate brown on their swirled-up tops and the spinach is green and tender. Mrs. Appleyard has a hot dish ready — probably it will be better if no one speaks to her just now (anyone who does is likely to get a dusty answer) — and she puts the spinach into the middle of it, with the rest of the butter. She makes a depression in the middle and into it puts half the beets. She puts the rings of sliced hard-boiled egg around on the spinach and surrounds it with the rest of the beets and the carrots, alternating them and sprinkling them with the chopped parsley.

Out of the way, everyone!

PEAS

You are lucky in Appleyard Centre if you get peas by the Fourth of July. Mrs. Appleyard has been known to transport most of a Penobscot salmon into the hills if it seems as if it were likely that there will be peas to go with it. She sees the noble fish packed into a thermos jar with cracked ice and it is never really out of her thoughts on the long trip. It is one of the few sadnesses of her life that salmon is not at its peak of perfection in the Green Mountains and that peas are never really peas in Boston. It is at times like these that she remembers that island off the coast of Maine where salmon and peas met together in a happy harmony never, she believes, duplicated anywhere else. However, she does her best.

The peas are picked just before she is ready to cook them and are shelled by everyone within range. Croquet-players must drop their mallets — though not on each other's toes. There must be no covers from cracker tins hurled from hand to hand. Sally must stop playing her flute and Tom must lay down his recorder. Mr. Appleyard must emerge from his book, for he has had a nice rest, it being fully twelve minutes since he stopped cleaning robins' nests out of the gutters. Hugh had better get off his hands the pitch from those logs he is hauling for his cabin — what else did his mother make that very powerful soap for? Put down your knitting, Cicely; wriggle out of those accordion straps, Stan. Leave the lawnmower where it is, Guilford, and, Paul, never mind pruning that apple tree. Dicky — this is no time for Southern languor. Nancy, stop squinting into that microscope. There are peas to shell!

'Always,' says Mrs. Appleyard, 'have the water boiling hard and have less than you think you need. You must cook it all out again and the peas are full of juice themselves. An inch at the bottom of the kettle is plenty. Eight minutes from the time you put the peas in is long enough to cook them. Stay right with them. Stir them so the same ones won't be on top all the time. If they are young — and why else are you cooking them, for goodness' sake? — five minutes, perhaps even less, after they start boiling again is long enough to cook them. Eat one every now and then and as soon as they are soft, put in what salt you like, stir them well, and begin ladling them out into a very hot dish with some butter in it. By all that you hold sacred — not too much salt. No sugar either. Peas cooked within three hours of the time they are picked have their own sugar in them, and when they have been off the vines only twenty minutes they are melting with it. When you have transferred the last of them to their mauve-and-ivory dish — you do this with a ladle with holes in it — there will still be a little juice at the bottom of the kettle. Cook this out rapidly over your hottest fire and just as it is down to the last teaspoonful pour it over the peas, which are waiting with big lumps of soft butter beginning to melt among the tender green globes.'

> *Now*
> Sound flutes and recorders,
> Thump the bass drum.
> PEAS ARE READY.
> Everyone come!

PEAS COUNTRY STYLE WITH NEW POTATOES

This assumes that the peas are not picked out of your garden. They will be good even if they came from a garden a little farther up the road, but they may perhaps lack just that last shade of delicate subtlety of your own.

The potatoes must be tiny new ones, the first digging of the season. Scrub them well but do not peel them. Have some boiling water ready and put into it two quarts of potatoes. Cut half a pound of salt pork into half-inch cubes and try them out until they are a delicate straw color. With them cook a small onion chopped fine. Do not let it brown. Add pork and onions to the potatoes and cook until the potatoes are done. Twenty minutes is all the cooking they need after the water starts boiling again. Do not use more water than will just cover them — you want it to cook away.

While the potatoes are cooking, shell the peas — there

should be at least a quart after they are shelled. Cook them in a very little rapidly boiling water for three minutes after they begin to boil. Add them, with any of their juice that has not cooked away, to the potatoes and pork, which you have just transferred to a big fireproof brown bowl. Now add a cup of thick cream. Put the bowl over a very low flame, where it will keep hot for a few minutes so that everything will blend. When the cream just begins to bubble around the edges, send the bowl to the table.

This is Mr. Appleyard's pet dish. For all anyone knows, this pampered creature, who has probably done nothing whatever all the morning except clean up the woodshed, get shingles for the church roof, inspire his sons to take the trash to the dump, and chase three Jersey heifers out of the corn, will get blueberry pudding for dessert. Even the peas, though, will make him smile with particular kindliness upon his little kingdom.

BROCCOLI

Broccoli is one of the few good things that have happened to the world in the last fifteen years, Mrs. Appleyard says. Before that it was just a luxury, and a joke about its being only spinach with a college education. Now it is available most of the year. Unlike most vegetables, broccoli is actually better in winter than in summer, and what travels over the continent from California is better than what grows nearer home. Broccoli has usually been sprayed, so be sure to stand it upside down for a while in plenty of water and rinse it well. Always cut off the tough part of the stems and if they are large, split them for most of their length. Always cook broccoli in plenty of boiling, salted water in a saucepan in which you can stand it with the flowers up. Have the water come well up around the stems and let the flowers cook in the steam. If they cook in the water with the stems they will be mushy. The water will stop boiling when you put them in. Time them when it starts boiling again. The broccoli should be tender in about twenty minutes. Serve it with Hollandaise Sauce (page 255) or with this Tomato Sauce.

Mrs. Appleyard learned this sauce from her fruit man. It was the way he used to have it at home — his mother made it. He told about it with such gusto that Mrs. Appleyard went right home and made it. She wishes she knew what army camp he is in now. She is afraid they haven't the rule.

JOHN'S TOMATO SAUCE

6 T. olive oil
2 carrots, sliced
1 stalk of celery, chopped
2 t. parsley, minced
1 bean of garlic, minced
2 onions, sliced
⅛ t. cinnamon
½ t. white pepper
¼ t. powdered thyme

½ t. red pepper
2 cloves
1 t. salt
1 green pepper, chopped
4 T. butter
4 T. flour
2 t. light-brown sugar
2 qts. fine red tomatoes

If the tomatoes are not really red and juicy, use two cans of tomatoes instead. They are better than the pallid, woody things that sometimes travel — and travel a lot too far — under the name of tomatoes.

Put the olive oil (or Wesson oil) into a large iron frying-pan and put into it everything else except the tomatoes, flour, and sugar. Stir carefully while the mixture cooks over a slow fire until the onions are soft. Shove the vegetables to one side and rub the flour into the hot fat. When it is well blended add a quart of cold water, slowly, and the tomatoes. Mix well and cover the frying-pan and set it where it will cook slowly for an hour and a half. The lower rack in the oven with the oven at 300° F. is a good place. Stir it from time to time and uncover it during the last half-hour.

Strain it through a fine sieve. This makes a lot of sauce It keeps well in the refrigerator and is good to use with spaghetti or to season soups or to pour over meat loaf.

Speaking of spaghetti, which Mrs. Appleyard supposes is a vegetable — anyway it's neither an animal nor a fruit and ought not to be cooked so that it seems like a mineral, although it sometimes does — this is the Appleyard Centre way of dealing with it; or rather two ways.

SPAGHETTI, APPLEYARD CENTRE NO. 1

1 package of spaghetti	1 lb. mild cheese
4 T. flour	1 t. finely scraped onion
4 T. butter	Crumbs from 2 Montpelier
3 c. milk	crackers
1 c. cream	Crumbs from 2 slices
1 t. salt	of French bread
½ t. pepper	

Mrs. Appleyard's project is to make enough spaghetti for ten people. She has her eye on a certain Bennington baking-dish, which she butters. First she cooks the spaghetti for ten minutes in rapidly boiling water. While she is cooking it she makes a white sauce of the butter, flour, season-

ings, and milk (method page 252) and adds the onion to it
and the cream. When the sauce is well blended she adds
to it the cheese, cut into small pieces. She saves some of the
cheese for the top of the dish. As soon as the cheese melts,
she stirs the cooked spaghetti into the sauce, lets it cook
slowly a minute or two, and then pours it into the baking-
dish. She scatters the crumbs over the top, adding the rest
of the cheese and a few dots of butter. Then she sets the dish
into the oven — 400° F. — and bakes the spaghetti until
the top is well browned — about fifteen or twenty minutes.

Don't try to scrimp on the cheese, she pleads. This is your
main dish for supper with a green salad and it had better
be good.

SPAGHETTI, APPLEYARD CENTRE NO. 2

This generally happens because Mrs. Appleyard is trying
to use up a jar of devilled ham to get the jar so she can serve
Vichyssoise in it. Make the spaghetti just as in the rule above,
only add two tablespoonfuls of devilled ham to the sauce.
Add also a can of thick vegetable soup, a can of tomato
soup, and some extra milk. Put the crumbs over it and
bake it until they are well browned. This will take the edge
off twelve hungry appetites. If Mrs. Appleyard has any of
her pet tomato sauce around she uses it instead of the soup.

Speaking of tomatoes, don't forget to broil some or fry
some on one of those cool September evenings.

FRIED TOMATOES

Choose tomatoes for this that are not too ripe. Slice them
rather thick, dip them in seasoned flour, fry them in some

fat from the Montpelier — or similar — sausage that you are cooking to go with them — Mrs. Appleyard hopes. There will be enough flour in the pan so that you can probably make your gravy with it, but be sure you rub it all smoothly into the fat — add some butter if you haven't enough fat. When your roux is ready, there should be about two tablespoonfuls of it, reduce the heat and add two tablespoonfuls of thick sour cream and a cup of rich milk, part sweet cream. Be sure your sauce is smooth — strain it if necessary — and add a tablespoonful of minced parsley. Serve it in a gravy tureen. New potatoes cooked in their jackets will be very good with this gravy mashed into them.

How about a little watermelon pickle (page 209) with this combination?

STEWED TOMATOES

Most stewed tomatoes, Mrs. Appleyard thinks, are not stewed nearly enough. They generally seem as if they had been in a can within fifteen minutes. This is, of course, all right if you like it, but she thinks it is better to put them, either fresh and cut up, or canned, into a shallow pan with a little onion, a little brown sugar and the same amount of butter, some salt and pepper, and either simmer them over a slow fire or put them into the oven. Use the oven if you have something else in it that takes long, slow cooking — a fruit cake, for instance. Stir the tomatoes occasionally. They should cook down to a rich dark red savory sauce. Serve them with rice or spaghetti. Baked pork chops with pineapple and rice are made even better if this kind of stewed tomato is present on the same plate.

STRING BEANS AND MUSHROOMS

1 qt. string beans	1 T. minced onion
1 lb. mushrooms — caps only	½ t. salt
1 c. cream	2 T. flour
4 T. butter	

Cut the string beans in long narrow diagonals, drop them into rapidly boiling water, and cook them until they are tender — about twenty-five minutes. Do not salt them until they are nearly done. By that time the water should be almost all cooked out. In the meantime you have peeled the mushroom caps (make stock out of the stems and skins for soup the next day — page 281) and cut them into medium-sized pieces. Fry them now with the onion in the butter until they are tender — about five minutes. Take them out and put them into the double boiler, rub the flour into the butter, and let it cook slowly for three minutes. Add the cream and the pepper, let the cream get hot, but not boil, and pour it over the mushrooms mixed with the beans in the top of the double boiler. Keep them hot until you are ready to serve them. Taste the sauce, add more salt if you like and a sprinkle of paprika. The beans should stand in the double boiler for at least twenty minutes before they are served, and standing longer does them no harm, so this is something that is good to have with broiled meat or fish that must be cooked at the last minute.

Frozen French-cut beans may be used if good fresh ones are not available.

RICE

For the way of boiling rice so that it is fluffy and the grains stand apart, see page 163.

A sauce to serve with rice that makes a little of several things go a long way is made as follows:

1 c. rice, boiled	2 T. butter
¼ lb. baked ham, cut in small cubes	1 c. cream
	2. T. paprika
1 c. meat from a roasted chicken, cut in squares	½ t. salt
	6 cakes of Montpelier sausage
½ lb. mushrooms	6 slices of bacon

Cook the onions in the butter. When they are tender add the mushrooms — caps sliced and stems chopped fine. Cook five minutes. Add the cream, seasonings, ham, and chicken. Put this all in the double boiler to blend. Cook the rice and while it is drying out cook the bacon and sausage cakes. When you are ready to serve the rice, stir about half the sauce into it and the rest on top. Add the sausages and the bacon.

A raw vegetable salad with a French dressing goes well with this. Shredded white cabbage, shredded purple cabbage, a little raw purple onion, carrot sticks, and watercress make a good combination.

BAKED BEANS

Even Mrs. Appleyard is a little hesitant about telling anyone else how to cook baked beans. Feelings run high on this point. Still, she was reminded by the Editor, suppose one of your great-grandchildren should say: 'I don't believe my Great-Grandmother Appleyard knew how to bake beans. There wasn't a word about them in her book.'

Thus challenged, and with an amount of humility that raised suspicions that perhaps she wasn't feeling quite well,

Mrs. Appleyard revealed her method for this controversial dish.

4 c. yellow-eye beans, soaked overnight	1 t. mustard
4 T. maple syrup	2 onions
½ t. salt	1 lb. salt pork

In the morning drain the beans. Cover them with fresh water and heat them slowly. Keep the water below the boiling point and cook the beans till the skins crack when you take some out on a spoon and blow on them. Drain them. You will like the flavor of your kitchen better if you don't pour the water down the sink. Perhaps you have a few plants outside that are yearning for a little bean water. Don't scald them, though. Few plants really enjoy being boiled.

Cut a thin slice off the pork and put it in the bottom of your bean pot. On it put the onions whole. You don't need to eat them and probably you will never know they are there — that is, not as onions; they just bring out the flavor of the beans. Now put the salt, mustard, and maple syrup into a cup of boiling water. Put some of the beans into the bean pot. Put in the pork, rind side up. There should be cuts in the rind about an inch deep. Surround it with the beans, letting the rind show at the top. Pour over the beans the water with the syrup and seasonings dissolved in it, and add enough water to cover the beans. Cover the bean pot and set it into a slow oven — 300° F. for eight hours. Add more water from time to time. The last hour uncover the beans and let the rind of the pork get brown and crisp.

Mrs. Appleyard, still in that gentle mood, says that you may use molasses instead of maple syrup if you like. Mr. Appleyard is not in favor of telling anyone about using maple syrup. There isn't enough to go around now, he points out. He likes chutney with his beans and he doesn't like his brown bread toasted. Mrs. Appleyard supplies some toasted — that is, spread with butter and heated in the oven for a few minutes — and some plain.

'Did you ever,' she inquired wistfully, 'have for breakfast the next morning brown bread that had been quickly fried in the fat from the sausages you had just cooked? Of course not, and probably no one ever will again,' she added, looking with disfavor upon her glass of spinach juice, and turned hastily to the more cheerful subject of Lima beans.

Dried Lima beans are very good baked, she says. Soak them overnight just as you would yellow-eye beans, drain and parboil them in the same way. Put some butter and a few slices of onion in a small bean pot; a small casserole will do. To a cup of beans add a cup of cream and half a teaspoonful of salt. Cover them and cook them in a slow oven until they are tender. Add more cream if necessary. Two hours should be enough.

LIMA BEANS AND MUSHROOMS

Fresh Lima beans, or frozen ones for that matter, are very good cooked with mushrooms in the same way as string beans (page 299) and in the same proportions.

MUSHROOMS IN CREAM

For this Mrs. Appleyard gets out her small covered glass casseroles. You may of course, she says, use a large casserole, but the mushrooms are really better in small ones. She allows a pound of mushrooms for three dishes — caps only

— and saves the skins and stems for soup. For six dishes:

2 lbs. mushrooms	¼ t. white pepper
3 c. heavy cream	¼ t. nutmeg
3 T. butter	2 t. minced onion
2 t. salt	1 bay leaf, cut into bits
½ t. paprika	3 T. sherry

Into each dish put the mushroom caps skin side down. The dishes are buttered and butter is dotted between the layers of mushrooms and over them. Put the seasonings, except the sherry, into a saucepan with the cream and heat it until it starts to bubble around the edges. Pour it over the mushrooms and put the dishes into a fairly hot oven — 425° F. — cover them tightly and cook until the mushrooms are tender. It will take about half an hour. The sherry is to be added just before the mushrooms are served. If the mushrooms are to be eaten from the dish in which they are cooked, have rounds of thin dry toast cut to fit the bottom of the dishes and when you put in the sherry, slip the toast under the mushrooms. If the mushrooms are to be taken out of the dishes, bring the dishes in on separate plates and have a pile of hot buttered toast to serve with them. Each person takes a piece of toast and spoons the mushrooms and the hot juice out onto it.

Don't, Mrs. Appleyard says, try to cook the toast in with the mushrooms all the time, because it soaks up all the liquid and gets mushy. The sherry has to be added last because it tends to make the cream separate.

GRILLED MUSHROOMS

Peel large mushroom caps. Into each one put a small lump of butter, 2 drops of Worcestershire sauce, ¼ t. of sherry, and ⅛ t. of salt. Place them in a buttered pan and broil them under a hot flame. If the broiler is well heated, two minutes is enough. This is a good way to make a meat loaf more interesting. Allow two large or three medium mushrooms for each person to be served. Pour the juice in the pan over the loaf and put the mushroom caps around it.

POTATOES (MRS. APPLEYARD)

Butter a large dripping-pan or a large iron frying-pan. Use at least two tablespoonfuls of butter, melt it and get it evenly distributed. Peel potatoes — allow one large one for each person to be served and one or two extra — and slice them very thin. Put a layer into the pan, dot it over thickly with butter, sprinkle it with crumbled soft cheese, finely minced onion, salt, pepper, and paprika. Do this until you have four layers. Put an extra amount of butter on the top layer. Now pour in a mixture of milk and cream — half and half into the pan. It should come up to the top layer but not cover it. Bake the potatoes for forty minutes at 450° F. When they are done they should be brown on top and a glazed brown underneath. They will absorb all the liquid. Serve them cut into serving portions on a hot platter. If you greased your pan well to begin with, you should be able to get them out neatly by using two pancake-turners or a turner and a spatula.

Even those who 'never eat potatoes' eat these.

POTATOES HASHED IN CREAM

6 baking-size potatoes, not too large	½ t. pepper
	3 T. butter
1½ c. cream	2 t. finely minced onion
2 t. salt	2 T. butter (extra)

Bake the potatoes for about half an hour at 450° F. Peel

them and chop them medium fine. Warm the cream, add the three tablespoonfuls of butter, the salt, pepper, and onion. Stir in the chopped potatoes. Melt the rest of the butter in the frying-pan. Put in the potato-and-cream mixture and cook over a slow fire until the cream is absorbed and you can see brown around the edges. Treat it as if it were an omelet: cut across at right angles to the handle of the pan, turn the top half over the other, and slide the whole thing out on a very hot platter.

CREAMED POTATOES

Never, NEVER, says Mrs. Appleyard, try to make creamed potatoes with cold potatoes. If she had any supply of larger letters she would print 'NEVER' bigger and blacker. If you do use cooked potatoes, you lose both the mineral salts and the taste. Besides, the way she approves is less trouble, though that's a detail.

Peel the potatoes, taking off the thinnest peel that you can manage. Cut them fine or chop them if you like. For each six potatoes use one large onion. Mince it fine and fry it in two tablespoonfuls of butter until it is a light straw color. Add another two tablespoonfuls of butter, stir in the chopped potatoes. Sprinkle over them two teaspoonfuls of salt and some paprika and stir some more. Pour in two cups of rich milk and 1 cup of cream. If you have a little sour cream that is unemployed at the moment, this is an excellent situation for it. Stir everything together, cover the pan, set it into a medium oven — 375° F. — and bake for forty–fifty minutes. If your oven is not going, you may do it on the top of the stove over a very low flame. The potatoes are not supposed to be brown on top. If you think they are drying up, add some more cream or rich milk. The dish will be a little like hashed brown potato except that it will be distinctly creamy. There will be a light golden crust on the bottom. Make plenty.

CANDIED SWEET POTATOES WITH PEANUTS

Parboil sweet potatoes twenty minutes. Let them cool. When they are cool enough to slice easily without breaking, cut them lengthwise into rather thick slices. Put them into a well-buttered baking-pan, dot each slice thickly with butter and light-brown sugar, put the pan into a moderate oven — 375° F. — and bake about fifteen minutes, by which time the sugar and butter should have melted and the potatoes have become tender. Allow a tablespoonful of chopped peanuts to each whole potato. Sprinkle them over the slices and cook a few minutes longer.

There is something about the young of the human species that makes it like marshmallows. Mrs. Appleyard outgrew this taste some years ago, but she sometimes caters to it by putting marshmallows on top of a dish of candied sweet potato. She parboils the potatoes, and slices them into a buttered baking-dish with lots of butter and sugar and just enough water to keep them from scorching before the butter melts. These get baked until they are sticky — about forty minutes. Then the marshmallows are put on and the dish returned to the oven until the marshmallows are a delicate brown.

INSIDE-OUT POTATOES

That's what they are called in the Appleyard family, although there is doubtless some more de luxe name for them.

Bake fine large potatoes until they are nearly done — about forty minutes at 475° F. Cut a piece off the side and scoop out the potato. Don't break the skin — you're saving it for a cold winter. Be sure to have the dish into which you scoop them hot and have in it for each potato ½ T. of butter, ¼ t. of salt, ¼ t. of paprika, and 1 T. of thick cream. Mash the potatoes thoroughly with the back of a fork into this mixture and beat them up light. Don't let the potato get cold. Pile it lightly back into the shells, sprinkle a little more paprika on it. Don't mash it down but make wavy lines on it with the tines of your fork if you like. Set the potatoes on a baking-sheet and put them back into the oven. If in ten minutes the tops are not a nice brown, slip them under the broiler flame for a minute. Watch it — no scorching allowed. Have some small sprigs of parsley ready to stick into the tops.

Mr. Appleyard considers this all nonsense. All he wants is a good baked potato — it doesn't have to come wrapped in pink tissue paper (we won't quote him directly on this point). Give him butter, salt, his pepper-grinder, fresh paprika, and a pitcher of cream, and he'll fix his own.

CAULIFLOWER BAKED IN TOMATO (E. K. T.)

1 cauliflower, parboiled	½ t. mustard
2 c. thick tomato soup	1 T. light-brown sugar
2 T. butter	½ c. grated cheese
2 T. flour	⅛ t. Worcestershire sauce
½ t. salt	1 t. grated onion
⅛ t. pepper	

Melt the butter. When it bubbles, work in the flour, cook three minutes slowly, add the canned soup, the seasonings, onion, and the grated cheese. Cook until the cheese melts — about two minutes. Grease a French earthenware casserole. Put the cauliflower into it, pour the sauce over the cauliflower, and on top put some buttered crumbs — half Montpelier or Common crackers and half dry French bread — and some more grated cheese. Bake it for half an hour at 400° F. or until the top is well browned.

22

The Most Important Ingredient. It will
be apparent to the thoughtful reader that there are strange
gaps in Mrs. Appleyard's cooking. What! An adopted
Vermonter and she never tells how to make doughnuts!
Where is her rule for griddle cakes? Can a woman who
doesn't mention French-fried potatoes really hold a good
man's affection?

These are all pretty sharp, pointed questions, and Mrs.
Appleyard's face — if not red — was at least a becoming
pink as she answered them. She had just taken a batch of
oatmeal cookies out of the oven, so it may have been only
her baking flush. Her hair net was broken because she had
just been chasing a Siamese kitten into a rosebush before the
urge to make cookies came upon her. She had on that
scarlet bandanna smock that makes her look like a fire
engine — on a small scale, of course. She had managed to
get a little flour on her nose. Mrs. Appleyard's nose is the
style that used to be called tip-tilted in the more sentimental

books of her youth. There's not room for much flour on it. Some was on her right cheek, too.

Still, in spite of these minor difficulties, Mrs. Appleyard preserved her poise. So does the Statue of Liberty, for that matter — in spite of this and that.

'I have seventeen wonderful rules for doughnuts and I never made one in my life,' she announced, apparently without shame. 'Why should I make them when my neighbors do it a lot better and send me in the results? Did you ever hear about the Covered-Dish Party in Gospel Hollow? You know everyone takes a covered dish and then at a moment of tense excitement, the covers are removed and the dishes are passed around. Usually one person has salad and another cake and another macaroni and cheese or baked beans. This time at Gospel Hollow when they opened the dishes everyone had brought doughnuts. Except the one who had marble cake. They have committees now. If I'd been there I'd probably have brought popcorn. As to griddle cakes,' Mrs. Appleyard went on, 'I am the sort of cook that sometimes has good luck with my griddle cakes — need I say more? Mr. Appleyard doesn't like French-fried potatoes. If he did I'd cut myself up into small pieces and fry the potatoes in it.'

Mrs. Appleyard made this somewhat obscure statement at a critical moment of taking cookies swiftly off a pan and did not seem to have time to explain it.

This was a favorable time to interview Mrs. Appleyard — for the interviewer — to whose share fell certain fragments of a quite exceptional character.

'Now, just one more question, Mrs. Appleyard,' the Editoi said, hoping she would break another cooky. 'I've heard it said that a well-known painter when asked what he mixed his paints with, said, "With brains." Now do you feel that — to sum up what you've told me — people should cook with brains? May I quote you?'

Mrs. Appleyard put another batch of cookies into the oven.

'Brains aren't enough,' she said. 'You have to like things: the dishes you cook with, the people you buy the butter from, the field where the crows fly over the corn and the wind that blows through their wings. You have to like the table you put the food on, and the people who sit around it. Yes, even when they tip back in your Hitchcock chairs, you have to like them. You don't just like how food tastes — you like how it looks and smells and how the egg-beater sounds. You like the rhythm of chopping and the throb of the teakettle lid. You like to test the frying-pan with water and see it run around like quicksilver. You like the shadows in pewter and the soft gleam of silver and the sharp flash of glass. You like the feel of damask napkins and the shadows of flowers on a white cloth. You like people eating in their best clothes in candlelight, and in their dungarees on a beach in the broiling sun, or under a pine tree in the rain.

'You like that last moment before a meal is served when the Hollandaise thickens, the steak comes sputtering out of the broiler, the cream is cooked into the potatoes and the last drop of water is cooked out of the peas.' Here she was silent long enough to take the correctly lacy and golden cookies off the pan. 'Not with brains,' she repeated, putting down the spatula. 'With love.'

Index